IMAGES
of America

FILIPINOS IN VENTURA COUNTY

I0807690

On the Cover: Pictured is a Filipino camp located at the Arneill Ranch in Camarillo (see page 22). (Author's collection.)

IMAGES
of America

FILIPINOS IN VENTURA COUNTY

Elnora Kelly Tayag

ARCADIA PUBLISHING

ISBN 978-0-7385-7473-8

Published by Arcadia Publishing
Charleston, South Carolina

Printed in the United States of America

Library of Congress Control Number: 2010939091

For all general information, please contact Arcadia Publishing:
Telephone 843-853-2070
Fax 843-853-0044
E-mail sales@arcadiapublishing.com
For customer service and orders:
Toll-Free 1-888-313-2665

Visit us on the Internet at www.arcadiapublishing.com

To my mom and dad, Victoria and Marner Tayag. This book would not have been possible without your love and support.

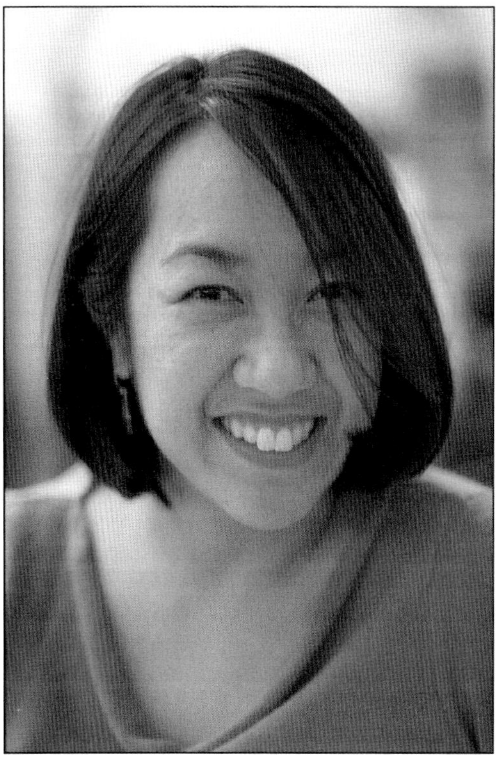

Elnora Kelly Tayag is a librarian and assistant professor at California State University Channel Islands, where she teaches critical thinking. She serves on the Filipino American Library (FAL) Board of Directors. A native Angelino and former middle school teacher with the Los Angeles Unified School District, Elnora earned her bachelor's degree in art history from UC Irvine, master's degree in religion from Claremont School of Theology, and master's degree in library information science from UCLA.

Contents

Foreword 6

Acknowledgments 7

Introduction 8

1. The Pioneers 9

2. Establishing Roots 23

3. Community 47

4. Military Life 69

5. Community Engagement and Creating Traditions 93

Bibliography 126

Index 127

FOREWORD

After several years of individuals expressing a desire to write the history of Filipino Americans in Ventura County, Ellie Tayag, a Filipina from Los Angeles, has compiled this excellent pictorial history of the FilAms in Ventura County. As a librarian, she recognized the lack of accessible resources documenting the history of this sizable, but often overlooked, population.

Through her perseverance, sincerity, and judicious treatment of available resources, she was able to obtain the cooperation and help of individuals whose families played integral roles in the history of Filipinos in Ventura County. This allowed her to collect personal accounts, pictures, newspaper clippings, and other primary sources. Compiling these resources required persistent hard work and several months of cultivating relationships with members of the Filipino community. Through these relationships she was able to cross reference the information provided by individuals, resulting in an accurate depiction and pictorial history that will serve as a great resource for those interested in Ventura County history and Filipino American migration and history.

In his book *America is in the Heart*, Carlos Bulosan wrote about the lives of Filipino migrants from the 1930s and 1940s, working the farms in California, including those in Ventura County. The Honorable Stanley J. Dailey, mayor emeritus of the City of Camarillo, affirms this in his book *Camarillo and Other Remembrances*, providing a detailed account of Filipinos working in the farms throughout the county and specifically those living at the Filipino camp at Arneill Ranch. Tayag depicted this history with 220 pictures ranging from the 1920s to the present.

I am delighted that future generations will have insight into the Filipino community's migration to Ventura County, the pioneers, their contributions, and the preservation of their traditions and values.

—Tony V. Grey
Executive Director, Filipino American Council

ACKNOWLEDGMENTS

I would like to express my deepest appreciation to the families who opened their hearts, homes, and albums and shared their stories and pictures for this project. I am grateful to Nora and Federico Talaugon Jr., Tony Baker, Tony V. Grey, Ellen and Chief Deputy Dante Honorico, Josie and Al Bautista, Cathy and Jim Ines, Nellie and John Obispo, Vicky Barretto, Vincent Ines, Dora Ines Vaca, Fe and Florentino "Toots" Vinzon, Irene and Eduardo Austria, Clara "Tawa" Montayre Desaucido, Julia Carrillo Macasieb and Ingemar Macasieb, Beatrice Talaugon-Dunn, Vic R. and Coring G. Mercado, Delia and Sid Cabran, Lisa and Domingo Dela Rosa Jr., Augie Castaneda Jr., Eloisa Gomez Borah, Delia and Bill Coleman, Lillian Omo Roman, George Omo III, Elizabeth and Mayor Emeritus Stanley Daily, Lynette and Robert Tayag, Monsignor Jon Marajucon, Marie and Judge Bernie LaForteza, Virginia LaForteza, Elaine and Jack Alpenia, Rosalina and Alejandro Sarreal, Darlene Johnson, Charleen Morla, Pete Villanueva, and Rosalie Marquez.

These families and photographs represent the leadership, members, and heart of the following organizations past and present: Filipino Brotherhood of Ventura County, Caballeros de Dimas-Alang, Jordan Lodge 604 Legionarios Del Trabajo, Filipino Optimist Club, Filipino Community of Ventura County Inc., Filipino Youth Club, Filipino Sports Club, Associated Farmers Ventura, Filipino American Social Club, Mabuhay Club and Ladies Auxiliary, Filipino American Military Retired Club and Ladies Auxiliary, Zambalas Association, Cavite Association, Visayan Association, Filipino American Council, Philippine Center, PINOYS, Anacapa Lodge 710, Knights of Columbus, American Legion No. 48, Filipino American Seniors, Philippine Patron of the Arts, *Kapitbahay*, *Filipinos on the Limelight*, Filipino American Golf Association, Rotary, Salin-Lahi, Mary Star of the Sea Church, Santa Clara Church, Simbang Gabi, Camarillo State Hospital, Ventura County Sheriff's Department, Filipino American National Historical Society California Central Coast, La Union Association, Filipinos Americans of Camarillo, and the Ilocano Association.

Thank you to my editor Jerry Roberts for his support and patience. I am grateful to my colleagues at local institutions Gina L. Nichols, US Navy Seabee Archives, Charles Johnson, Ventura County Museum and Library, Dow Jarvis, Oxnard Public Library, and Dr. Pat Lyons, St. John Seminary Library.

These photographs and many more that were not included because of space restrictions will be part of a community-based Filipino photo digital collection at the John Spoor Broome Library at California State University Channel Islands. I hope this collection of primary sources will provide historical insight for future generations. Thank you to library dean Amy Wallace for giving me the green light on this digital project and to my colleagues at the library for their support. I work at the best library and have the best colleagues!

I would also like to thank my mentors Eloisa Gomez Borah and Dr. Clara M. Chu for their guidance and support these past years and for planting the seeds to create this collection. Thank you to Dr. Jose Alamillo for always pointing me to new resources and discoveries. Thank you to Florante Peter Ibanez for all his support, editing, and guidance throughout this process. Thank you to my dearest grandpa and grandma, Ken and Elnora Kelly, and my dear friends Zarina Iqbal and Martha Reyes for their love and support. Thank you to Janet Pinkley for her love and support with covering classes, editing, compiling the index, and for being my best compadre at work. Thank you to Jason De Castro for his love and support with continuously editing, brainstorming ideas for all my projects, the late night pep talks, and for being my partner-in-crime best friend. Most of all thank you to my mom and dad, Victoria and Marner Tayag for all their love and encouragement and always being my biggest cheerleaders.

Unless otherwise credited, images are from the author's collection.

INTRODUCTION

Early Filipinos in the United States fell into one of the two categories: *pensionados* or migrant farm laborers. Pensionados were government-sponsored students from the Philippines sent to the United States for a college education and then returned to the Philippines to occupy government positions. Migrant laborers provided cheap labor for the Hawaiian sugar cane fields, California farms, and Alaskan canneries. The first pensionados arrived in 1903, while the *sakadas*, a term used to describe unskilled Filipino labor imported by the Hawaiian Sugar Planters Association, arrived in Hawaii in 1906. Not all laborers arrived in California via Hawaii; eventually, Filipinos arrived directly from the Philippines to ports in San Pedro, San Francisco, and Seattle. There was a high demand for Filipino labor, especially with the Immigration Act of 1924 that excluded the Japanese and Chinese, whereas Filipinos, at the time, were US nationals and could freely travel to the United States. Of the two groups, it was the migrant farm laborers that eventually settled in the United States.

The earliest documentation to date of Filipinos living in Ventura County, California, is that of four pensionados who stayed at the home of Mrs. H.H. Arnold in Hueneme from 1903 to 1904. In 1903, the first 104 pensionados arrived in the United States, and 4 of them were assigned to Principal Charles F. Blackstock in Hueneme. Ranging from 16 to 17 years old, they were Silvino Gallardo from Rizal, Segundo Hipolito from Manila, Jose G. Sanvictores from Pampanga, and Hillario Valderas from Tayabas. In 1904, Mrs. H.H. Arnold threw a farewell party at her home in June with plans for the young men to attend the Louisiana Purchase Exposition, in St. Louis, and Eastern colleges under the new charge of Mr. Sutherland.

Ventura County was the home to many farm laborers who settled in La Conchita del Mar, Oxnard, Ventura, Santa Paula, and Camarillo. Filipinos worked at farms throughout the area, such as the Arneill Ranch (on Arneill Road), Springville Ranch (at Las Posas and Pleasant Valley Roads), Ocean View (on Laguna Road), Campo Blanco (at Cawelti and Las Posas), and El Rio (in Oxnard) to name a few. I hope to identify more labor camps and employers as my research progresses. There is still much more to uncover, and the challenge ahead lies in the urgency to document and capture as much information before it is lost in order to provide primary source material for historical research.

Filipinos in Ventura County serves as an introduction to (re)discover, (re)capture, and (re)visit our place in the history of the region.

One

The Pioneers

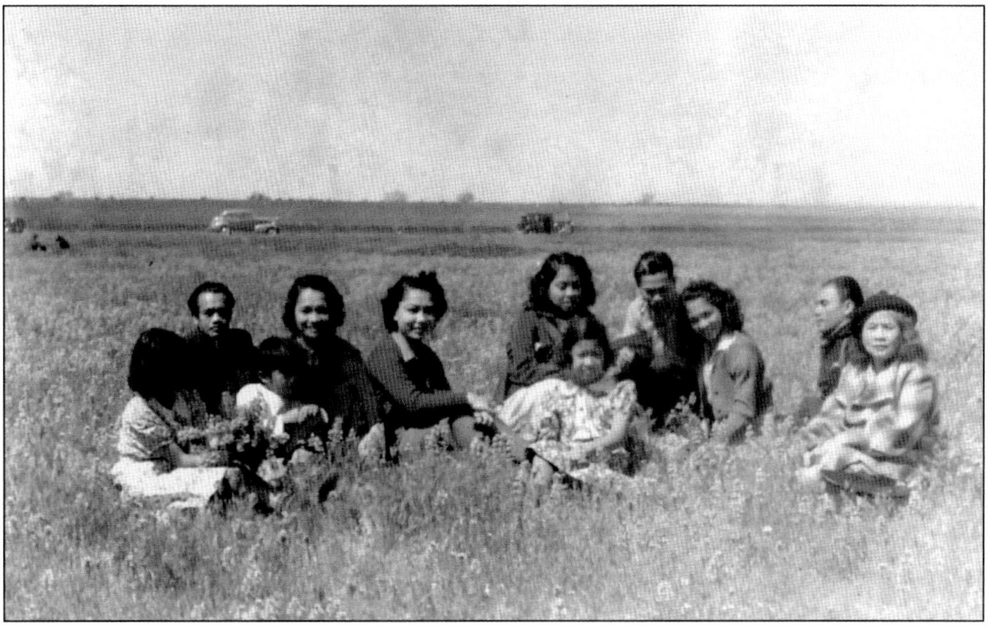

Filipinos originally came to the United States in the 1920s looking for work and greater opportunities. Most Filipinos arrived in northern ports like Seattle or San Francisco, worked as laborers, and followed the crop rotations and seasons, traveling from California to Alaska and back. It was very common that Filipinos arrived in Ventura County by way of Stockton, California, a major Filipino hub for new immigrants at the time. Discrimination was very real and educated Filipinos worked as laborers, houseboys, and cooks because no one would hire them otherwise. Despite being socially excluded from mainstream America, Filipinos organized and created social networks, played sports, established fraternal orders, and nurtured their communities. In Ventura County, they started two homegrown organizations, the Filipino Brotherhood Association of Ventura County in 1928 and the Filipino Community of Ventura County Inc. in 1931. The Tydings McDuffie Act of 1934 changed Filipino immigrant status from US nationals to aliens and limited new entry to only 50 Filipinos per year. At the time, the ratio of Filipino men to women was 14 to 1. Coupled with antimiscegenation laws, most Filipino men married women of Mexican, White, and Native American heritage, resulting in a new generation of mestizos. They put down roots, started families, and contributed to American society in positive ways. Here the Talaugons and relatives enjoy a meadow of wild flowers and California poppies in 1937. (Courtesy of Nora and Federico Talaugon Jr.)

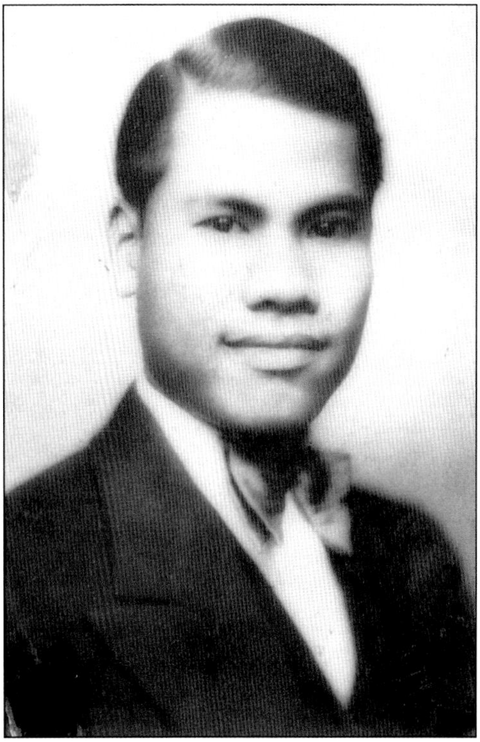

George Omo Sr. was born in 1904 in Balaoan, La Union, Philippines. He immigrated to Kialia Kauia, Territory of Hawaii, and arrived in San Francisco in 1926. In 1929, Omo married Sarah Guitierrez, whom he hired at the Sunshine Café in Los Angeles, and they finally settled in Oxnard in 1932. (Courtesy of Lillian Omo Roman.)

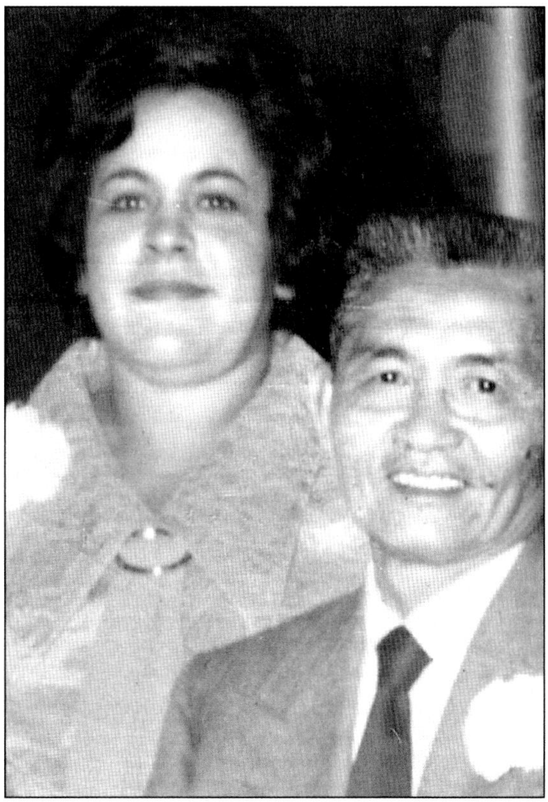

Valinte P. Ines was born in 1912 in the Philippines and decided to come to the United States when he saw a flyer recruiting laborers with the promise of $2 a day. Seven cockfight wins later, Ines won his passage to the United States at age 17 and arrived in San Francisco in 1929. Like many early immigrants, officials altered his last name from "Inis" to "Ines" upon entering the United States. Valinte briefly worked in Stockton before settling in Oxnard in the 1930s. (Courtesy of Vincent Ines and Isidora Ines Vaca.)

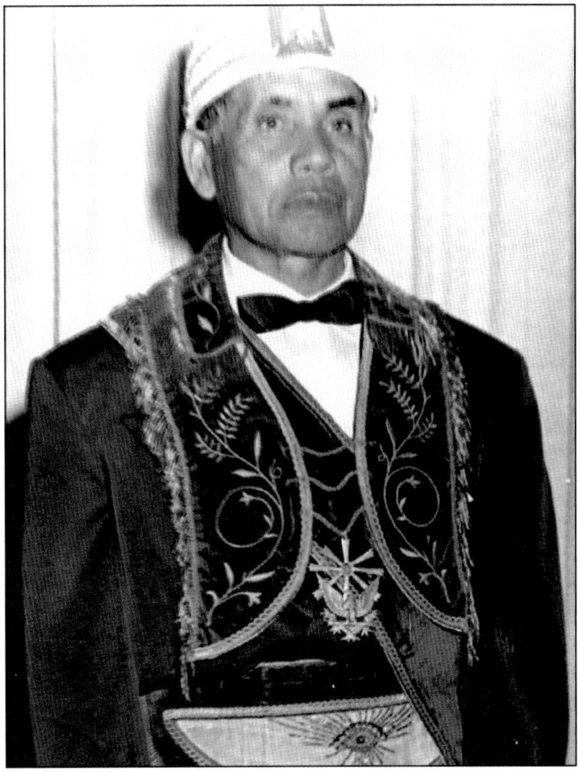

Domingo Dela Rosa, born in 1900 in Ilococos Sur, Philippines, was a former schoolteacher before he arrived in Seattle, Washington, in 1927. Initially working in Alaska before settling in Oxnard in 1928, Dela Rosa was a pioneer, father figure, and advocate for the early Filipinos in Oxnard. Dela Rosa translated, advocated, and intervened on behalf of Filipinos when disputes arose. He was a farm laborer and entrepreneur and owned a dozen businesses in his lifetime, including the Plaza Restaurant at 301 South C Street, Shipside Café in Port Hueneme, a pool hall, a hamburger stand, bars, a barbershop, rental properties, and gift shops, as well as multiple business incarnations at his storefront at 127 Enterprise Street in Oxnard. (Courtesy of Lisa and Domingo Dela Rosa Jr.)

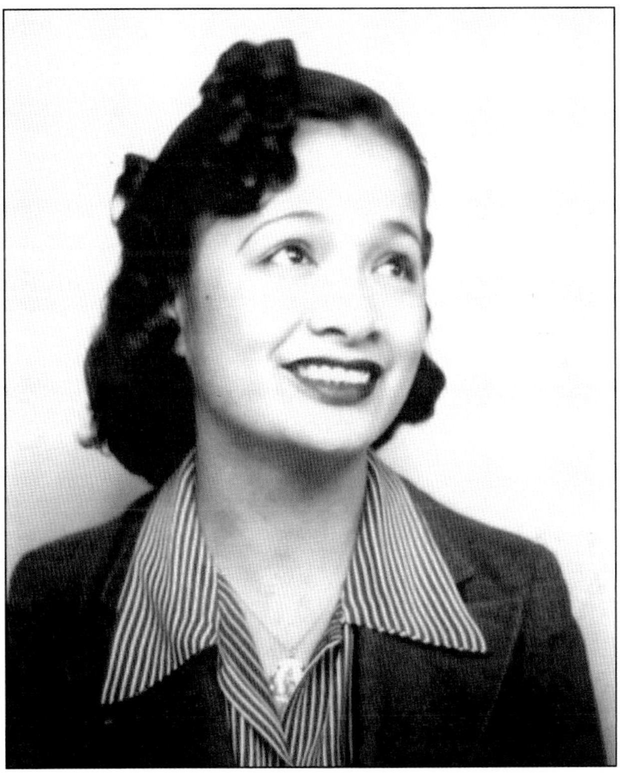

Asuncion Villano (Talaugon Wisco) was born in Cebu City, Cebu, Philippines in 1906 and arrived in San Francisco with her sister Remedios Villano, aunt Fortunata Arandan, and uncle Minico Arandan on board the SS *Hoosier State* in 1922. She was 15 years old. Her family went to Stockton. Later, Asuncion would arrive in Ventura County in the early 1930s. (Courtesy of Nora and Federico Talaugon Jr.)

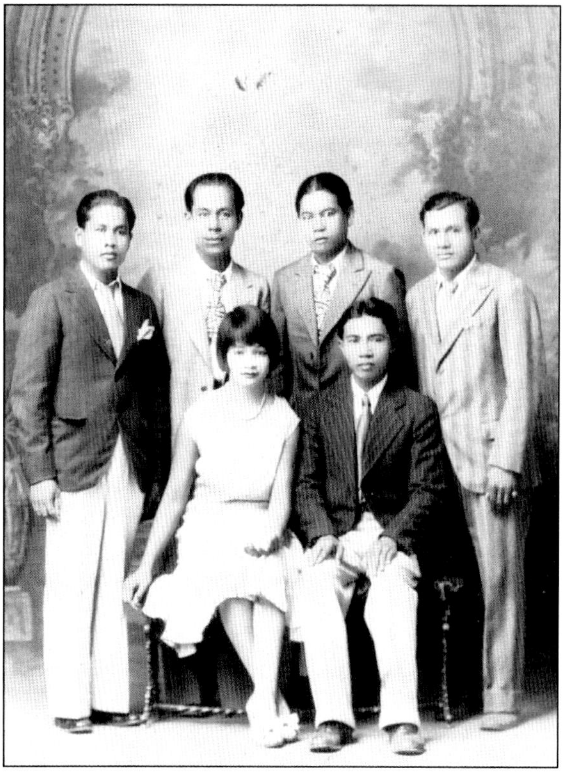

This 1920s photograph shows Asuncion Villano and Federico Talaugon Sr. seated in the first row. Federico Talaugon Sr. was born in 1902 in Tuburan, Cebu, Philippines. He arrived in the United States in 1922 on board the SS *Cleveland*. It is unknown how, when, and where Federico and Asuncion met, but it is possible that they met in Stockton. The Talaugons moved to La Conchita del Mar in the 1930s. (Courtesy of Nora and Federico Talaugon Jr.)

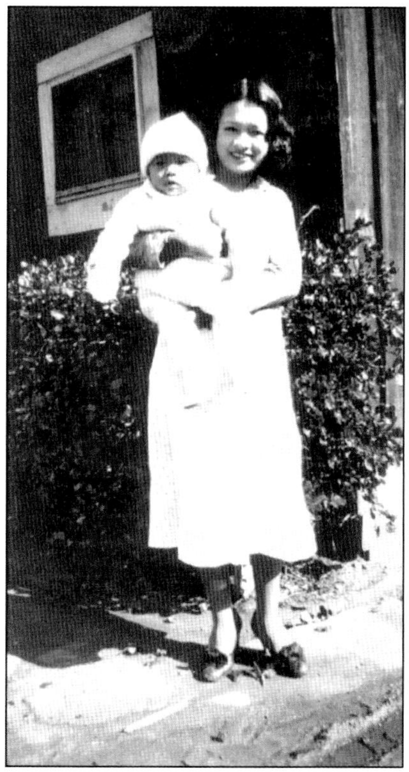

Asuncion Talaugon (Wisco) holds Federico Jr. "Dickie Boy" in front of 55 South Ventura Avenue in Ventura in 1932. (Courtesy of Nora and Federico Talaugon Jr.)

Felipe Ventura was a farm worker in the San Fernando Valley before he settled in Santa Paula. Here he became a foreman at Briggs Lemon Association, which was owned by Sunkist. First only managing Filipinos, Felipe also began managing *braceros* (contracted laborers from Mexico) after World War II. Pictured in 1936, Ventura family members include, from left to right, Trinidad Ventura, Nora Ventura, Phil Ventura, and Felipe Ventura. (Courtesy of Nora and Federico Talaugon Jr.)

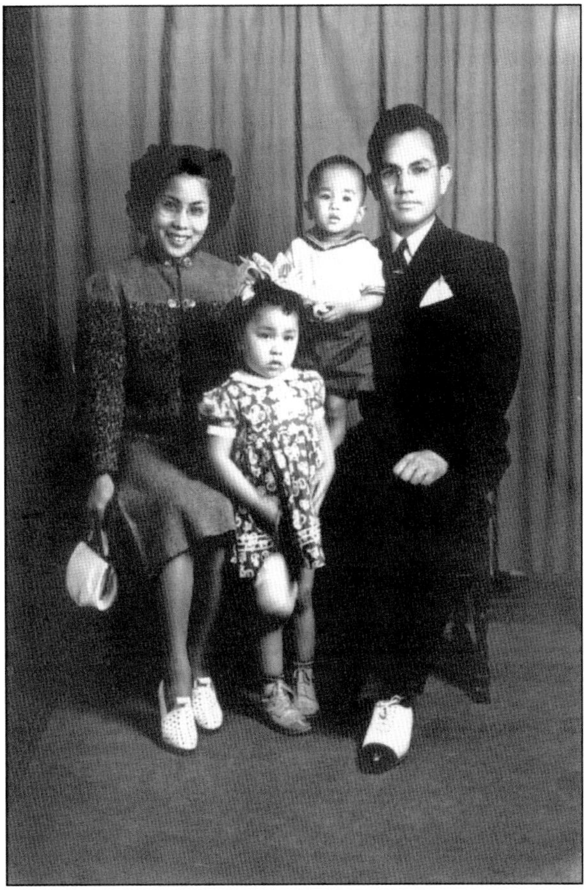

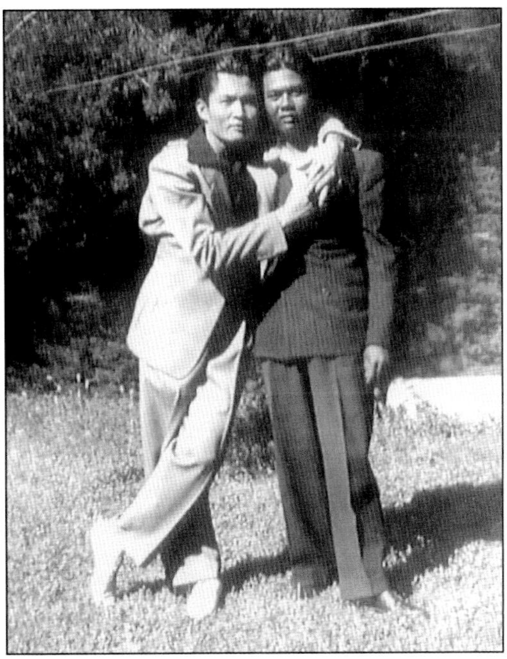

Valinte Ines and Leon Ines pose in their suits at the Springville Ranch in the 1930s. Valinte and Leon were farm laborers at Springville, which was located on Las Posas and Pleasant Valley Roads in Camarillo. (Courtesy of Vincent Ines and Isidora Ines Vaca.)

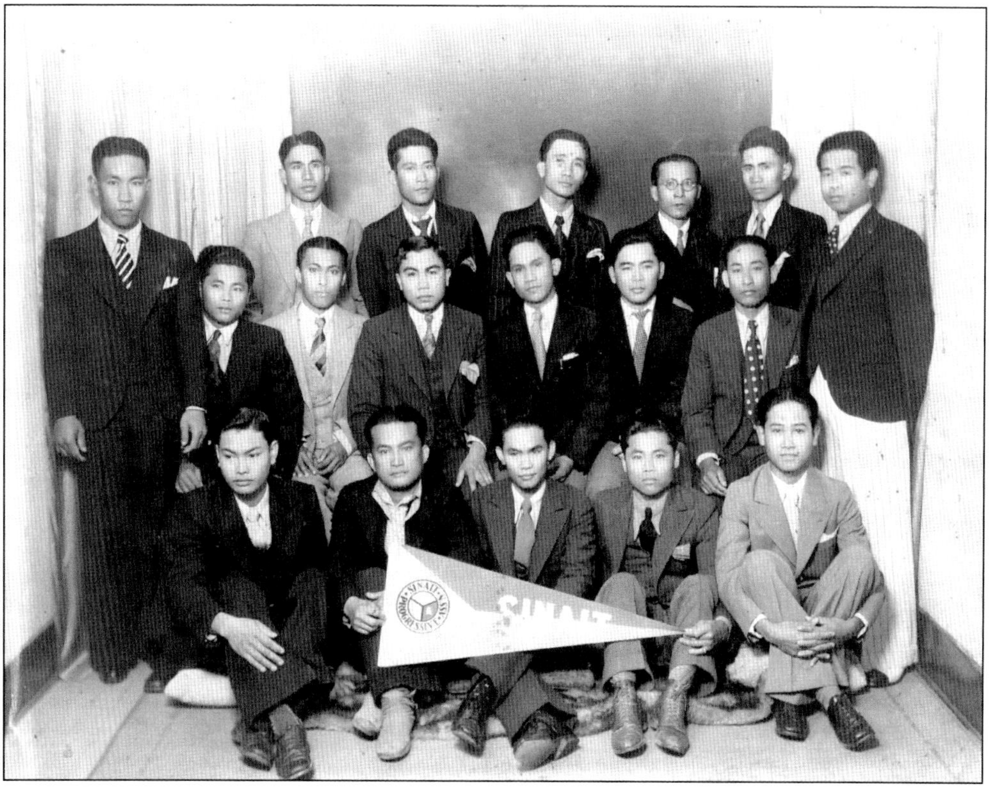

Young Filipinos pose for a Sinait Progressive Association group shot in the 1930s. Identified on the far right is Fred Sotelo. (Courtesy of Lillian Omo Roman.)

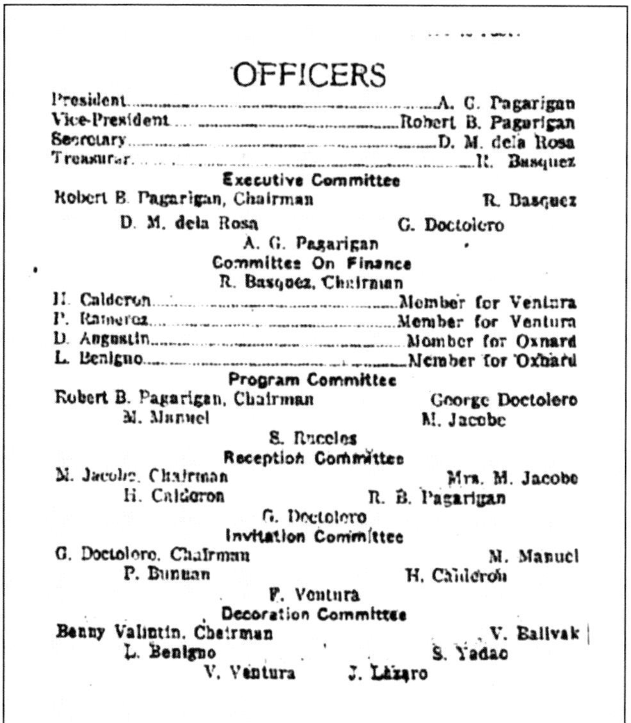

OFFICERS

President .... A. G. Pagarigan
Vice-President .... Robert B. Pagarigan
Secretary .... D. M. dela Rosa
Treasurer .... R. Basquez

Executive Committee

Robert B. Pagarigan, Chairman — R. Basquez
D. M. dela Rosa — G. Doctolero
A. G. Pagarigan

Committee On Finance

R. Basquez, Chairman
H. Calderon .... Member for Ventura
P. Ramerez .... Member for Ventura
D. Angustin .... Member for Oxnard
L. Benigno .... Member for Oxnard

Program Committee

Robert B. Pagarigan, Chairman — George Doctolero
M. Manuel — M. Jacobe
S. Ruccles

Reception Committee

M. Jacobe, Chairman — Mrs. M. Jacobe
H. Calderon — R. B. Pagarigan
G. Doctolero

Invitation Committee

G. Doctolero, Chairman — M. Manuel
P. Bunuan — H. Childeron
F. Ventura

Decoration Committee

Benny Valintin, Chairman — V. Balivak
L. Benigno — S. Yadao
V. Ventura — J. Lázaro

The *Oxnard Daily Courier*, dated Friday December 30, 1927, reports the Filipino Brotherhood Association of Ventura County hosted an event to commemorate the 31st anniversary of the death of Dr. Jose Rizal, the national hero of the Philippines. It was stated that over 150 Filipinos were in attendance. The evening's program included George Doctolero's biography of Rizal and steel guitar performances by Domingo Dela Rosa and Mariano Unciano. Listed are the officers and committee members.

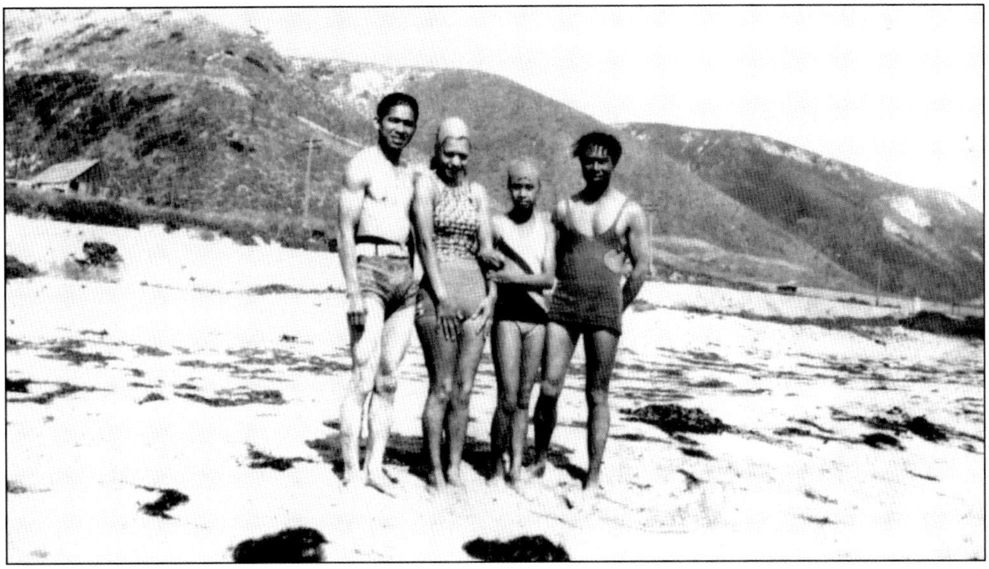

Four friends are pictured in the 1930s at Faria Beach, located just south of La Conchita del Mar. From left to right are Kading Jacobe, mechanic for Buick in Ventura; two unidentified ladies; and Severo Talaugon, laborer and farmer who leased land on the Gaynor Ranch with his brothers Federico Sr., Andres, and Paulino. Passenger list records indicate that Severo Talaugon sailed from Honolulu, Territory of Hawaii, to San Pedro in 1925 on the SS *Utacarbon*. (Courtesy of Tony Baker.)

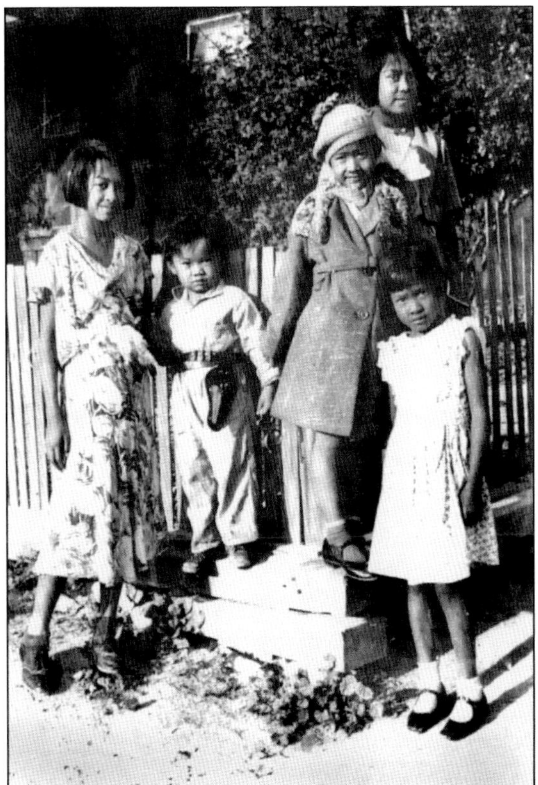

Like many children in La Conchita in the 1930s, the Talaugons and family relatives attended the Punta Gorda School, a one-room schoolhouse that was utilized from 1883 to 1941. From left to right are Gloria Talaugon, Federico Talaugon Jr., Marcy Jacobe (hat), Pacita Montayre (behind), and Tawa Montayre. (Courtesy of Tawa Desaucido.)

THE CHAMPIONS

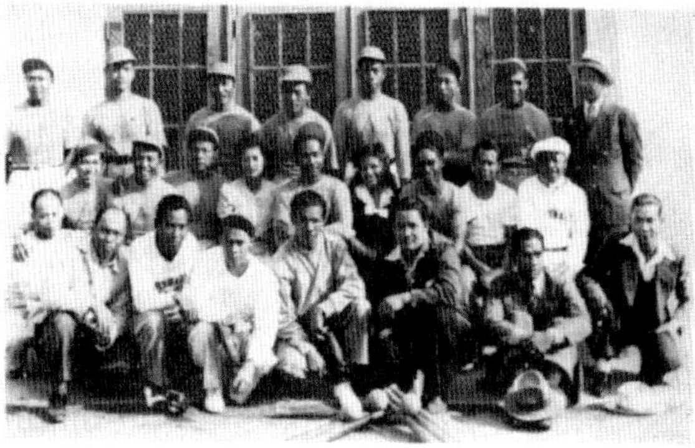

LEGIONARIOS DEL TRABAJO TEAM
(Represented by the Wor.'. JORDAN Lodge 604, Oxnard)

Front row, l to r: George Lapastora, team treasurer; Mariano M. Mendoza, assistant coach; George P. Rebudos, manager; Johnny Lamatao, co-captain; Amado E. Dino, social chairman and co-manager; Paul Garcia, assistant manager; Jose Loreto; Mamerto S. Miguel. Middle row: Melquiades Jacobe, 1b. and star home-runner; Feding Talaugan, p(4); Zacarias Lazaro, 3b; Zoraida Loreto; Pete Tagayuna, c and captain; Virginia Parong; Cayetano Raciles, lf; Larry S. Santos; Juan Gulmayo, coach and co-catcher. Rear row: Lolong Talaugan, p(2); Paul Almirol, p(1); Fred Talaugan, sub-catcher; Epifanio Sinfuego. ss; Cenon Guanzon, 2b; Eustaquio Duldulao, cf; Julian Simon, p(3); Raymond Basquez.

GOOD LOSERS

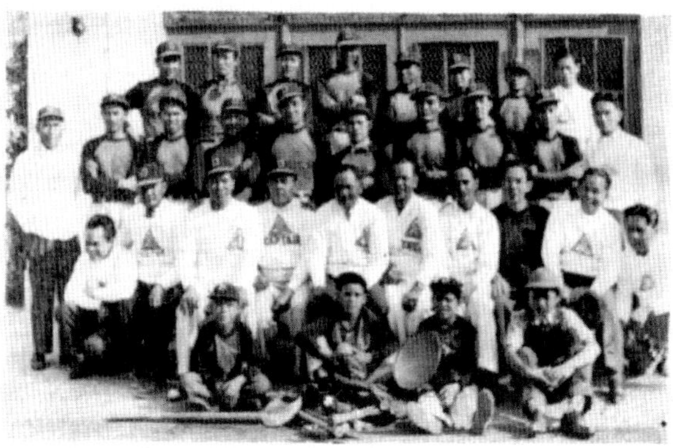

CABALLEROS DE DIMAS-ALANG TEAM

Front row, l to r: T. Magdaluyo; Eustaquio J. Amplayo; Severino Moya, coach; Agapito R. Flores, captain; Felipe Inocencio, Grand Master; Parin P. Colombo, social chairman and manager; Lamberto Malinab, Grand Secretary; Dr. J. M. David-Malig, assistant manager; Pete Guzman; Juan Razonable. Second row: P. Calmarin, assistant coach; Vicente Vito,c; Benny Inocencio, cf; Dionisio Cruz, 2b; Monico Gonzales, p and captain; Eddie Caballero, c; Natalio Panimdim, p; Ciriaco "George" Sabolbora, 1b; Dick Santiago, p; George Raymundo. Rear row: Jimmy Reynoso, lf; Mario Encarnacion, rf; Amado Aurora, 3b; Panilo "Blackie" Libre, ss; Quintin Monces, rf; Luis Tupaz, 1b; M. Calos, cf; R. Cardinales. Mascots: Vincent Vito, Moning Gonzales, Danny Cartagena, Davey Malig.

— 166 —

This image was taken from the *Legionarios Del Trabajo Blue Book*, summer of 1949 issue. It depicts the winning team with an accompanying article on the baseball series and championship game between the Jordan Lodge 604 Legionarios Del Trabajo (LDT) and the Caballeros De Dimas-Alang. The LDT team is composed mostly of laborers from Oxnard. (Courtesy of the Eloisa Gomez Borah Research Collection.)

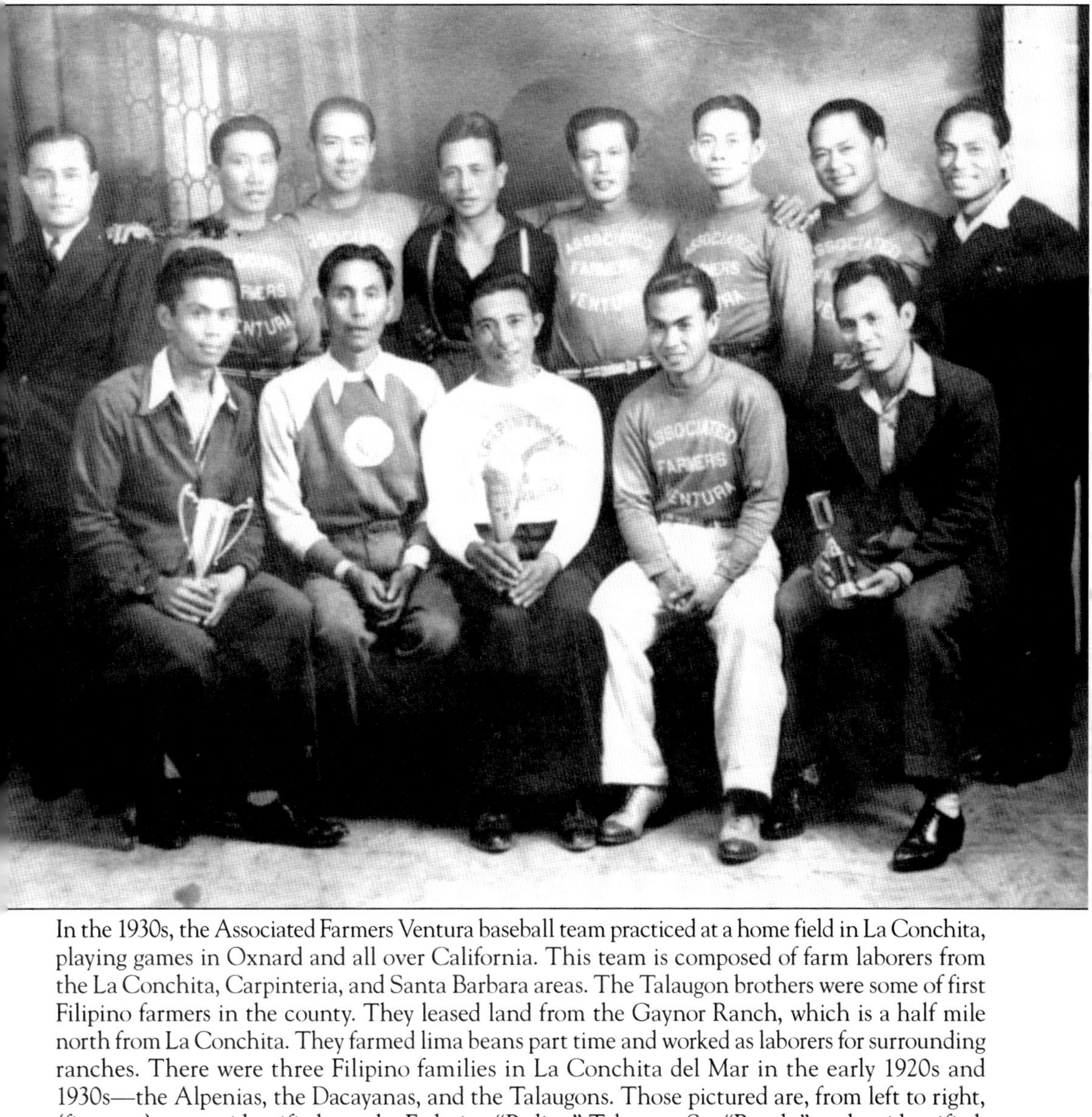

In the 1930s, the Associated Farmers Ventura baseball team practiced at a home field in La Conchita, playing games in Oxnard and all over California. This team is composed of farm laborers from the La Conchita, Carpinteria, and Santa Barbara areas. The Talaugon brothers were some of first Filipino farmers in the county. They leased land from the Gaynor Ranch, which is a half mile north from La Conchita. They farmed lima beans part time and worked as laborers for surrounding ranches. There were three Filipino families in La Conchita del Mar in the early 1920s and 1930s—the Alpenias, the Dacayanas, and the Talaugons. Those pictured are, from left to right, (first row) two unidentified people, Federico "Peding" Talaugon Sr., "Bundy," and unidentified; (second row) unidentified, Paulino "Nenong" Talaugon, Severo "Lu-long" Talaugon, unidentified, Venancio Dacayana, unidentified, Lauriano "Aloy" Alpenia, and unidentified. (Courtesy of Nora and Federico Talaugon Jr.)

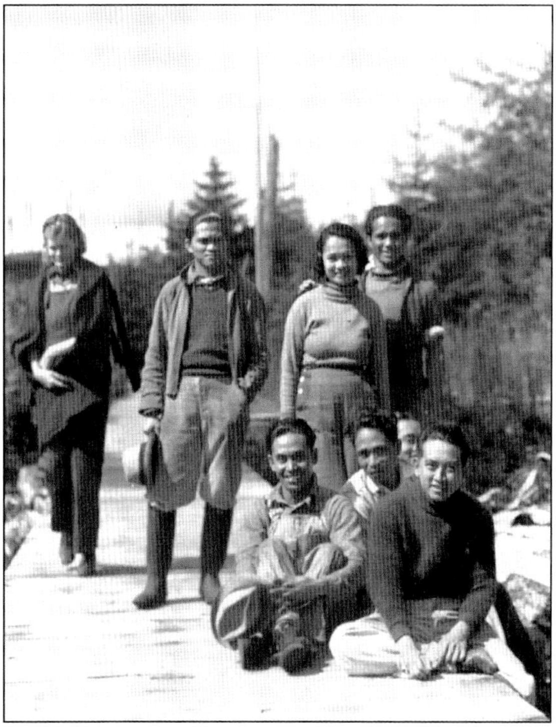

Like many Filipinos since the 1920s, the Talaugons traveled from California to Alaska to work in the fisheries and canneries from 1935 to 1936. After working for a year, the gang at Beele Packing Company wished Asuncion Talaugon (center) "boundless happiness and luck" on her journey back to Ventura County. (Courtesy of Nora and Federico Talaugon Jr.)

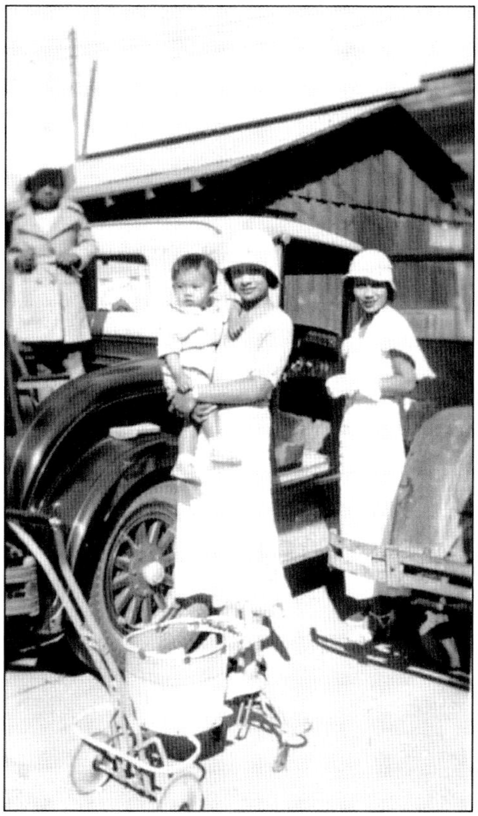

Asuncion Talaugon (Wisco) holds baby Dickie around 1932 in Ventura, California. Despite humble wages, Filipino men and women were so fashionable that one never would have guessed that they labored in the fields. (Courtesy of Nora and Federico Talaugon Jr.)

The Talaugons departed Ketchikan, Alaska, aboard the SS *Victoria* and were bound for Seattle, Washington, with plans to return to La Conchita del Mar in Ventura County. Taken on September 15, 1936, this picture shows Federico Talaugon Sr. and Jr. (Courtesy of Nora and Federico Talaugon Jr.)

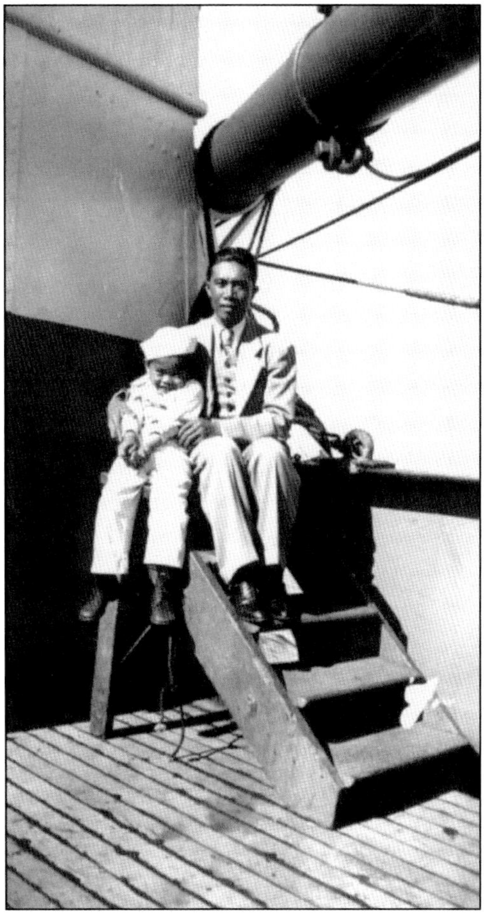

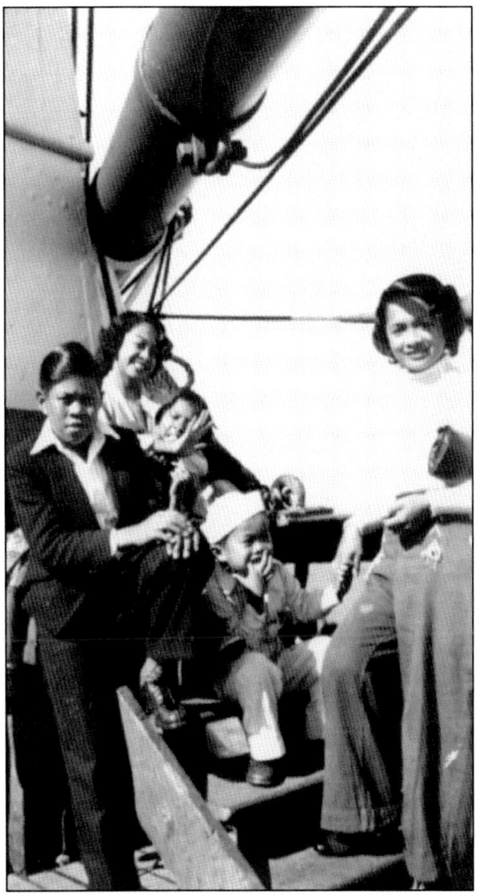

Gloria Talaugon, Marcy Jacobe, Federico Jr. (sailor hat), and Asuncion Talaugon are pictured on board the SS *Victoria* in 1936 heading for California. Similar to the crop rotations of fields in the Central Coast and Central Valley, work in the Alaskan fisheries and canneries were also seasonal and required families to migrate. (Courtesy of Nora and Federico Talaugon Jr.)

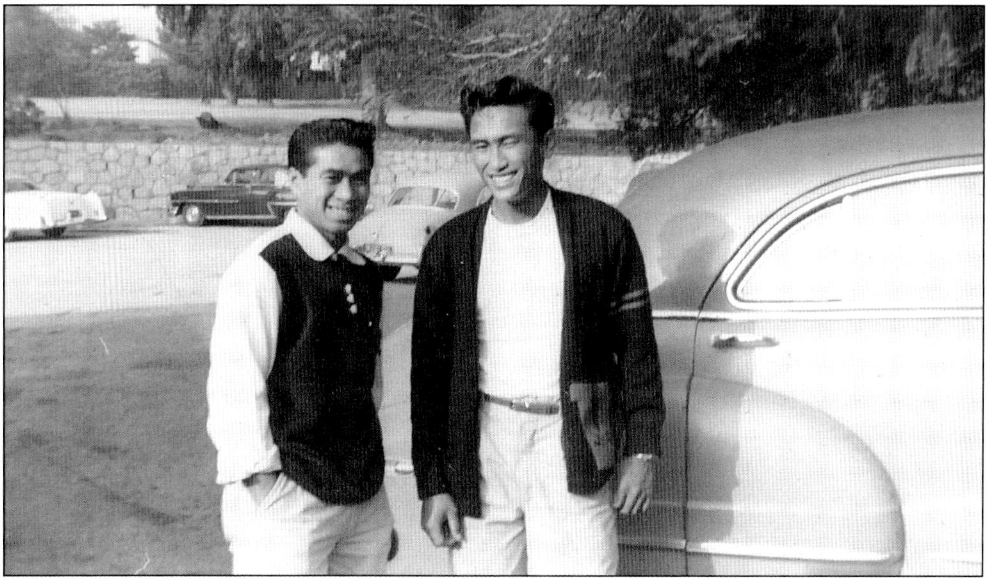

In 1952, teenagers residing in La Conchita del Mar, such as Bobby Decayana and Jack Alpenia, attended Ventura High School. Due to La Conchita's unique location, students typically rode the train to attend high school in Ventura. Bobby's parents, Venancio and Pelagia Dacayana, and Jack's parents, Lauriano and Paulina Alpenia settled in La Conchita in the early 1930s. (Courtesy of Tony Baker.)

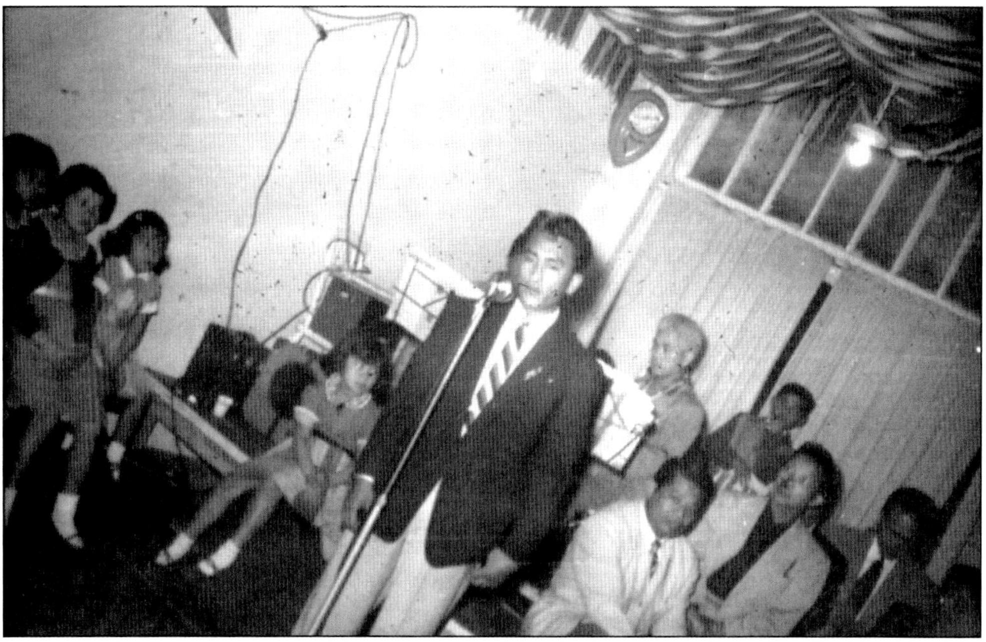

With bandleader Demo Sancha in the background, Jack Alpenia sings at the Filipino Youth Club in 1954. Many Filipinos in La Conchita attended functions with the Santa Barbara Filipino community because of the proximity and because they worked at the same agricultural farming areas of La Conchita, Carpinteria, and Santa Barbara. The Filipino Youth Club was a Santa Barbara organization that held dances and socials. Filipinos also traveled as far as Santa Maria and Guadalupe for family festivities, gambling, and recreation. (Courtesy of Tony Baker.)

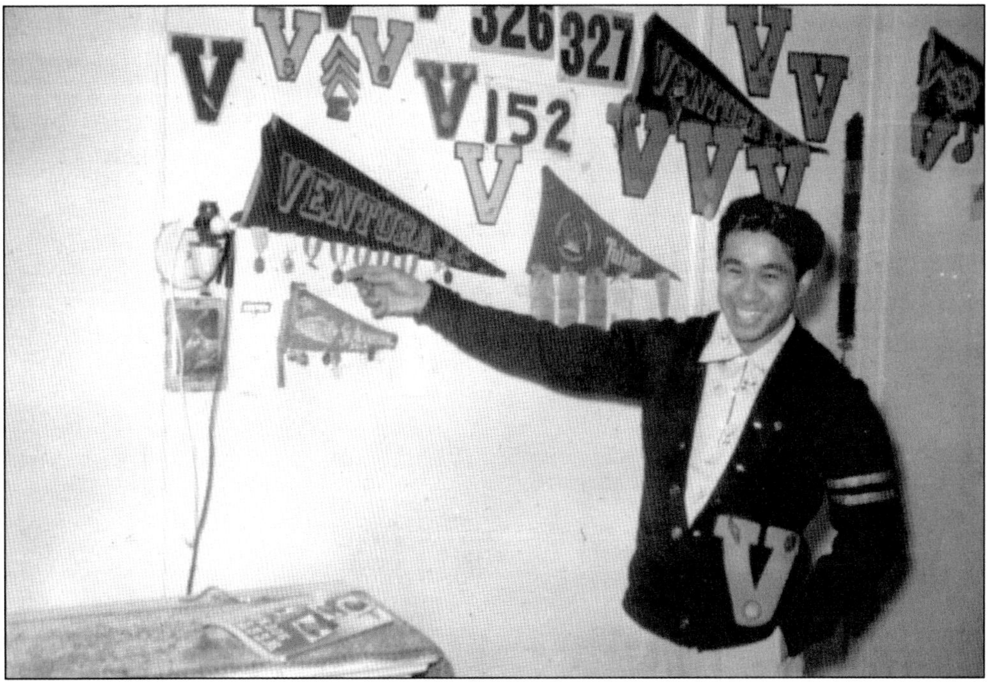

Bobby Dacayana shows off his Ventura High pride in 1954. Bobby's father, Venancio Decayana, was 22 when he arrived in the Territory of Hawaii on board the SS *Ecuador* in 1920. He worked as a laborer in the sugar cane plantations. Venancio met Pelagia Putane in Hawaii, and they married in the 1920s then settled in La Conchita in the 1930s. (Courtesy of Tony Baker.)

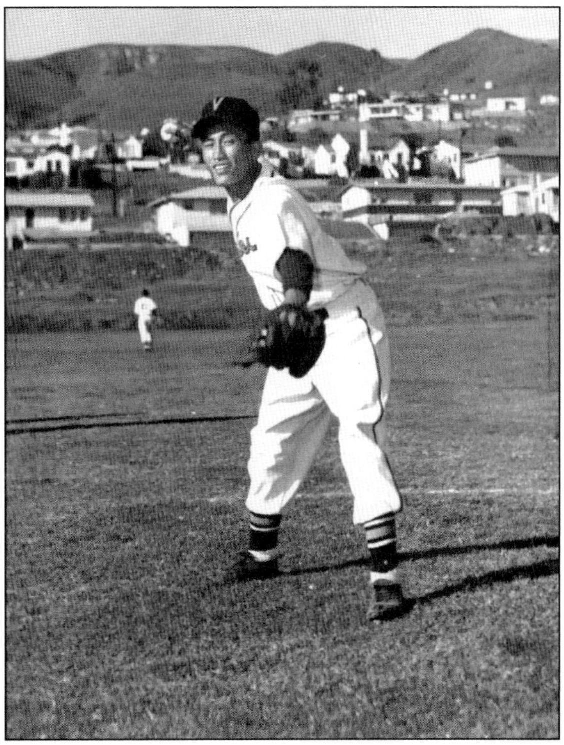

Jack "Strap" Alpenia poses in his Ventura Junior College baseball uniform in 1951. The Alpenias and Talaugons are relatives; in particular, Jack and Dick (Frederico Jr.) are cousins who grew up together. After Dick's parents separated, Dick Talaugon moved with his mom to Long Beach but he always spent his summers with his dad in La Conchita. (Courtesy of Tony Baker.)

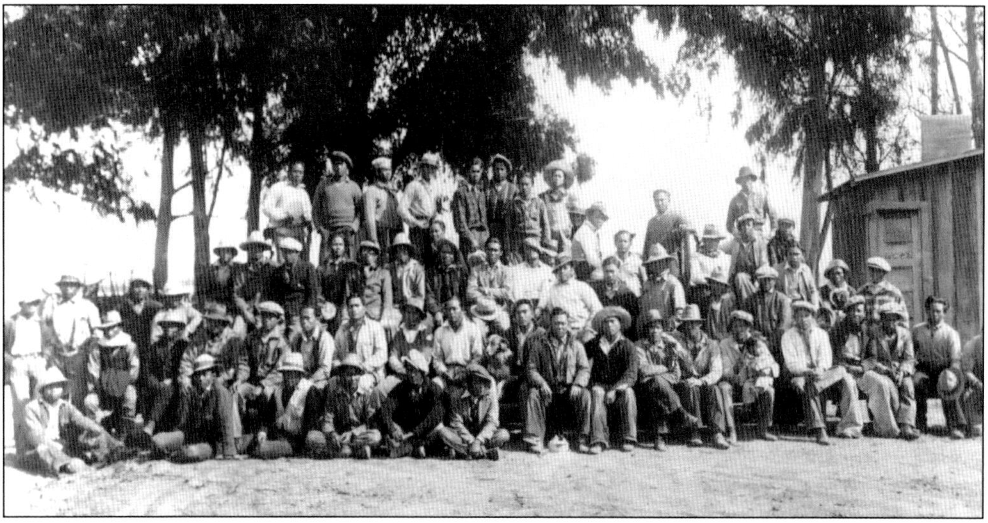

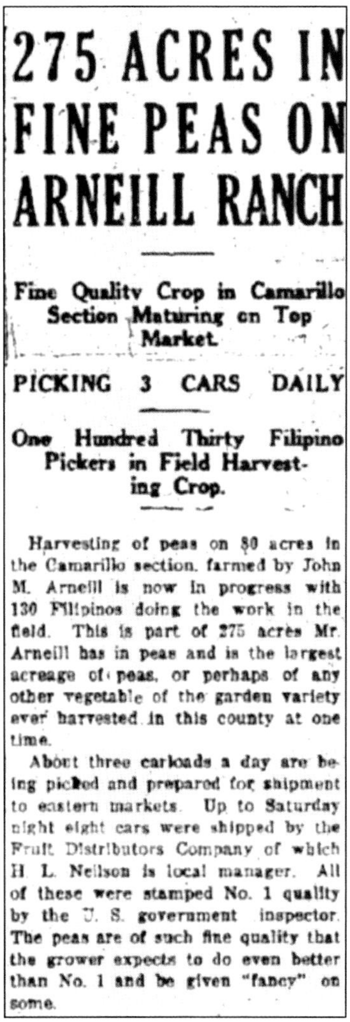

275 ACRES IN FINE PEAS ON ARNEILL RANCH

Fine Quality Crop in Camarillo Section Maturing on Top Market

PICKING 3 CARS DAILY

One Hundred Thirty Filipino Pickers in Field Harvesting Crop.

Harvesting of peas on 80 acres in the Camarillo section, farmed by John M. Arneill is now in progress with 130 Filipinos doing the work in the field. This is part of 275 acres Mr. Arneill has in peas and is the largest acreage of peas, or perhaps of any other vegetable of the garden variety ever harvested in this county at one time.

About three carloads a day are being picked and prepared for shipment to eastern markets. Up to Saturday night eight cars were shipped by the Fruit Distributors Company of which H. L. Neilson is local manager. All of these were stamped No. 1 quality by the U. S. government inspector. The peas are of such fine quality that the grower expects to do even better than No. 1 and be given "fancy" on some.

The *Oxnard Daily Courier*, dated January 7, 1929, reported that 130 Filipinos harvested peas at the Arneill Ranch in Camarillo. Lima beans, walnuts, lemons, and oranges were also grown at the ranch. Filipinos worked the fields and lived at the labor camp on the ranch. According to Arneill Ranch Superintendent Frank Daily's pay ledgers for 1937–1938, a 12-hour day shift driving a CAT (Caterpillar tractor) paid $3.50, and a 12-hour night shift driving a CAT paid $5. Sunday afternoons at the camp included picnics (roasted pig or goat) and cockfighting, which drew the occasional police raid. Stanley Daily, mayor emeritus of Camarillo, grew up on the Arneill Ranch in the 1930s and 1940s and fondly remembers in particular Yoro, Ted, and Phillip, who taught him Filipino dances and the skills needed to drive a tractor. Also, they made lovely kites for his sister Jean.

Two

Establishing Roots

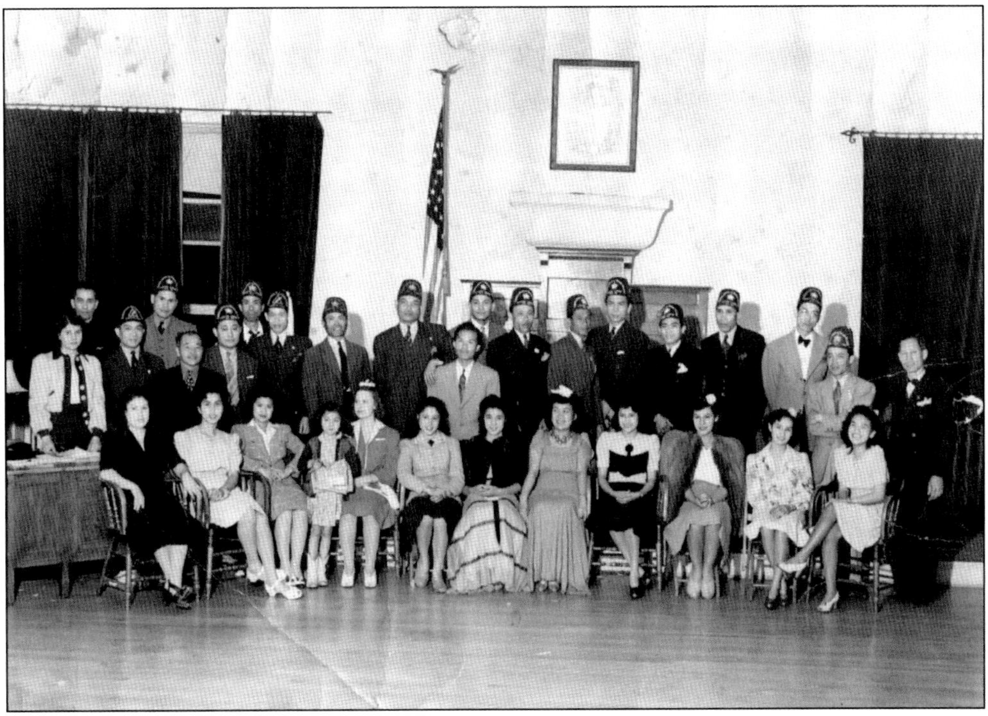

The 1940s and 1950s saw an explosion of social activity and families in the Filipino community. Association membership was high and community involvement included the neighboring counties of Los Angeles and Santa Barbara. Antimiscegenation laws were repealed in 1948, and interracial couples were now allowed to marry in California. The Luce-Cellar Act of 1946 also gave Filipinos the right to naturalize and become citizens. They were now able to purchase homes and own property. Business entrepreneurship was also significant, as families who labored in fields were now business owners. The War Brides Act of 1945 enabled servicemen to marry and bring home their spouses and adopted children. In Ventura, three of the big four Filipino fraternal organizations were represented and flourishing, Jordan Lodge 604 Legionarios Del Trabajo, Caballeros de Dimas-Alang, and the Filipino Federation of America. In 1955, the Filipino Community of Ventura County incorporated, and members actively engaged in fundraising to purchase their own building. Also, after World War II, there were three military bases in the county that contributed to the influx of families and a military workforce, Port Hueneme, Point Mugu, and Camarillo. Shown are the Caballeros de Dimas-Alang at a community social. (Courtesy of Lillian Omo Roman.)

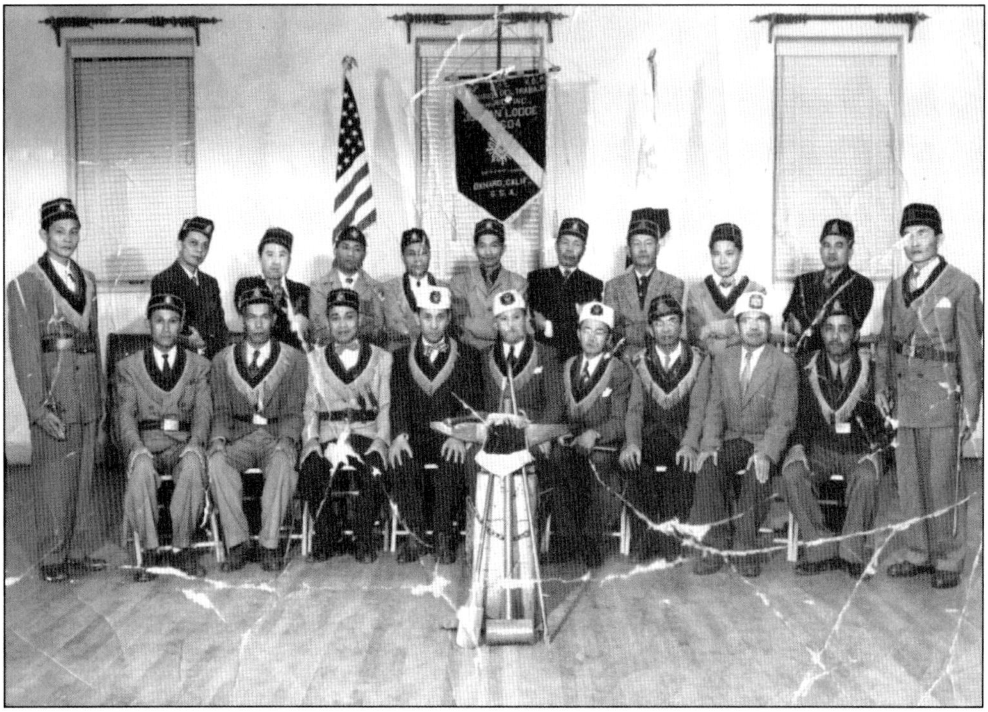

The Legionarios del Trabajo is a fraternal order founded in the United States in the early 1920s. The Jordan Lodge 604 Legionarios del Trabajo in Oxnard was established in 1937. The 1949 leadership included Fred M. Estavillo, the worshipful master; George C. Doctolero, the venerable secretary; and Antonio Estilery, the venerable treasurer. Standing on the far right is Valinte Ines. (Courtesy of Vincent Ines and Isidora Ines Vaca.)

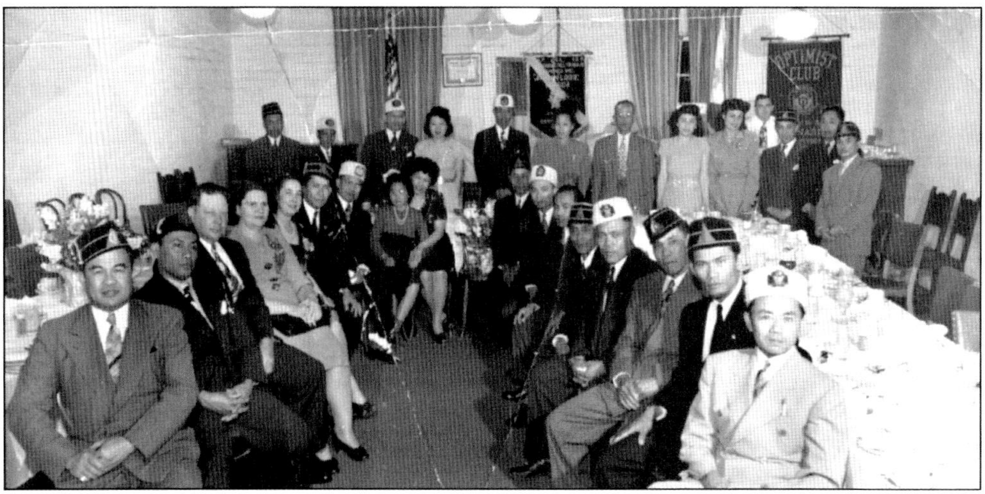

The Filipino Optimist Club pose for a group shot in the 1940s in Oxnard. Those standing are, from left to right, Nick Kote, Domingo Dela Rosa, three unidentified people, Trinidad Ventura, Felipe Ventura, Agnes Doctolero, Laura Yabes, unidentified, George Doctolero, Joe Yabes, and Valinte Ines. Those sitting on the left side are, from left to right, seven unidentified people, Cathy Omo, and Bening Omo. Those sitting on the right side are, from right to left, Tony Estilery, unidentified, Julian Simon, and five unidentified people. (Courtesy of Vincent Ines and Isidora Ines Vaca.)

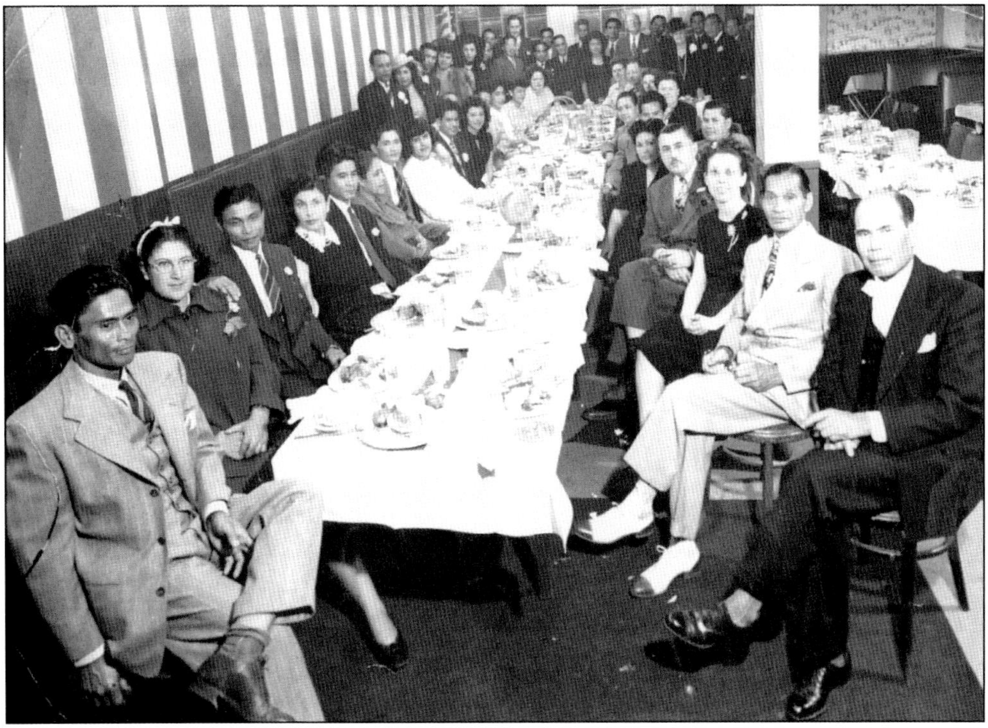

Filipinos celebrate Philippine Independence on July 4, 1948, at the Tom Tom Café in Oxnard. Those pictured sitting on the left side of the table are, from front to back, five unidentified people, Margarita Rodriguez, Valinte Ines, Mary Rodriguez, George Omo Jr., Carmen Omo, two unidentified people, Lillian Omo, Linda Franco, Domingo Dela Rosa, unidentified, and Virginia Salinas. Those pictured sitting on the right side of the table are, from front to back, Julian Simon, three unidentified people, Sarah Omo, George Omo Sr., and six unidentified people. (Courtesy of Vincent Ines and Isidora Ines Vaca.)

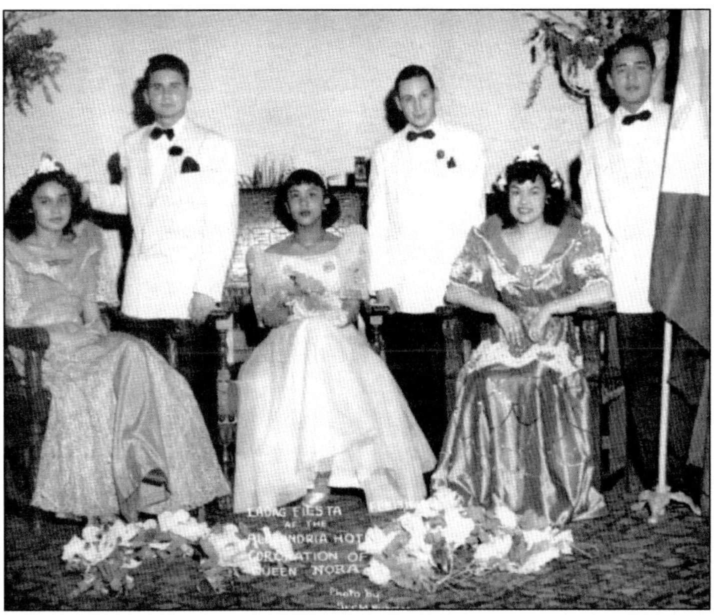

Queen Nora Ventura (Talaugon) and her entourage, Doris Yabes on the left and Lillian Omo on the right, celebrate the Laoag Fiesta at the Alexandria Hotel in Los Angeles on February 13, 1949. Nora Ventura grew up in Santa Paula and graduated from Santa Paula High School, Lillian Omo was from Oxnard and graduated from Union High School, and Doris Yabes lived in Oxnard. (Courtesy of Lillian Omo Roman.)

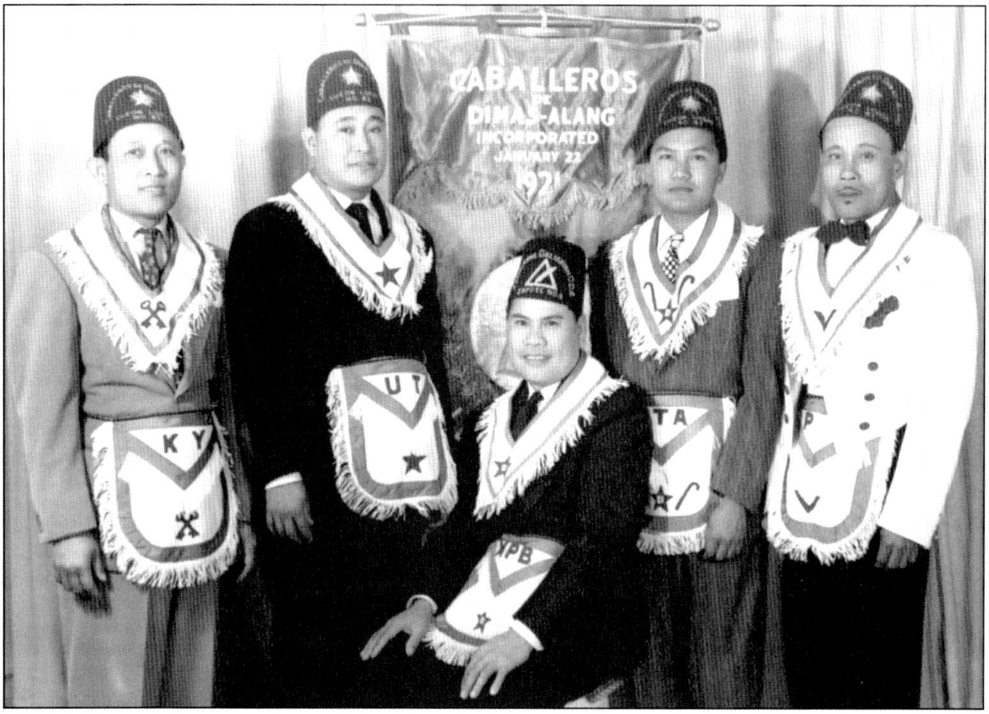

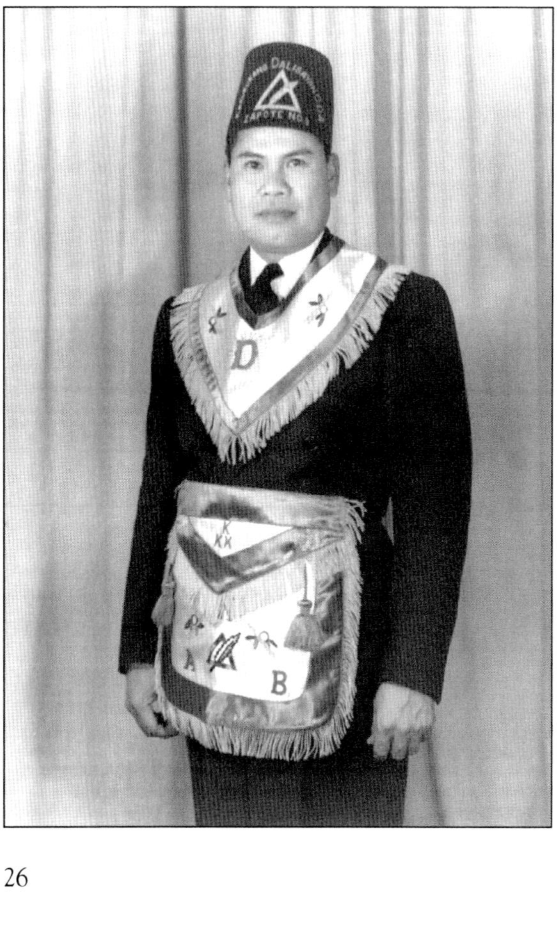

The Caballeros de Dimas-Alang was founded in 1921 and considered one of the big four Filipino fraternal organizations, along with the Legionarios Del Trabajo, Filipino Federation of America, and Gran Oriente Filipino. The second and third gentlemen from left are Joe Yabes and George Omo Sr. (Courtesy of Lillian Omo Roman.)

George Omo Sr. poses in his Caballeros de Dimas-Alang regalia in the 1930s. (Courtesy of Lillian Omo Roman.)

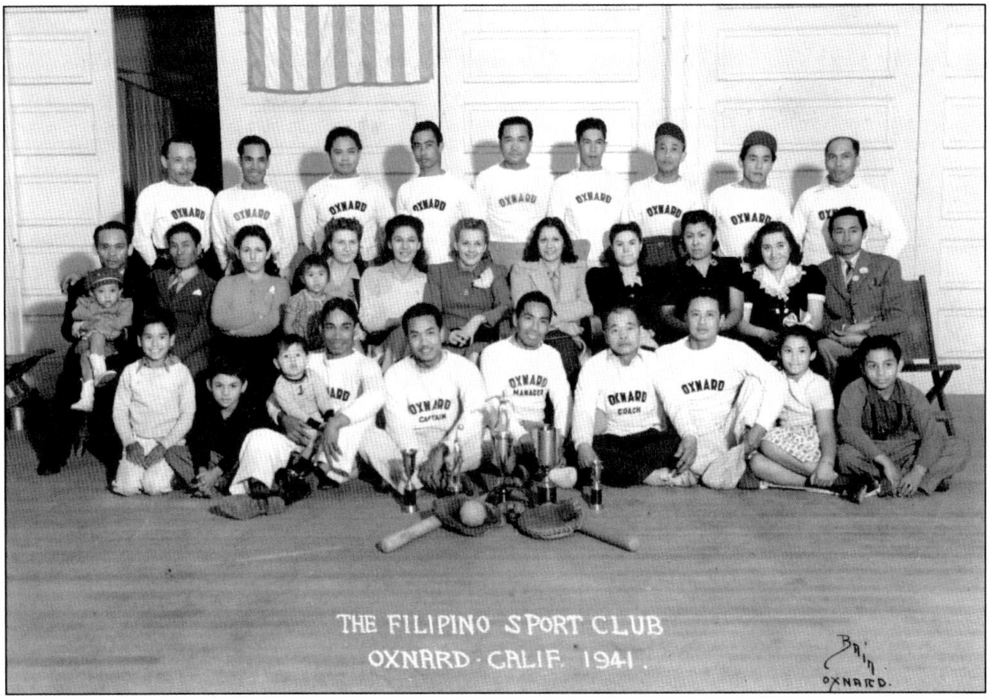

The Filipino Sport Club of Oxnard poses in 1941 with their trophies and softball gear. Identified in the first row and on the far left is George Omo Jr. In the second row and forth from the right is Frances Ilar, and third from the right is Sally Larizabal. (Courtesy of Lillian Omo Roman.)

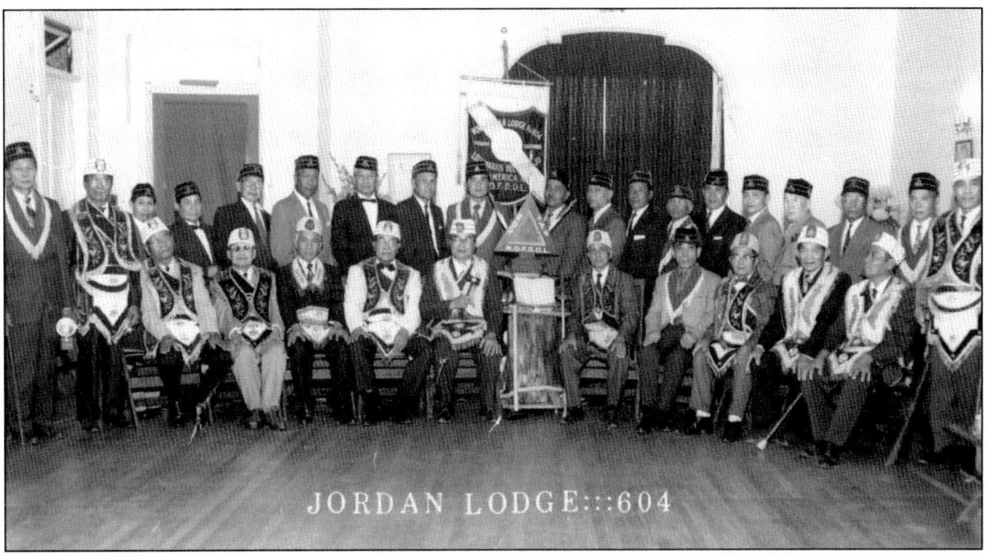

The Jordan Lodge 604 Legionarios del Trabajo owned a building at 737 West Sixth Street where they held meetings and offered space to other community groups until it was sold in the 1980s. Pictured from left to right are (first row) unidentified, Aquilino Bagay, George Doctolero, two unidentified people, Domingo Dela Rosa, Augie Castaneda Sr., Tony Estilery, unidentified, and Albert Sindayin; (second row) three unidentified people, Monico Olivares, three unidentified people, Ricky Ilar, two unidentified people, Silver Ines, three unidentified people, Valinte Ines, and Julian Simon. (Courtesy of Vincent Ines and Isidora Ines Vaca.)

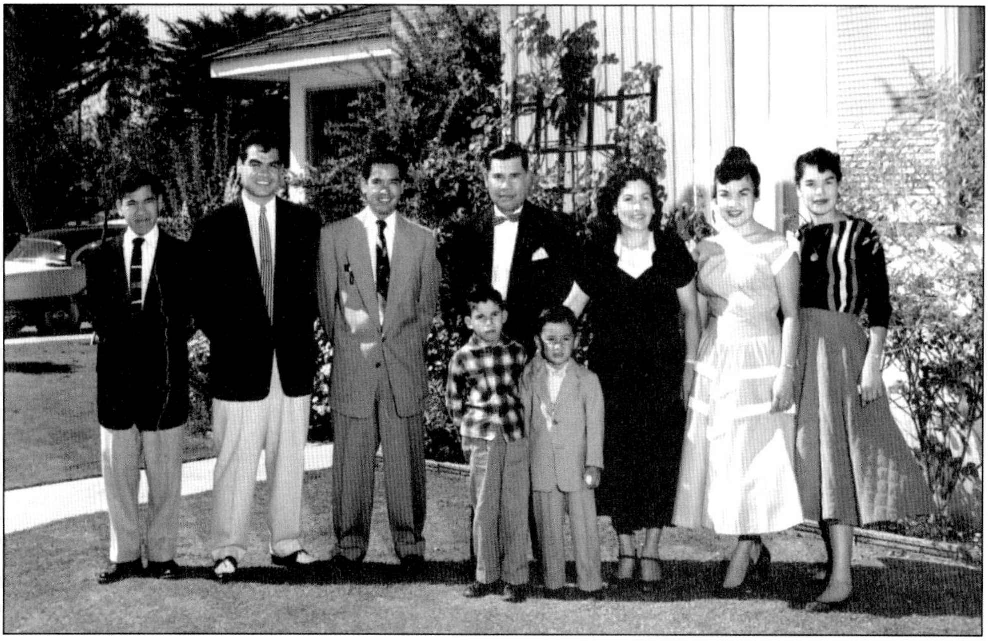

This Omo family portrait was taken in the 1950s in front of the Omo home at 1447 Beverly Drive in Oxnard. This was the third and final residence of George Sr. and Sarah. Prior to Beverly Drive, they lived on Hayes Avenue and later on Colonia Road. The adults are, from left to right, Larry Omo, James Omo, George Omo Jr., George Omo Sr., Sarah Omo, Lillian Omo Roman, and Christina Omo. The youngest two of the family are, from left to right, Vincent Omo and Manuel Omo. (Courtesy of Lillian Omo Roman.)

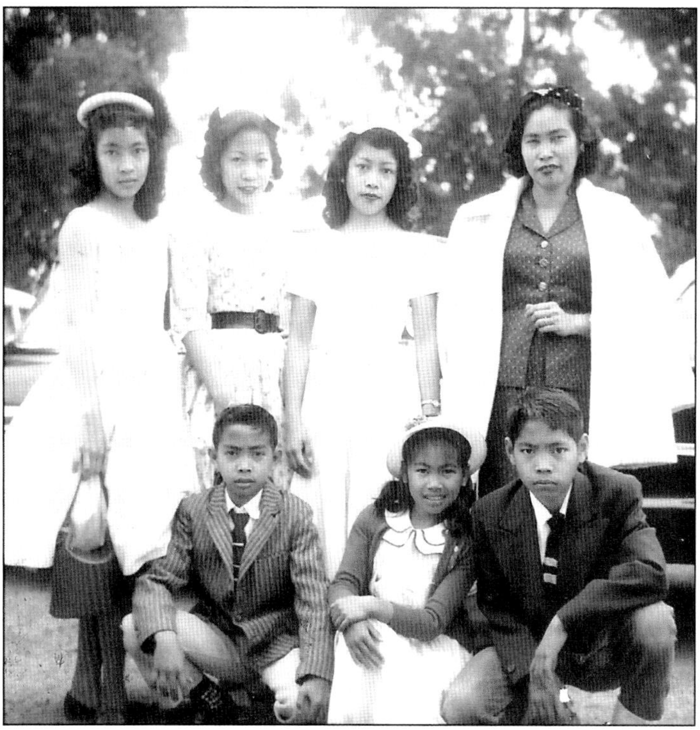

In 1959, the Castaneda family at Sunday church in the Hamoja Housing complex, located inside the Naval Center Port Hueneme. Pictured from left to right are (first row) Augie Castaneda Jr., Virgie Castaneda, and Albert Castaneda; (second row) Josie Castaneda, Millie Castaneda, Edith Castaneda, and Belen Castaneda. (Courtesy of Augie Castaneda Jr.)

The Castanedas grew up at 660 Tamarac Street in Oxnard and were neighbors with the Dela Rosa family. This picture shows the children on the front yard at home with Augie Castaneda Sr.'s 1957 Chevy in the background. Pictured from left to right are (first row) Albert Castaneda and Valentine Dela Rosa; (second row) Augie Castaneda Jr., Millie Castaneda, Josie Castaneda, Edith Castaneda, and Virgie Castaneda. (Courtesy of Augie Castaneda Jr.)

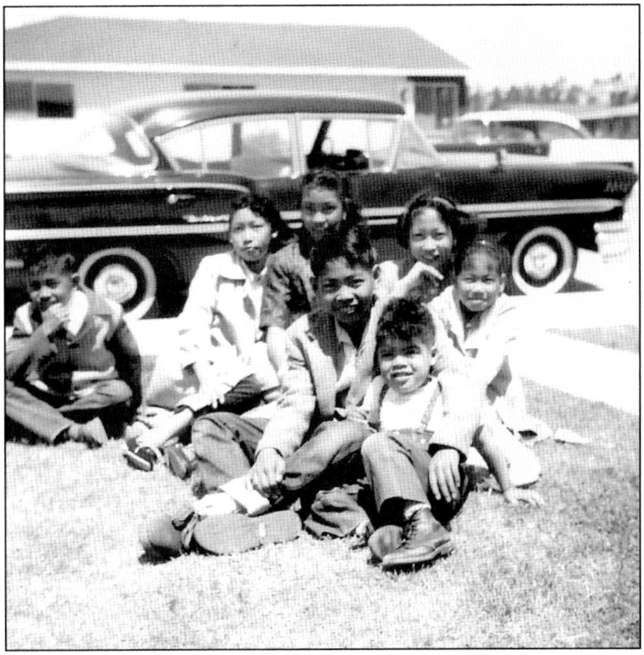

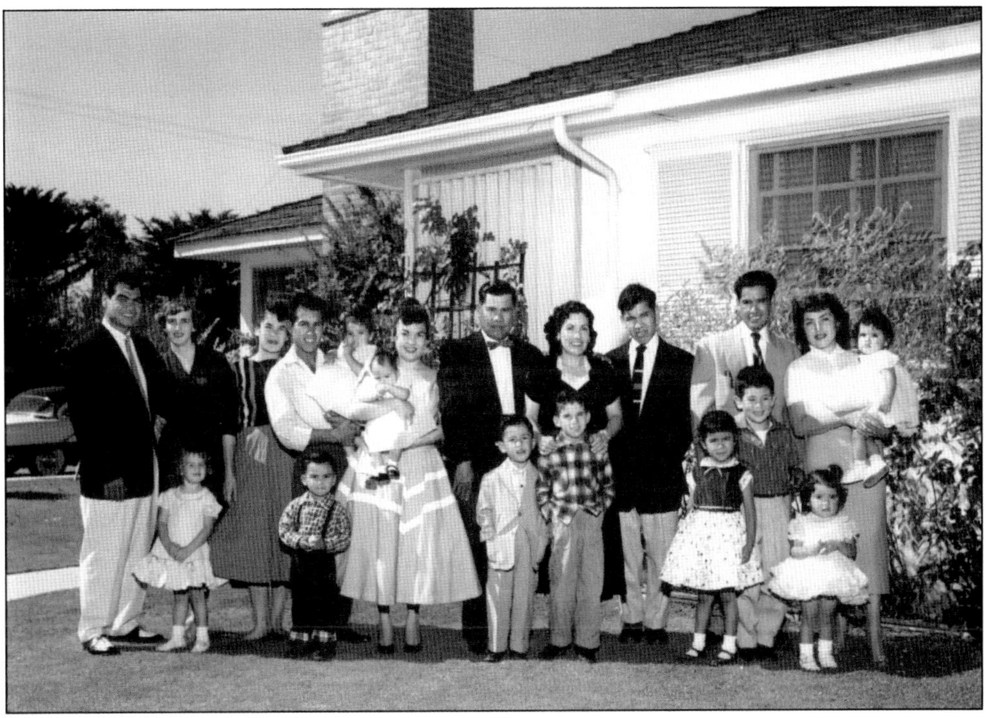

This Omo family portrait includes George Sr. and Sarah's children, sons-in-law, daughters-in-law, and grandchildren in the 1950s. Pictured from left to right are (first row) Terry Omo, Richard Omo, Manuel Omo, Vincent Omo, Judy Omo, George Omo III, and Peggy Omo; (second row) James Omo, Joyce Omo, Christina Omo, Rudy Roman, Debbie Roman, Ruth Roman, Lillian Omo Roman, George Omo Sr., Sarah Omo, Larry Omo, George Omo Jr. Carmen Omo, and Georgina Omo. (Courtesy of Lillian Omo Roman.)

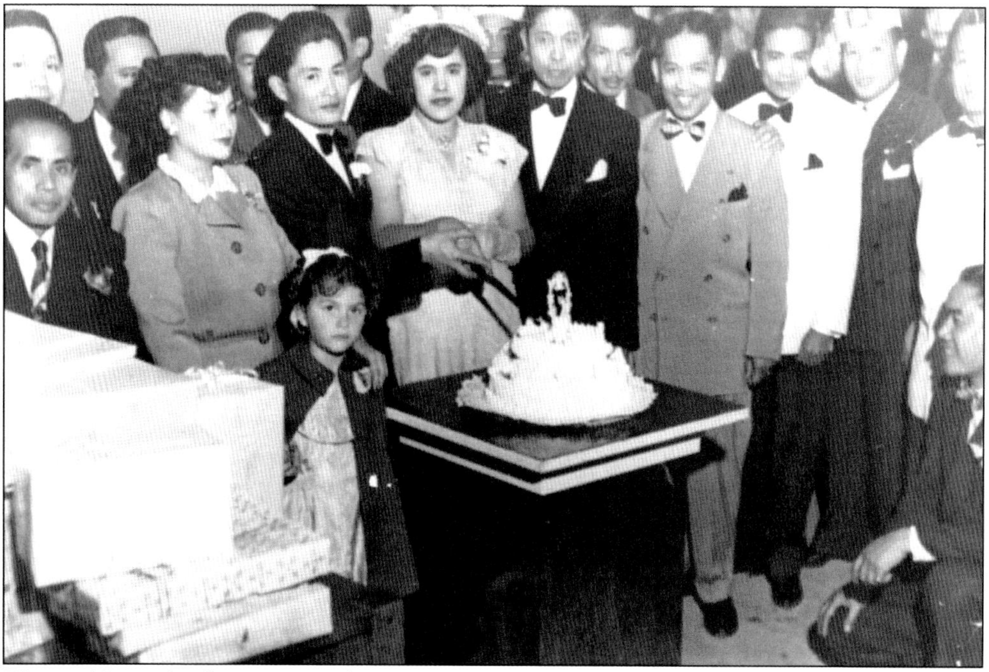

The wedding of Valinte Ines and Mary Louise Rodriguez took place in Camarillo on January 31, 1949. Valinte and Mary were residents of Oxnard and met while working in the fields and orchards of Bard's Burlwood Investment ranches (BI) in Camarillo and Somis. Their wedding caused a stir in the local paper and described Valinte as the first Malaysian man to marry a white woman in the county. (Courtesy of Vincent Ines and Isidora Ines Vaca.)

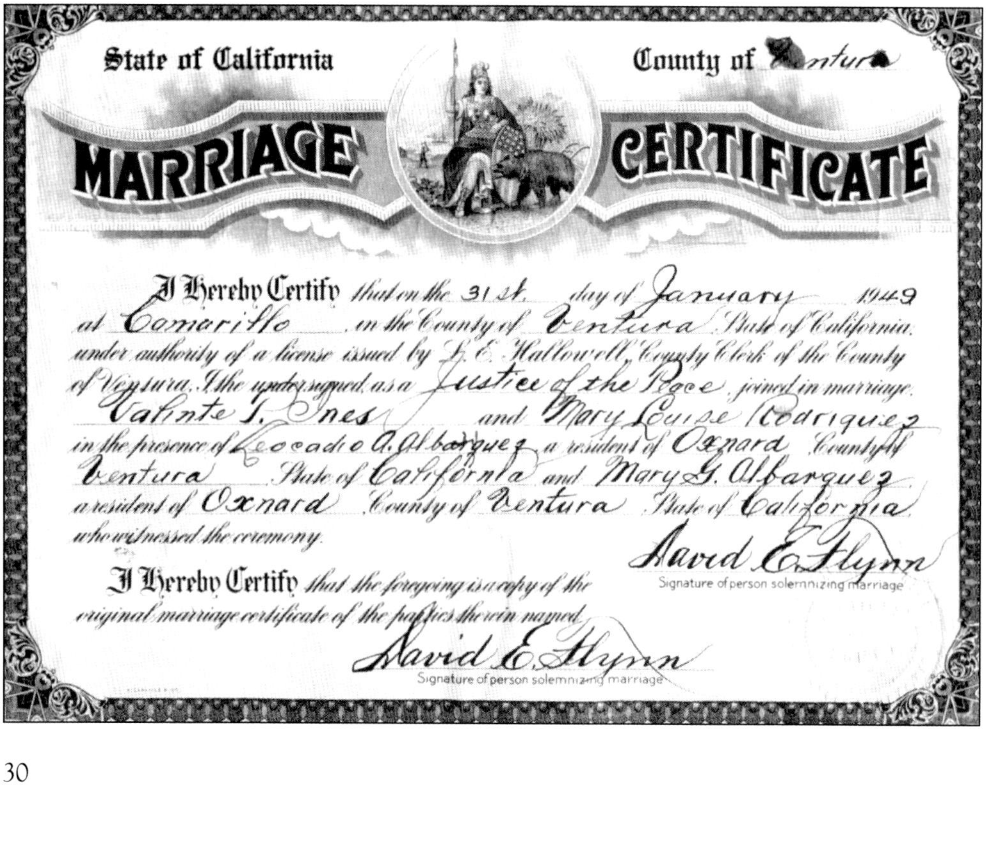

State of California — County of Ventura

MARRIAGE CERTIFICATE

I Hereby Certify that on the 31st day of January 1949 at Camarillo in the County of Ventura State of California under authority of a license issued by L. E. Hallowell, County Clerk of the County of Ventura, I the undersigned, as a Justice of the Peace joined in marriage Valinte I. Ines and Mary Louise Rodriguez in the presence of Leocadio A. Albarquez a resident of Oxnard County of Ventura State of California and Mary G. Albarquez a resident of Oxnard County of Ventura State of California who witnessed the ceremony.

David E. Flynn
Signature of person solemnizing marriage

I Hereby Certify that the foregoing is a copy of the original marriage certificate of the parties therein named.

David E. Flynn
Signature of person solemnizing marriage

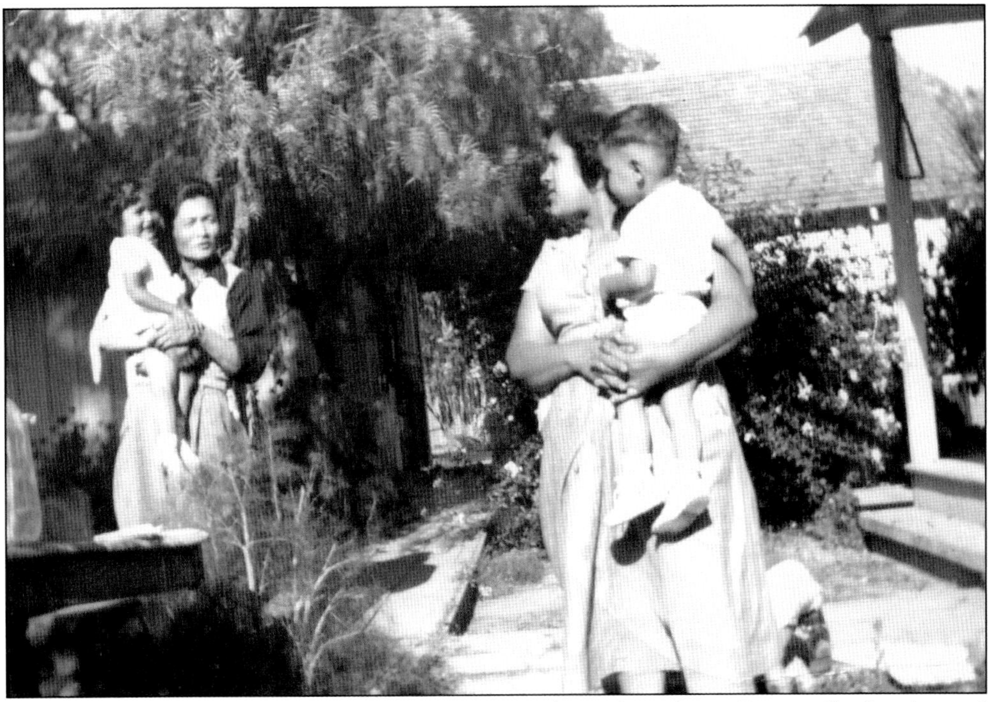

Valinte carries Dora, while Mary holds Vincent in the early 1950s at Springville. Just beyond the doorway are the labor camp living quarters and rooster coops. The path on the right of the porch led to the kitchen, and the triangle shown on the porch was rung at meal times. The Ines family lived in project housing at the Colonia Village in Oxnard, not at the ranch, but they were at Springville every weekend for gambling at the game room, cockfights, and picnics. (Courtesy of Vincent Ines and Isidora Ines Vaca.)

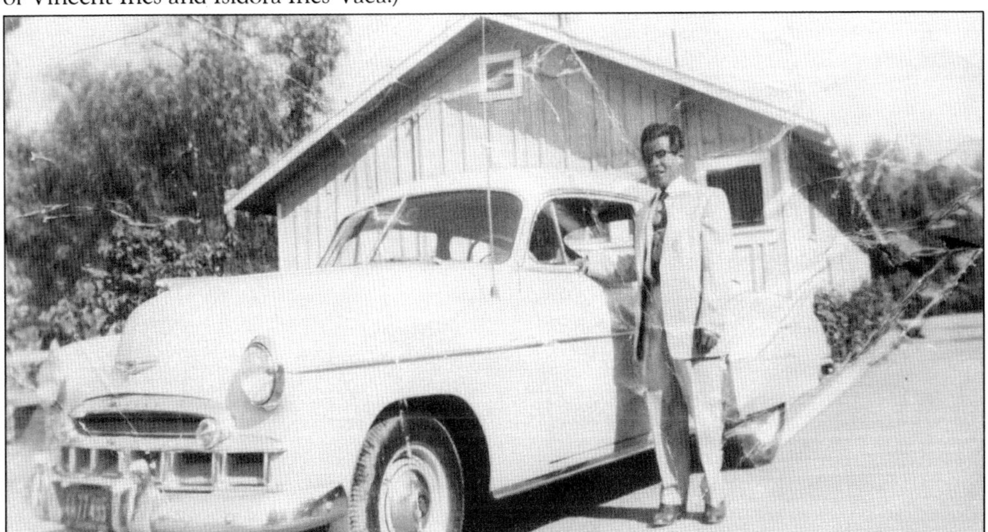

Frank Ines, Vincent Ines's *ninong* (godfather), is pictured at the Springville Ranch in Camarillo in this damaged image from the 1950s. Frank's car is parked in front of one of the labor camp living quarters, which housed 10 units. The living quarters at Springville totaled 20 units for single males and 7 homes for families. (Courtesy of Vincent Ines and Isidora Ines Vaca.)

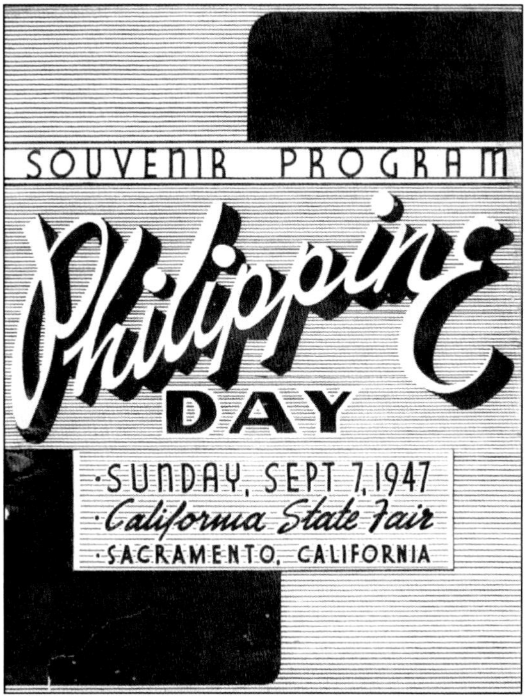

Philippine Day took place on Sunday, September 7, 1947, at the California State Fair in Sacramento. The Omos and other Filipino families traveled up and down the state to raise money for this event. The program contains advertisements from Filipino businesses all over the central valley, including a tribute advertisement from the Filipino Labor Foremen Contractors. (Courtesy of Lillian Omo Roman.)

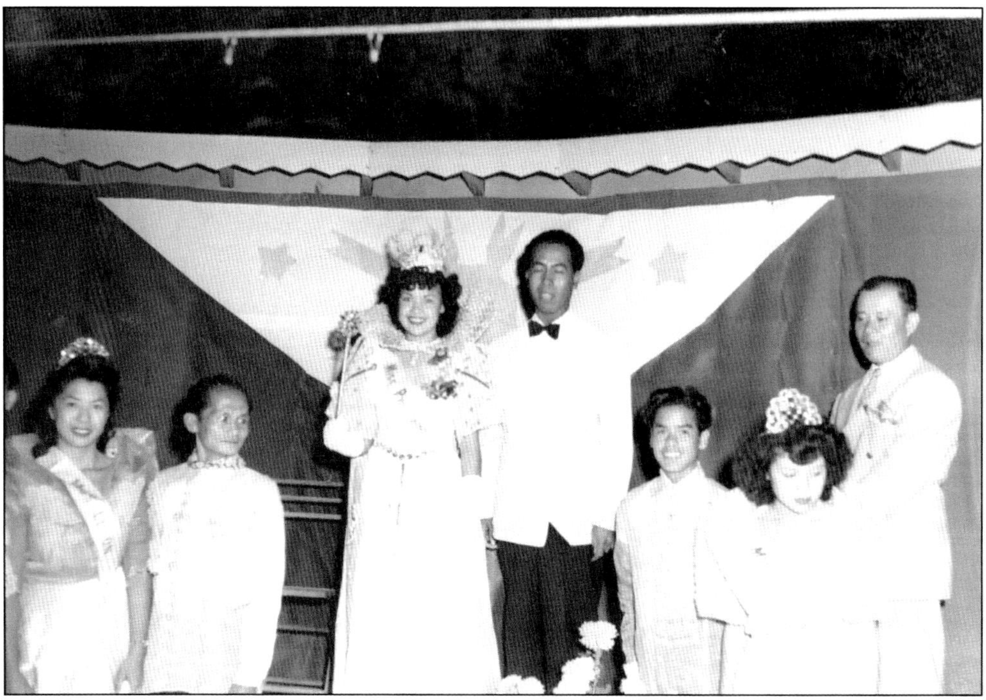

This picture captures the coronation ceremony of queen Lillian Omo at the California State Fair's Philippine Day celebration. The couple in the bottom right corner are identified as Lillian's brother George Omo Jr. and Carmen Valdez, who was crowned Miss Visayas. Carmen Valdez, also from Oxnard, eventually married her escort, and they had a son named George Omo III. (Courtesy of Lillian Omo Roman.)

Lillian Omo was crowned queen to reign over the Philippine Day's festivities. The 16-year-old Lillian was a student at Union High School in Oxnard and did the bookkeeping for her father's businesses. (Courtesy of Lillian Omo Roman.)

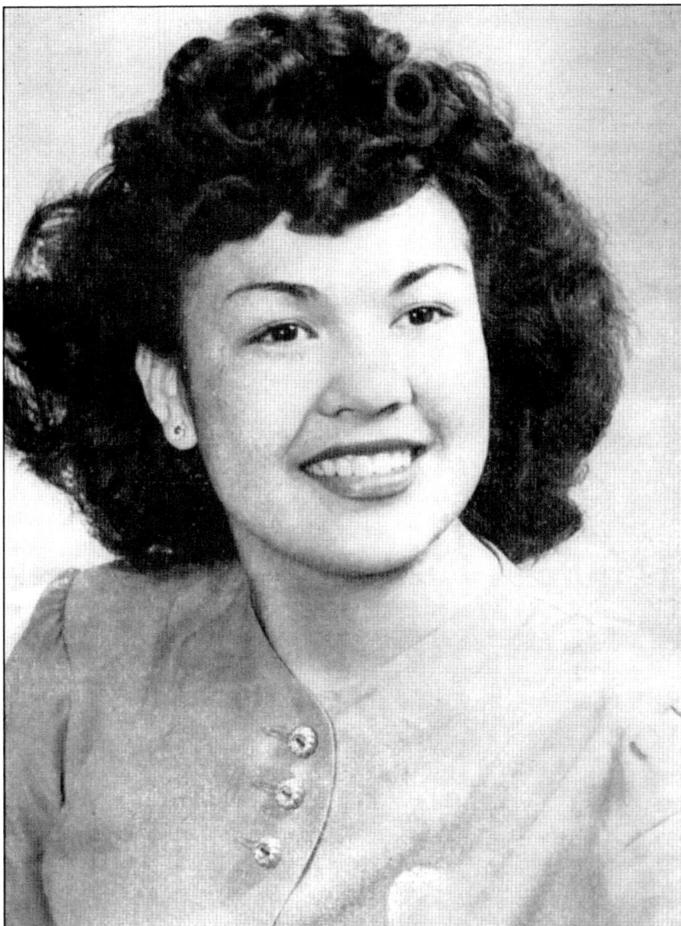

Queen Lillian I

A teenager at the time, Lillian Omo recollects making preparations to recite a short speech during the Rizal Celebration in Oxnard in the 1940s. Standing in the back row are Lillian Omo, Domingo Dela Rosa, unidentified, George Omo Sr., and Sarah Omo. Seated in front of Lillian are George Omo Jr. and Carmen Valdez Omo. (Courtesy of Lillian Omo Roman.)

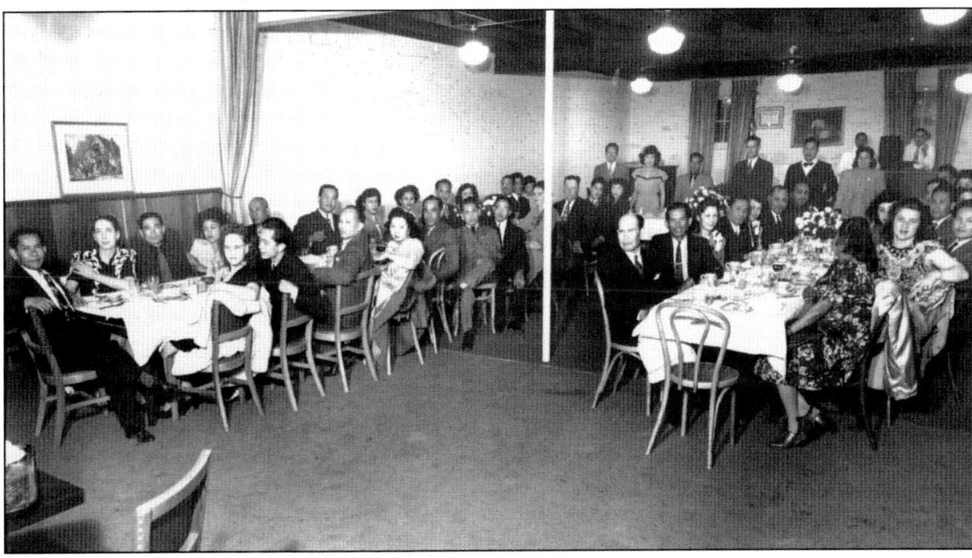

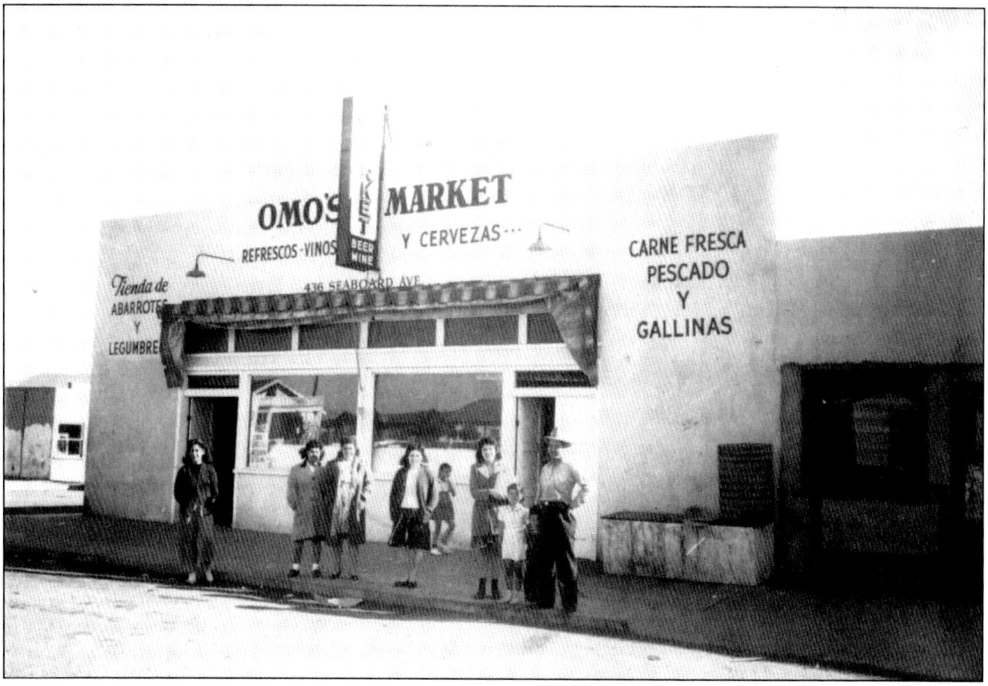

George Omo Sr. opened the original Omo's Market in 1943 at 436 Seaboard Avenue in Oxnard. A few years later the street was renamed, and the new address became 436 Colonia Road. By 1949, Omo opened Omo's Market No. 2 on 508 East Date Street at the corner of California Street in Oxnard. They sold groceries, meats, produce, delicatessen, frozen foods, and beer and wine. The *Oxnard Press Courier* reported Omo's Market No. 2 opened on Friday July 22, 1949, boasting the latest in refrigeration technology, two check stands, and six employees. Pictured from left to right are Amelia Lopez (clerk), two unidentified, Sarah Omo, unidentified, Christine Omo, Larry Omo, and George Omo Sr. (Courtesy of Lillian Omo Roman.)

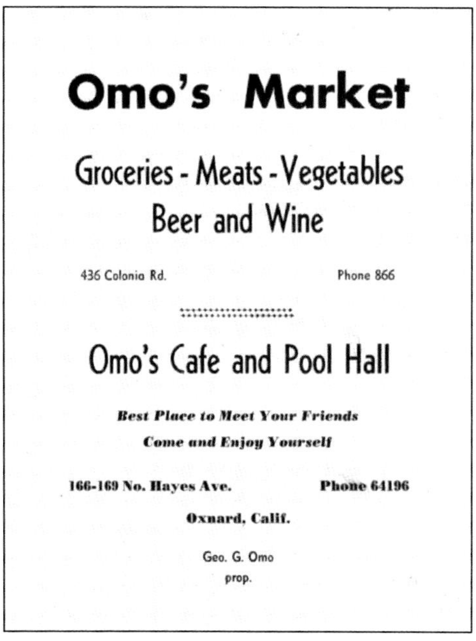

This 1947 full-page advertisement in the California State Fair's Philippine Day program promotes three of Omo's many businesses, Omo's Market, Omo's Café, and the Pool Hall. In his lifetime, George Omo Sr. owned ten businesses including two pool halls, two markets, two restaurants, two motels, rental property, and a motorcycle shop. (Courtesy of Lillian Omo Roman.)

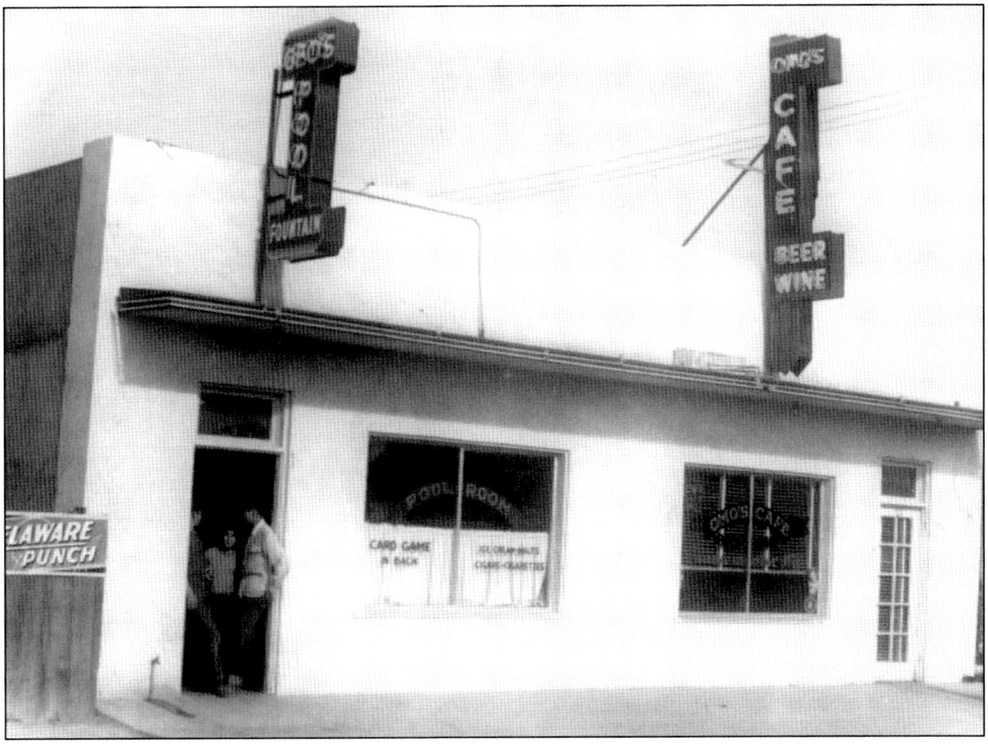

In 1945, Omo opened the Pool Hall and Omo's Café located on 166–169 North Hayes Avenue in Oxnard. The café served American and Spanish food during this period and later Chinese food. Omo purchased his first business in 1941, a former Japanese fish market on Oxnard Boulevard, and transformed it into a restaurant and pool hall. (Courtesy of Lillian Omo Roman.)

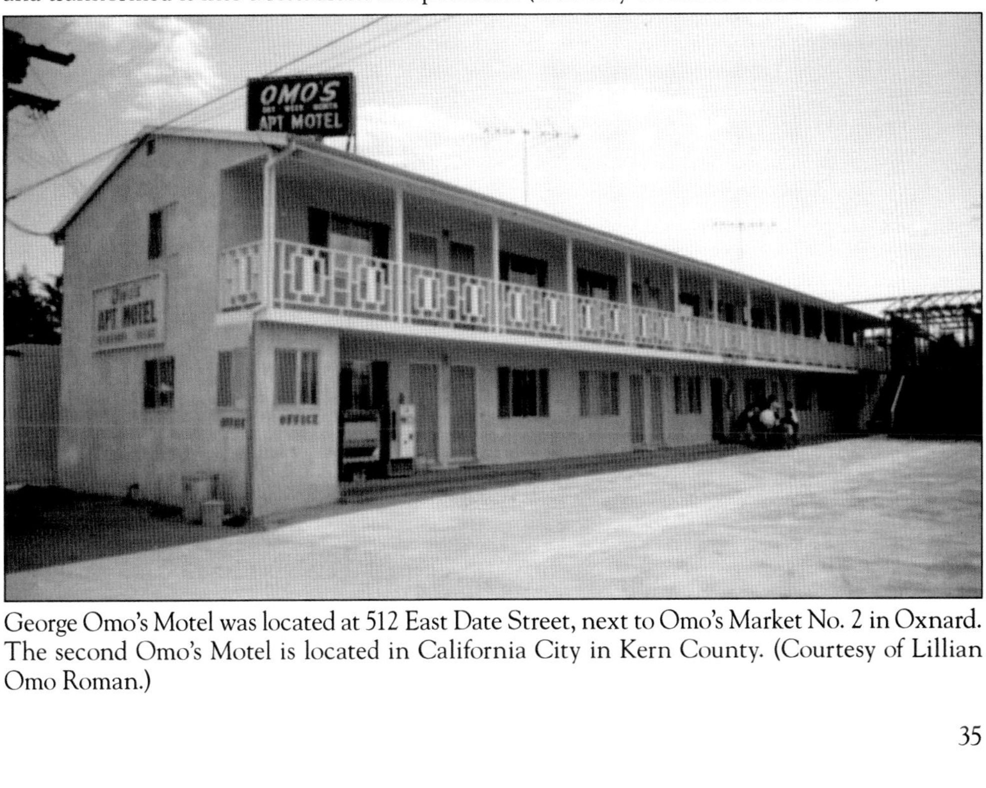

George Omo's Motel was located at 512 East Date Street, next to Omo's Market No. 2 in Oxnard. The second Omo's Motel is located in California City in Kern County. (Courtesy of Lillian Omo Roman.)

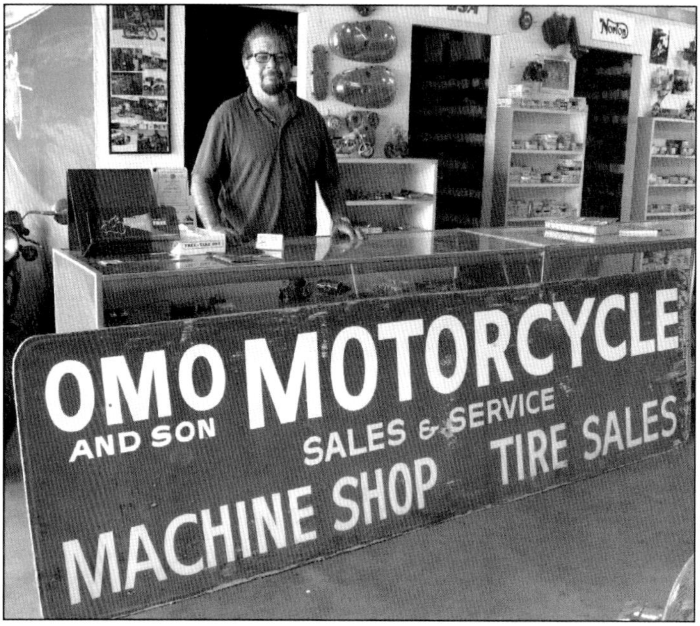

Omo & Son Motorcycle Shop is located at 1570 Pine Street in Oxnard and has been in business since 1969. It was previously located on Ventura Avenue in Ventura (1969–1972) and Oxnard Boulevard in Oxnard (1972–1982). George Jr. asked George Sr. for startup money for a motorcycle shop, and George Sr. agreed on the condition the business carries the name "Omo." Today, George Omo III owns and operates Omo & Son Motorcycle Shop.

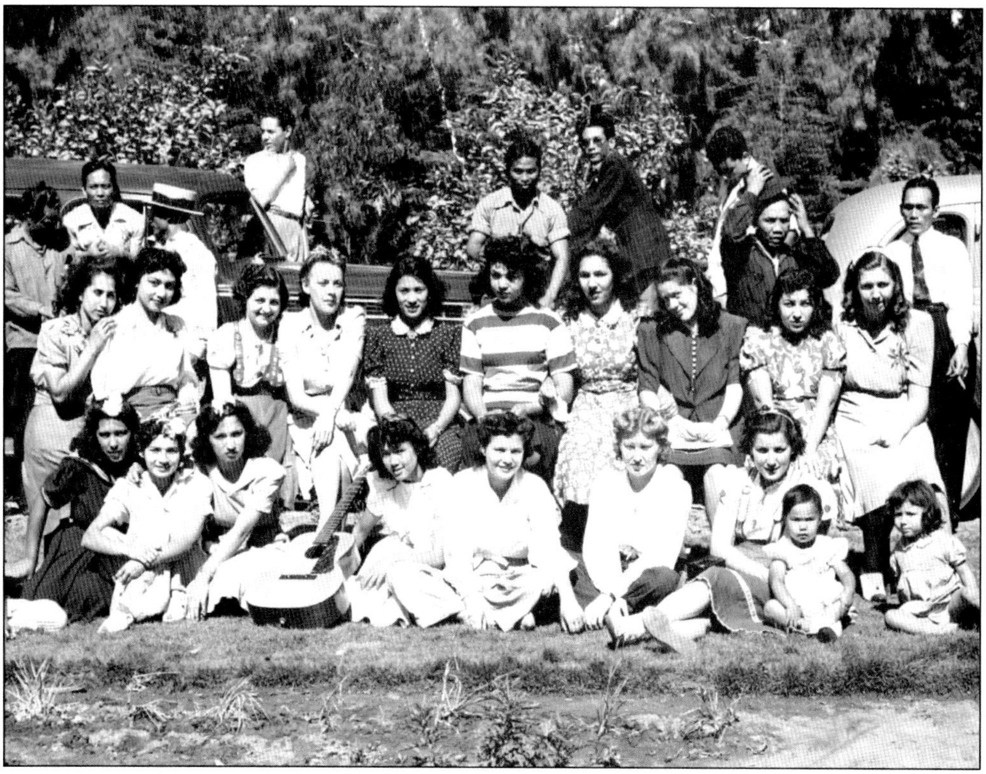

Young men and women gather for a picnic in the 1940s. This photograph reflects the courtships typical of the time when Filipino men courted women with Mexican, Caucasian, or Native American heritage. Sweethearts experienced racism and antimiscegenation laws that forced many couples to marry outside of California until 1948, when such laws were repealed. (Courtesy of Lillian Omo Roman.)

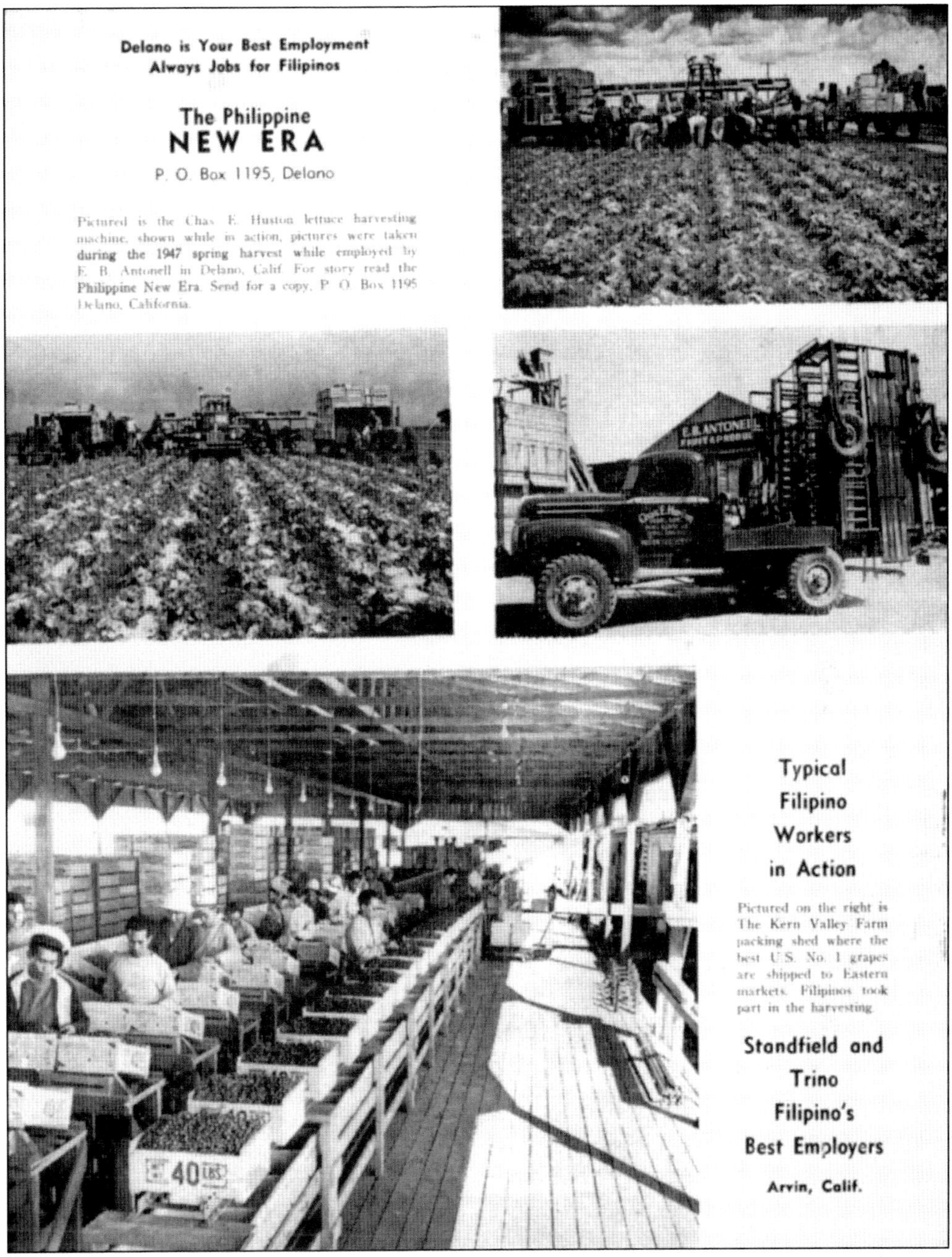

The *Philippine New Era* full-page advertisement recruits Filipino labor for jobs in Delano and Arvin and promotes employment with Stanfield and Trino. The *Philippine New Era* describes itself as an independent paper dedicated for the welfare of Filipinos according to its May 1947 issue. This advertisement was located at the back of the Philippine Day program for the California State Fair on Sunday, September 7, 1947, in Sacramento, California. (Courtesy of Lillian Omo Roman.)

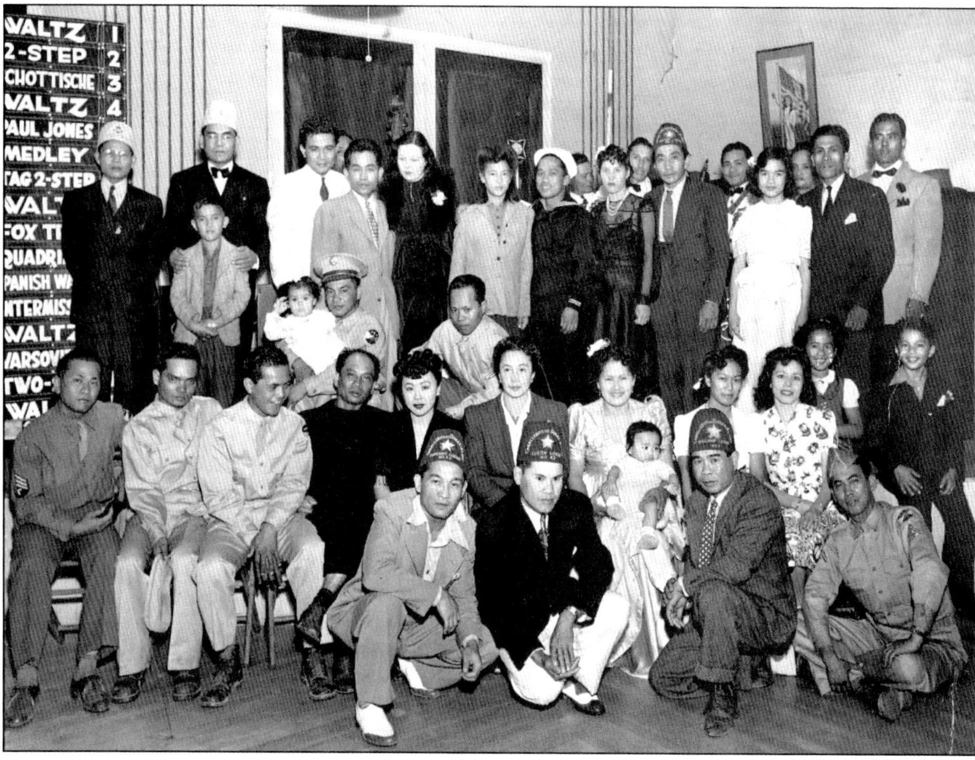

This photograph depicts a Caballeros de Dimas-Alang dinner and dance in the early 1940s. The two gentlemen in Army uniforms wearing their hats have the insignia of the 1st and 2nd Filipino Infantry Regiments of World War II on their sleeves. The insignia has a volcano representing the area where units were stationed, and the three stars represent the three Philippine islands from the Philippine Coat of Arms. Standing in the fourth row and forth from the right is Lillian Omo (wearing a white dress). Sitting in the second row are, second and fifth from right, Delia Sotelo and Sayong Sotelo. Kneeling in the first row and second and third from the right are Fred Sotelo and George Omo Sr. (Courtesy of Lillian Omo Roman.)

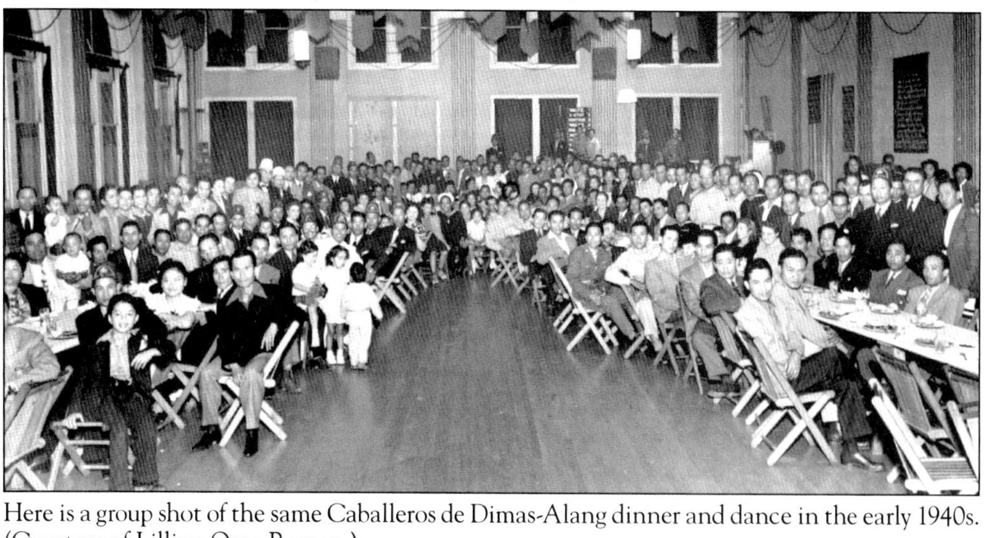

Here is a group shot of the same Caballeros de Dimas-Alang dinner and dance in the early 1940s. (Courtesy of Lillian Omo Roman.)

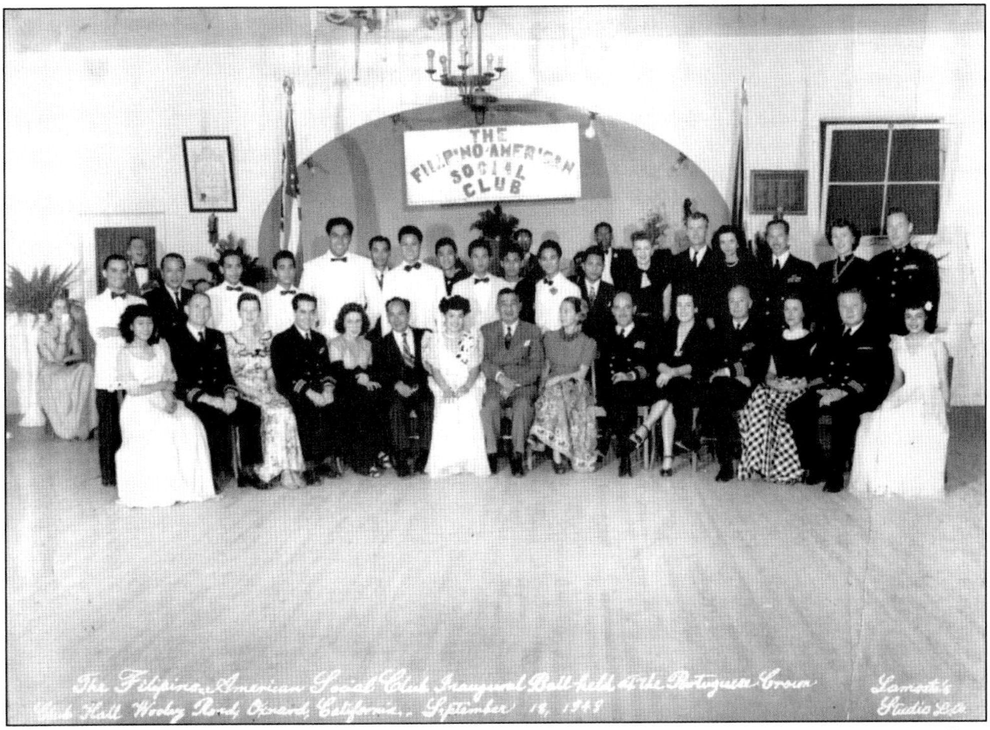

The Filipino American Social Club Inaugural Ball was held at the Portuguese Crown Hall at 750 West Wooley Road in Oxnard on September 18, 1948. The Filipino American Social Club provided social events and dances, and its male membership was comprised of Navy servicemen. (Courtesy of Lillian Omo Roman.)

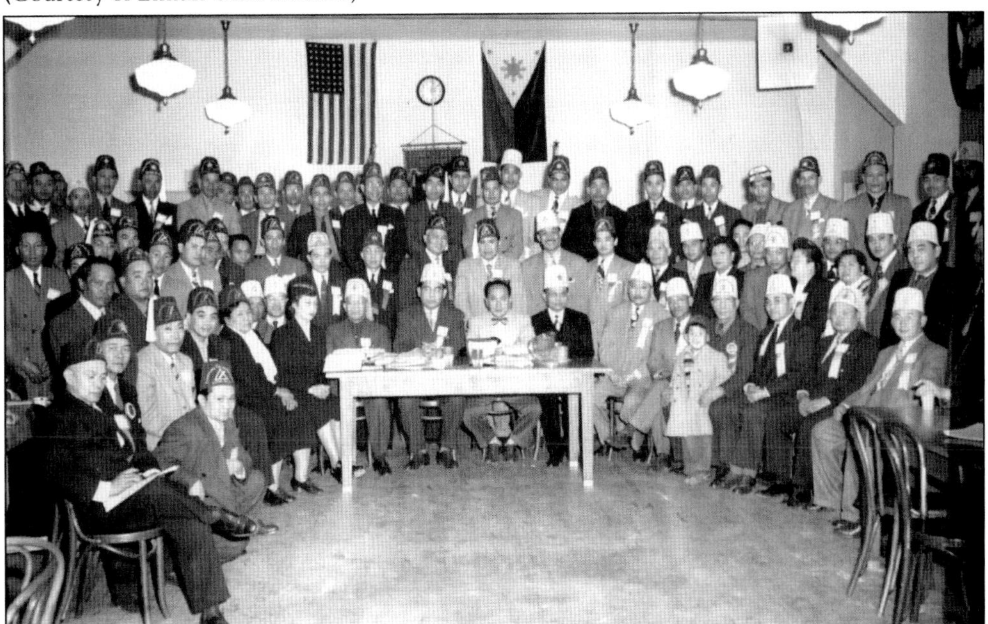

Caballeros de Dimas-Alang members gather in the 1940s in Oxnard, possibly at the Moose Hall. (Courtesy of Lillian Omo Roman.)

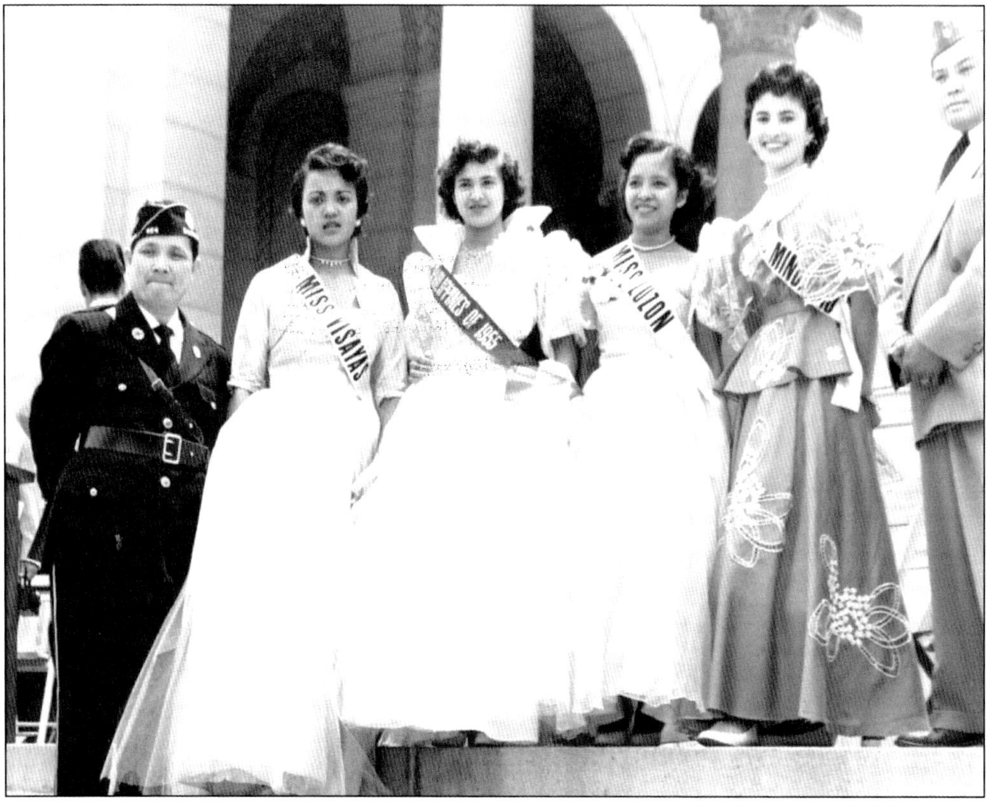

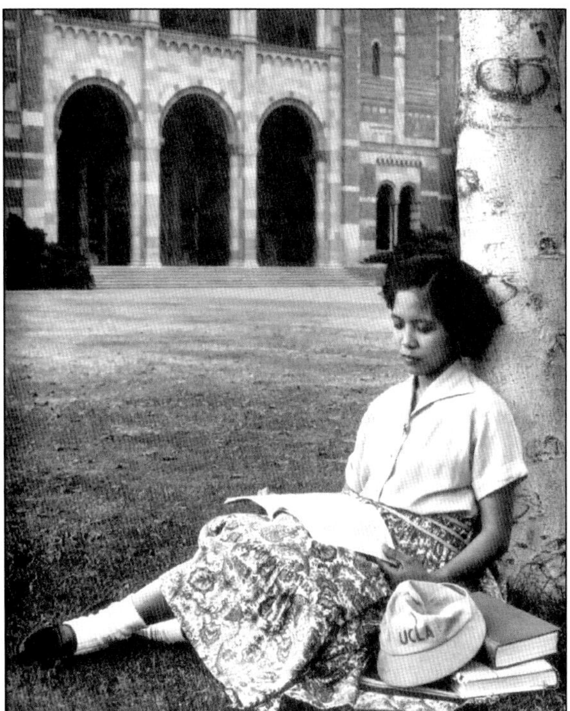

Miss Luzon 1955, Josie Rivera (Bautista), is shown standing on the steps of Los Angeles City Hall during a fundraising event for the Filipino community. (Courtesy of Josie and Al Bautista.)

Josie Rivera (Bautista) is from Salinuyan, Cotabato, Philippines, and came to the United States in 1953 and attended UCLA, where she studied nursing. She was a nurse at the Camarillo State Hospital in Camarillo until it closed its doors in 1997. (Courtesy of Josie and Al Bautista.)

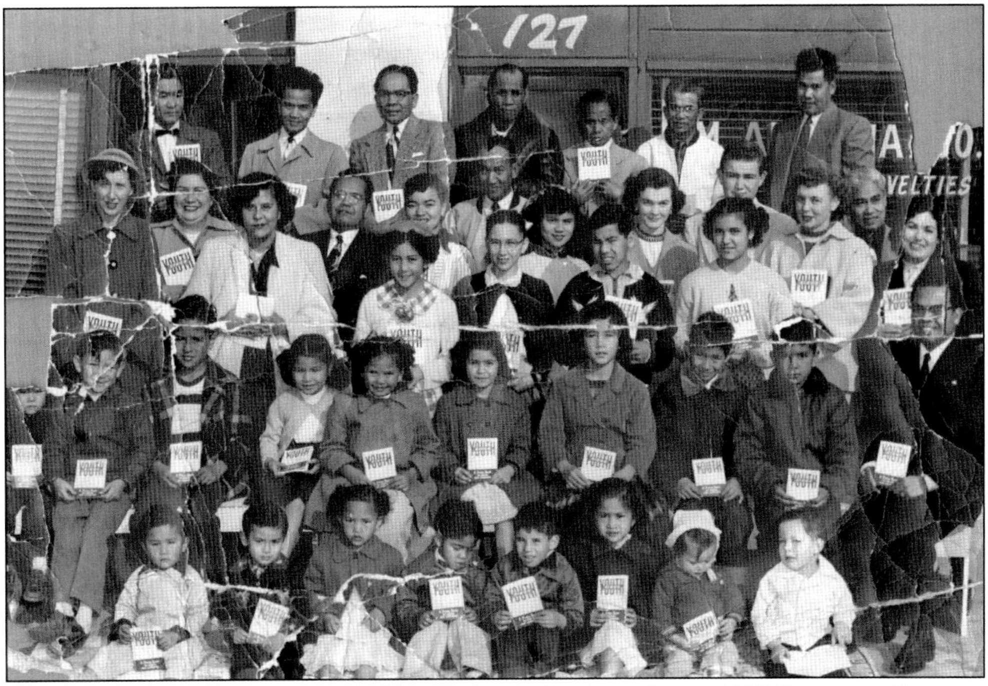

In this tattered and torn image, children hold songbooks in front of 127 Enterprise Street in Oxnard. Domingo Dela Rosa Sr. owned The Enterprise, a complex that included the storefront at 127 Enterprise, the big house behind it, and apartment units in the back. A total of 24 residential units were rented out to Filipinos, who worked as laborers, barbers, and chauffeurs. Units were also rented out to non-Filipinos, and that is how Domingo Dela Rosa met his wife, Mary. (Courtesy of Lisa and Domingo Dela Rosa Jr.)

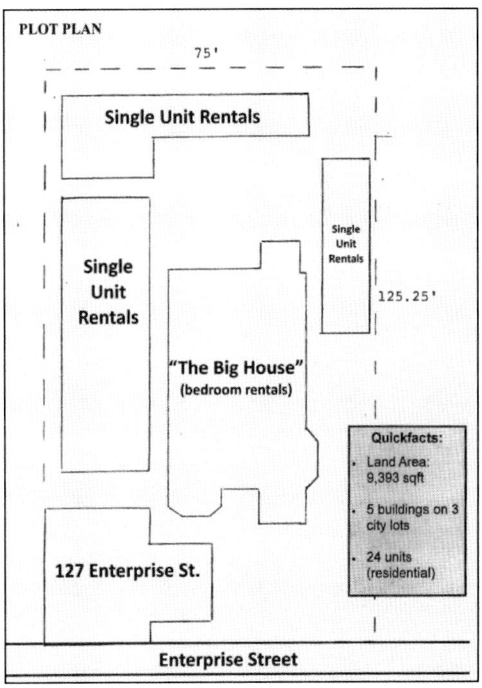

Domingo Dela Rosa owned 127 and 131 Enterprise Street, which included five buildings on three city lots. The diagram illustrates the plot plan of 127 Enterprise Street. (Courtesy of Lisa and Domingo Dela Rosa Jr.)

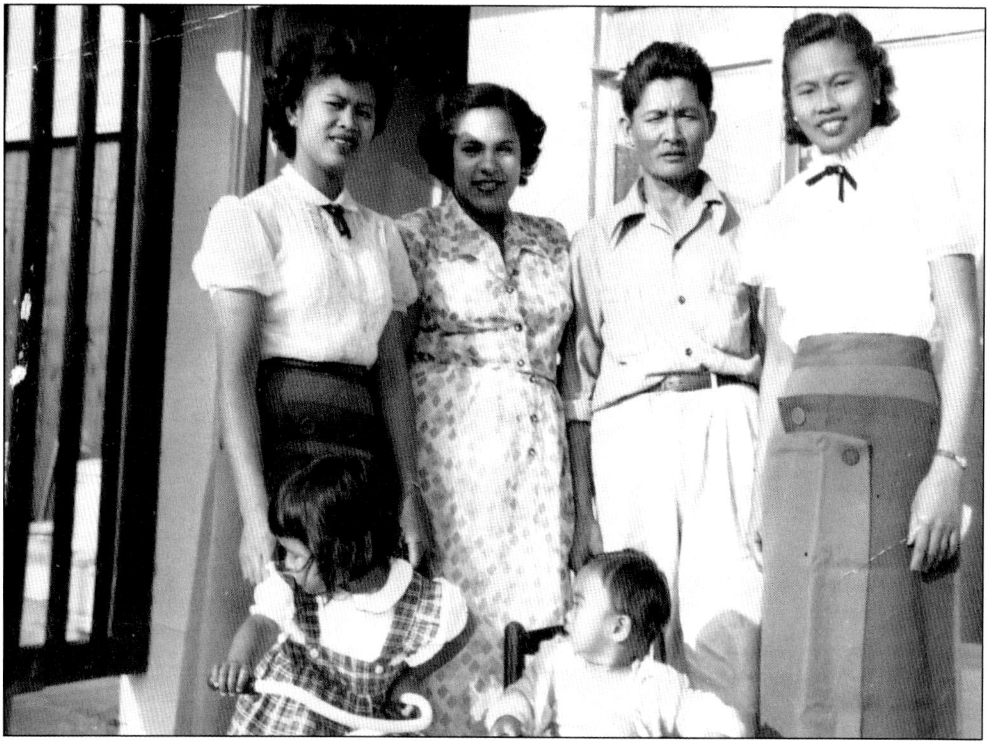

This Ines family picture was taken at 173 North Garfield Street in the Colonia in Oxnard. In June 1952, the *Oxnard Press Courier* reported the Colonia Village project-housing complex opened with 104 brand new units and listed their new tenants including the Ines family. From left to right are Laura Ines, Mary Ines, Valinte Ines, and Ana Ines with children Dora Ines and Sylvestre Ines Jr. (Courtesy of Vincent Ines and Isidora Ines Vaca.)

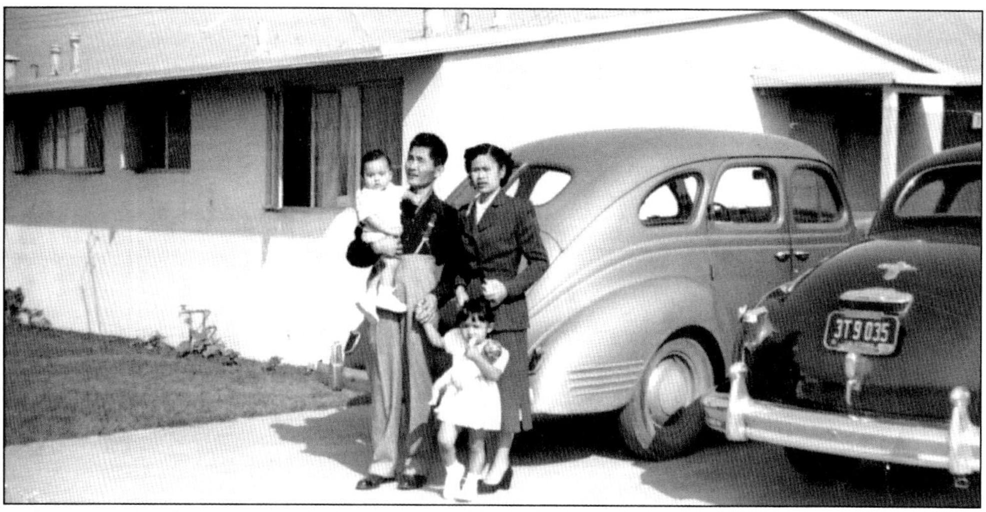

Valinte Ines holds his son Vincent Ines and his daughter Isidora "Dora" Ines by the hand in 1953. Valinte is standing next his niece Laura Ines in front of the Colonia Village project-housing complex in Oxnard, where the whole family lived. Isidora is named after her maternal grandmother, and Vincent is named after his fraternal grandfather. (Courtesy of Vincent Ines and Isidora Ines Vaca.)

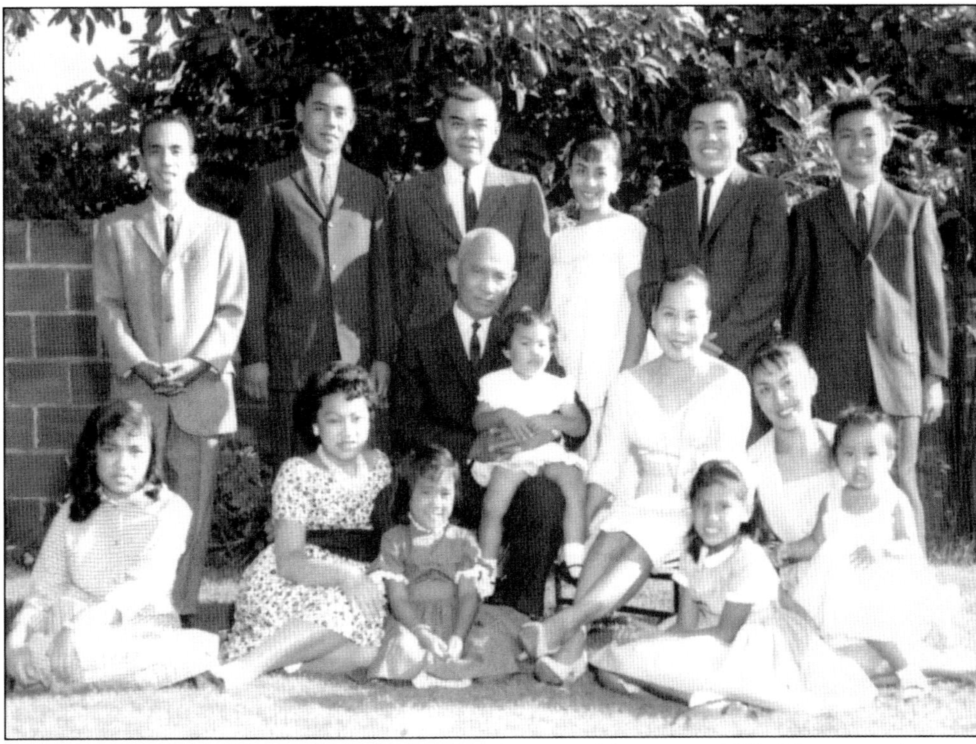

The Ventura family portrait was taken at their home in Ventura in 1959. Those standing are, from left to right, Jim Ventura, Eddie Ventura, Federico (Dick) Talaugon Jr., Nora (Ventura) Talaugon, Phil Ventura, and Tom Florin Jr. The three people sitting on the chairs are, from left to right, Felipe Ventura, Kristina Urbano, and Trinidad Ventura. Those sitting on the grass are, from left to right, Julie Florin, Pauline Panetto, Noree Urbano, Valerie Ventura, Nena Ventura, and Vanessa Ventura. (Courtesy of Nora and Federico Talaugon Jr.)

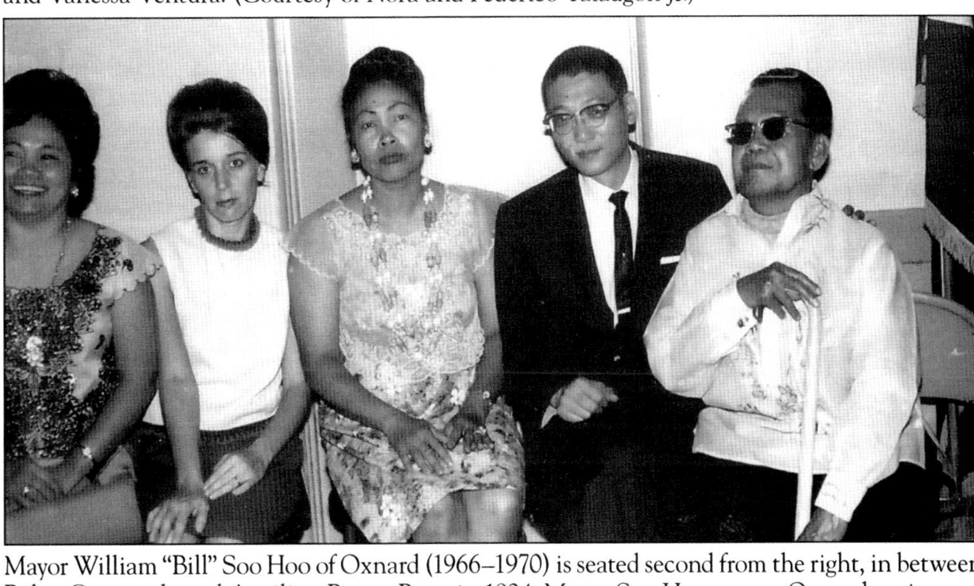

Mayor William "Bill" Soo Hoo of Oxnard (1966–1970) is seated second from the right, in between Belen Castaneda and Aquilino Bagay. Born in 1924, Mayor Soo Hoo was an Oxnard native and the first Chinese American mayor. (Courtesy of Augie Castaneda Jr.)

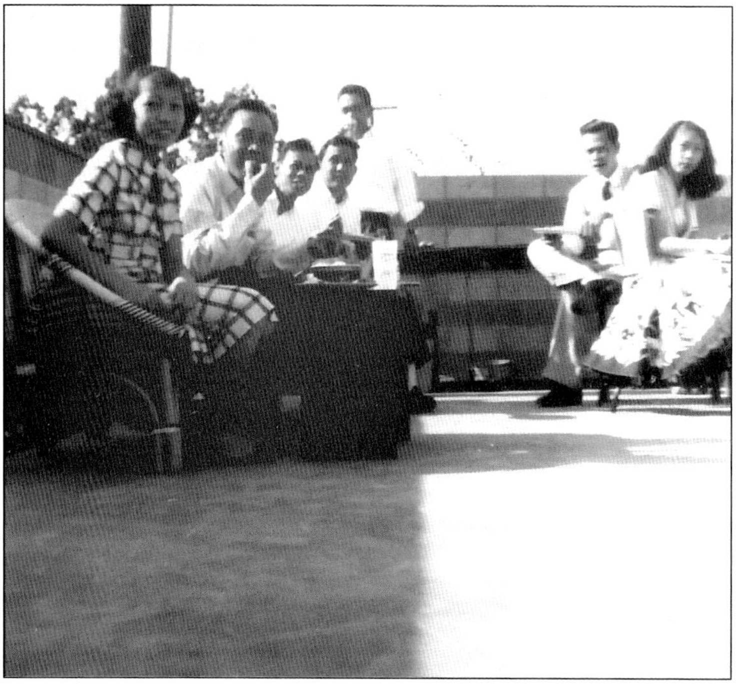

The Castaneda family Thanksgiving took place in their backyard at 660 Tamarac Street in Oxnard in 1959. The family drove to Santa Paula to buy a pig for slaughter and prepared *lechón* (roasted pig) for the holiday. Once they returned home, the kids took shifts to cook the meal over several hours. (Courtesy of Augie Castaneda Jr.)

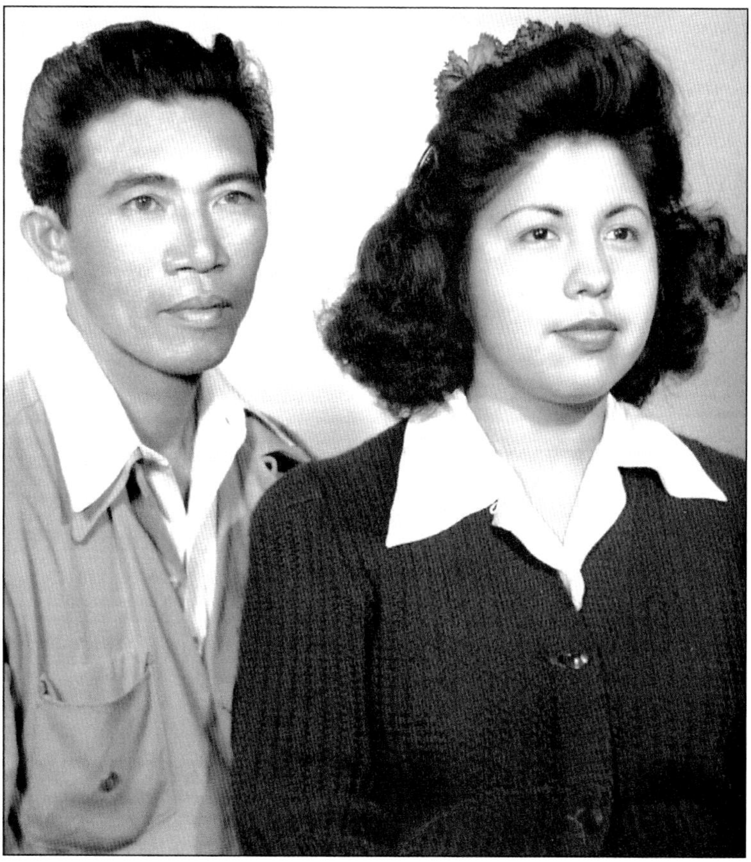

Since his return from Alaska in 1937, Federico Talaugon Sr., with his brothers Servero and Andres, continued to lease and farm the land on the Gaynor Ranch. When Federico Sr. married Catalina Razo in 1953, he quit the lease, and they moved to Carpinteria, where they had two daughters, Beatrice and Rebecca. (Courtesy of Beatrice Talaugon-Dunn.)

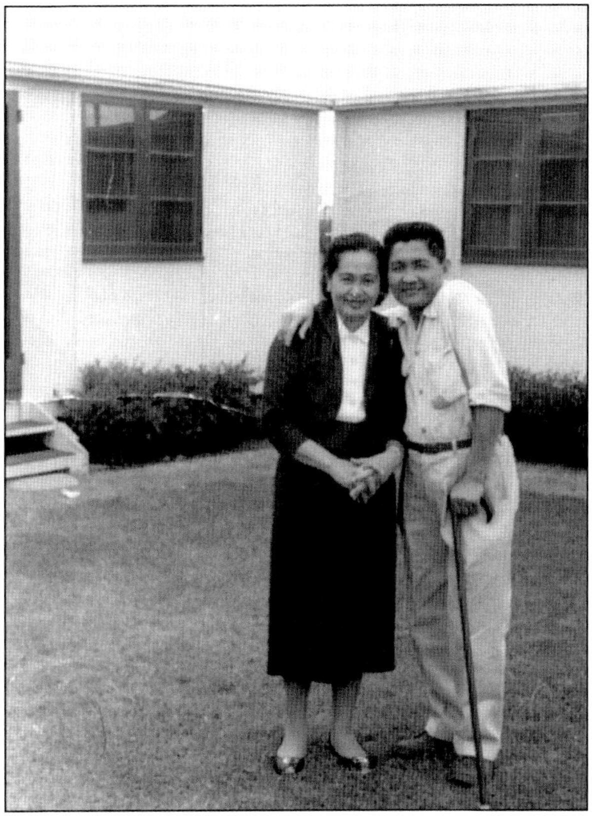

These pictures were taken in 1957 during an Ines family visit to see Grandpa Ciano Ibarra at the Ocean View Farm on Laguna Road in Oxnard. Right, Amalia Ines and Valinte Ines pose in front of the labor camp living quarters at Ocean View. Below, Paulino Ines is photographed at Ocean View Farm during the visit. Local ranches brought their peas to Ocean View, where Filipinos operated the thrasher machines. Afterward, the Ines children snacked on sweet peas all afternoon. (Courtesy of Vincent Ines and Isidora Ines Vaca.)

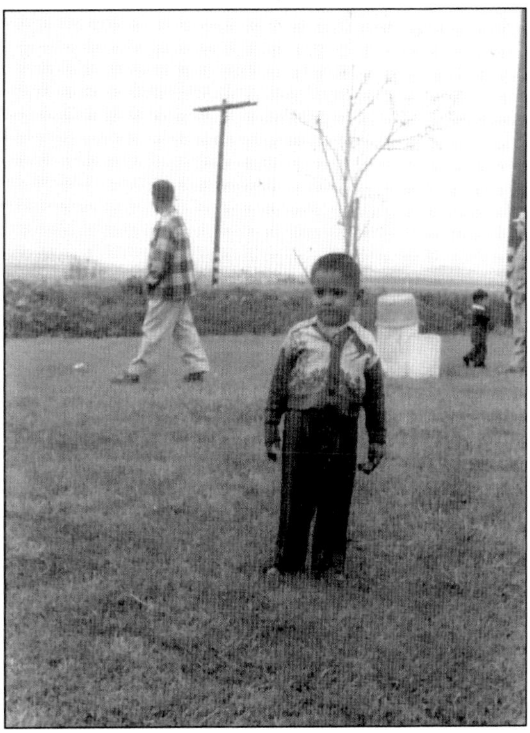

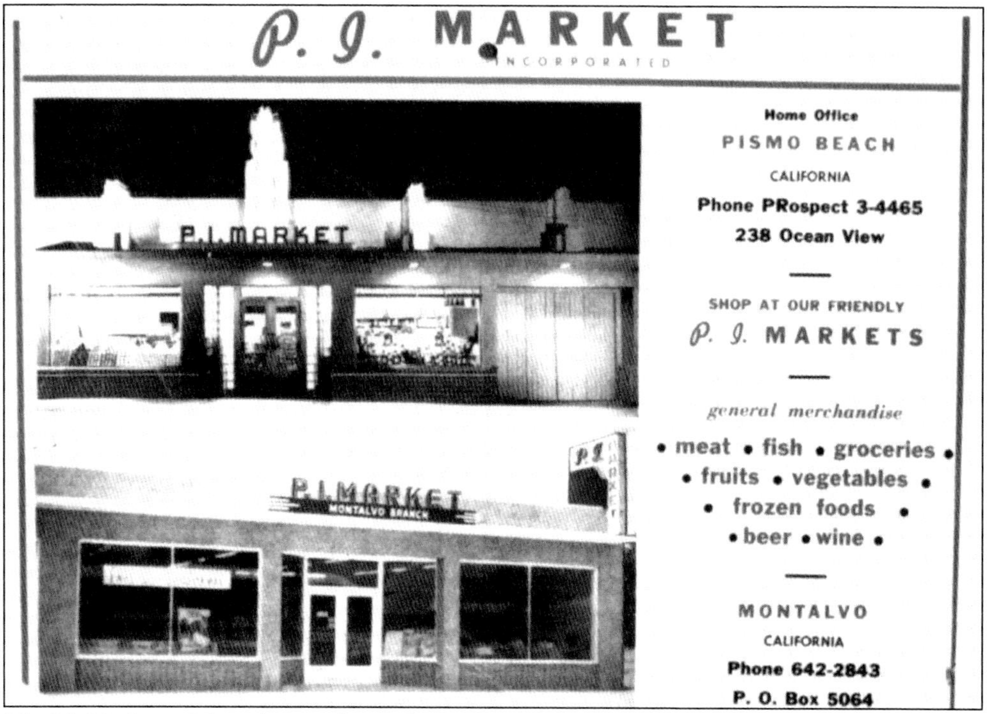

The P.I. Market at Montalvo was located at 2531 South Grand Avenue in South Ventura. The P.I. Market was a social networking hub and pit stop where Filipinos traveling between Northern and Southern California could find jobs in the area, locate families, and make travel arrangements. The market offered groceries, a butcher shop, fresh fish, and homegrown Philippine vegetables not found in American grocery stores. There were a total of four stores in the following four cities: Pismo Beach (1936–1989), Salinas Beach (1939–1944), Los Angeles (1939–1941), and Montalvo (1955–1972). (Courtesy of Filipino American National Historical Society California Central Coast.)

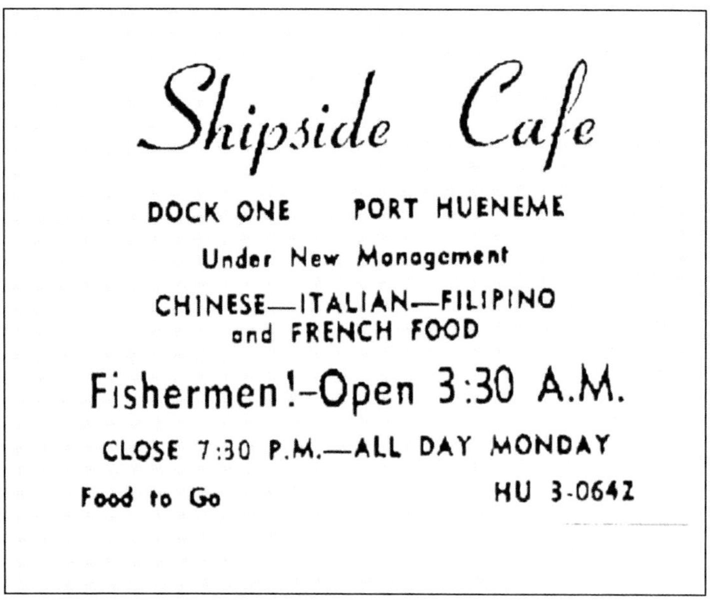

The Shipside Café was located at the east end of Dock 1 in Port Hueneme. This advertisement is from the *Press Courier*, dated Saturday, October 24, 1959. The café was only one of the dozen businesses that Domingo Dela Rosa Sr. owned and operated. Dela Rosa's first business was a barbershop he purchased in Oxnard in 1929.

Three

Community

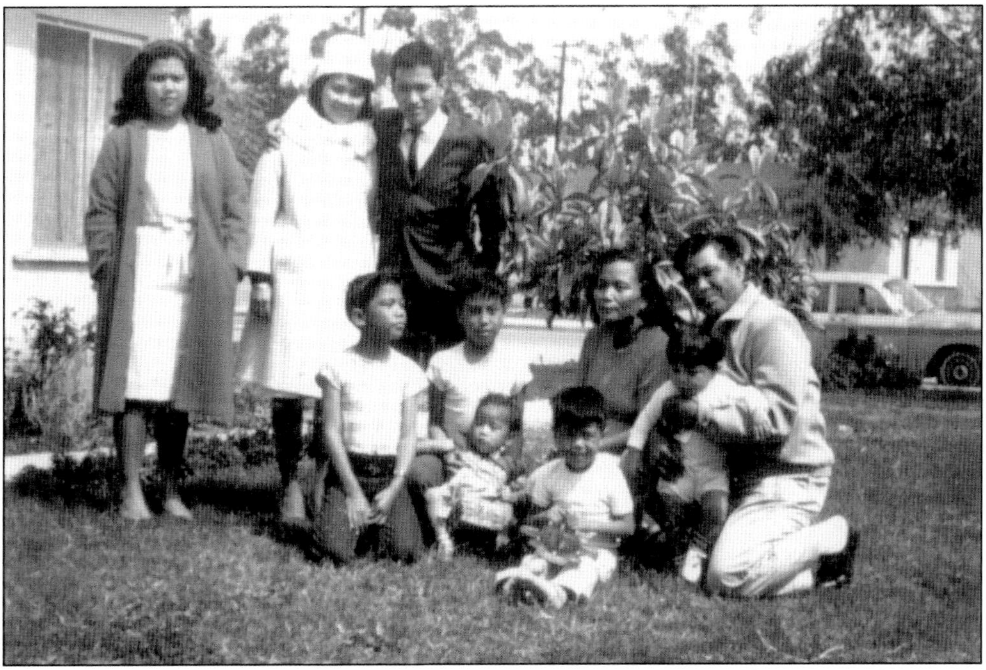

Many Filipino families began settling in Oxnard and Port Hueneme in the 1960s and 1970s, as the Navy Base Ventura County Construction Battalion at Port Hueneme and Air Station at Point Mugu were the largest employers in Ventura County. Filipino military families purchased homes in the Pleasant Valley Estates, Lemonwood Estates, Oxnard Estates, College Estates, Strawberry Fields, and Seabreeze developments. The influx of new residents called for the building of new schools, such as Hueneme High School in 1959 and Channel Islands High School in 1966. Even as the number of Filipino servicemen increased, some serving multiple tours of duty in the Vietnam War, the farms were still very much operational throughout the county and Filipino labor camps continued to exist, such as the one at Springville Ranch in Camarillo. Pictured above, the Babautas, a typical military family, settled in 1958 when Chief Joe Babauta Sr. was stationed at the US Navy Construction Battalion Center (USN-CBC) at Port Hueneme. Mary Babauta, his daugther, attended the newly built Hueneme High School and was part of the second class to graduate. Standing are, from left to right, Terry Babauta, Mary (Babauta) Grey, and Tony Grey. Seated on the grass are, from left to right, Henry Babauta, Joe Babauta Jr., Kim Babauta, Johnny Babauta, Peter Babauta, and Joe Babauta Sr.

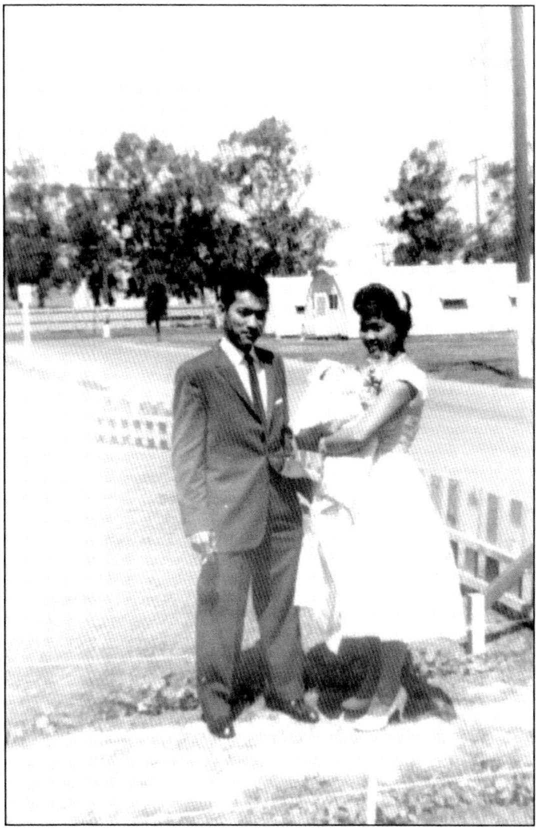

In 1960, Tony and Mary Grey are pictured after a baptism, with the Hamoja Housing complex at Port Hueneme Naval Center in the background. Hamoja Housing was comprised of quonset buildings that were divided inside. (Courtesy of Tony V. Grey.)

Tony Grey purchased his first American car with money from his *ninong* (godfather). Grey stands in front of his brand new Kaiser in 1960, with the Hamoja barracks behind him. (Courtesy of Tony V. Grey.)

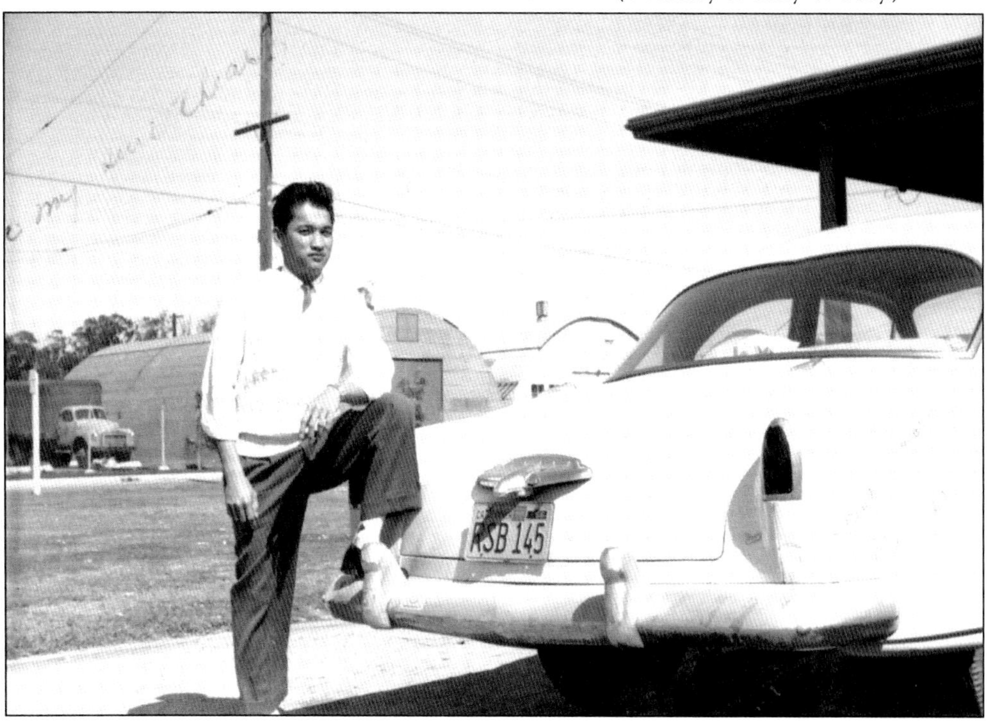

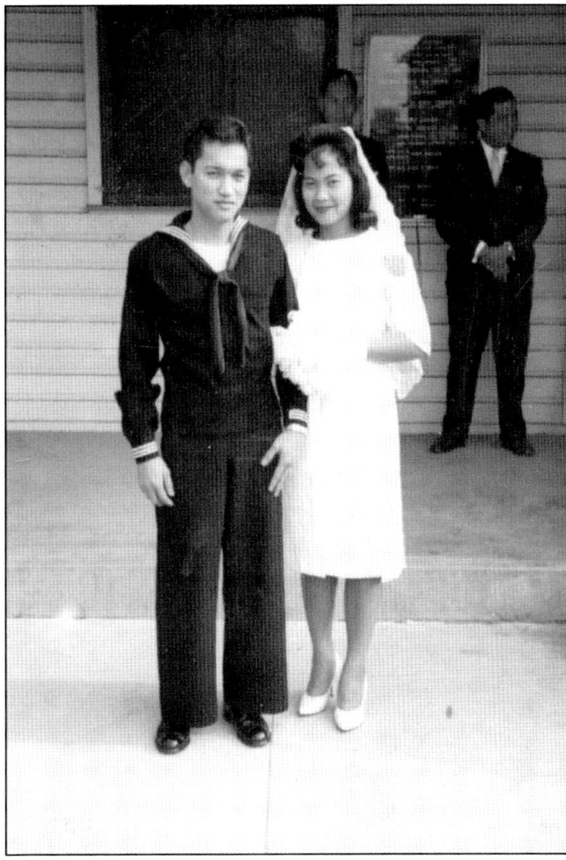

The wedding of Tony Grey and Mary Babauta took place on December 26, 1961, at the US Navy Construction Battalion Center (USN-CBC) Station Chapel at Port Hueneme. (Courtesy of Tony V. Grey.)

The Grey wedding party included, from left to right, Marie Connolly (maid of honor), Lil Gonzaga, Chaplain Aldrich, Mary Babauta Grey, Tony Grey, Ernie Atiano (best man), and unidentified. (Courtesy of Tony V. Grey.)

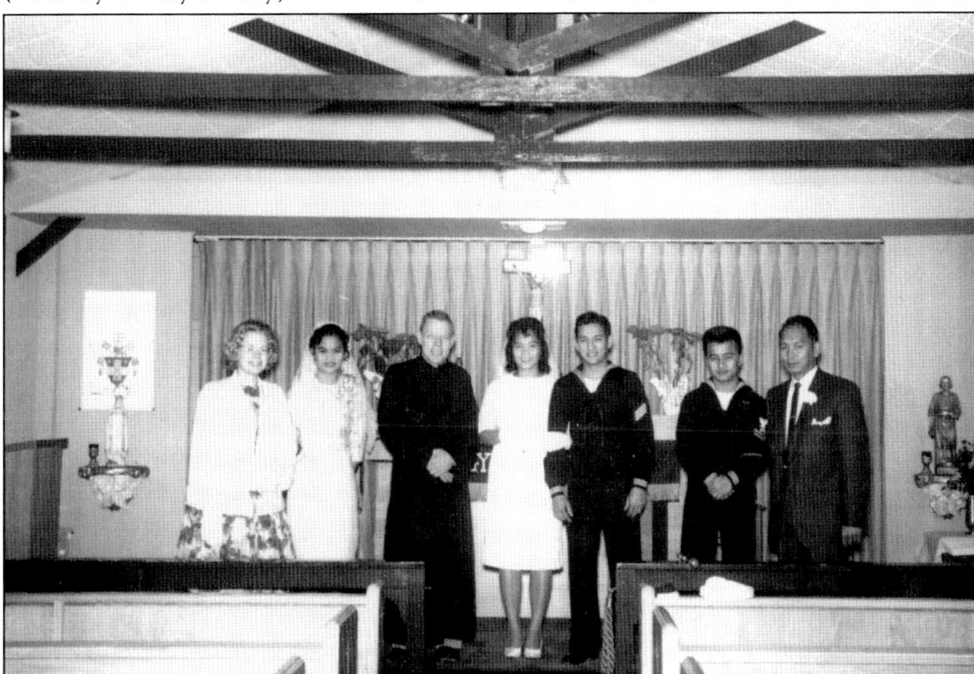

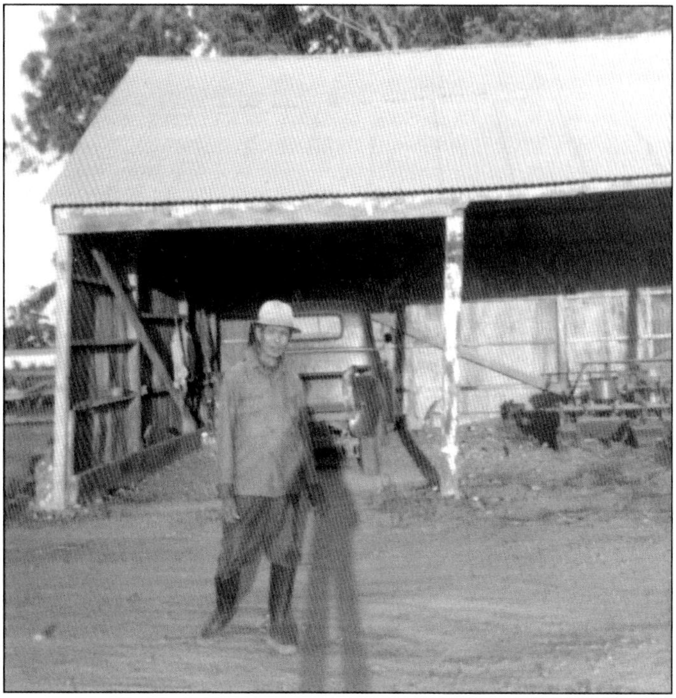

Uncle Tom Torres stands in front of the carport at Springville Ranch in 1963. Torres arrived in the United States in the 1930s as a farm laborer. He lived at Springville Ranch where he was allowed to plant his own vegetables, such as bitter melon and cabbages. He would invite Filipino families and friends to come pick them. Tom Torres was a lifelong vegetarian, who never married, but saved his earnings to send to students in the Philippines. (Courtesy of Vicky Barretto.)

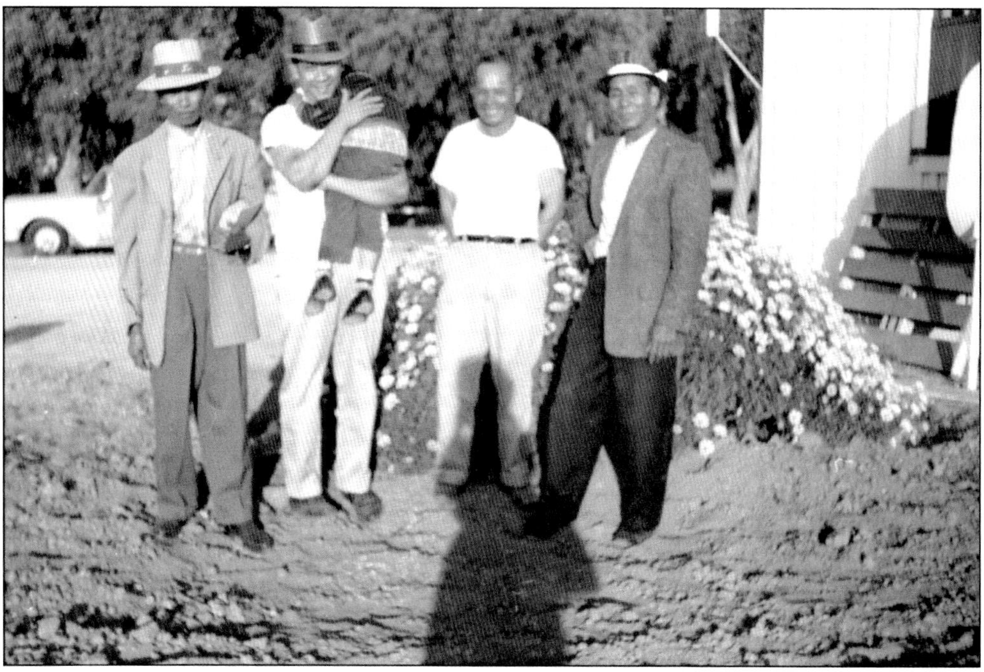

The Barretto family visits Uncle Tom Torres at the Springville Ranch in 1965. One day, Leopoldo Barretto met Tom Torres at a gathering and made the discovery that Torres was Vicky Barretto's uncle. Unaware she had any relatives in Camarillo, Vicky met her Uncle Tom for the first time in 1963. Torres was a first cousin to Vicky's mother, Teodora Agbisit De Ocampo. From left to right are Uncle Tom Torres, Leopoldo Barretto, Michael Barretto, and two of Uncle Tom's roommates. (Courtesy of Vicky Barretto.)

The Barrettos brought their friends from out of town to Springville to visit Uncle Tom and pick vegetables. The road behind the group of friends is Pleasant Valley Road. Uncle Tom Torres is on the far right, wearing a hat. (Courtesy of Vicky Barretto.)

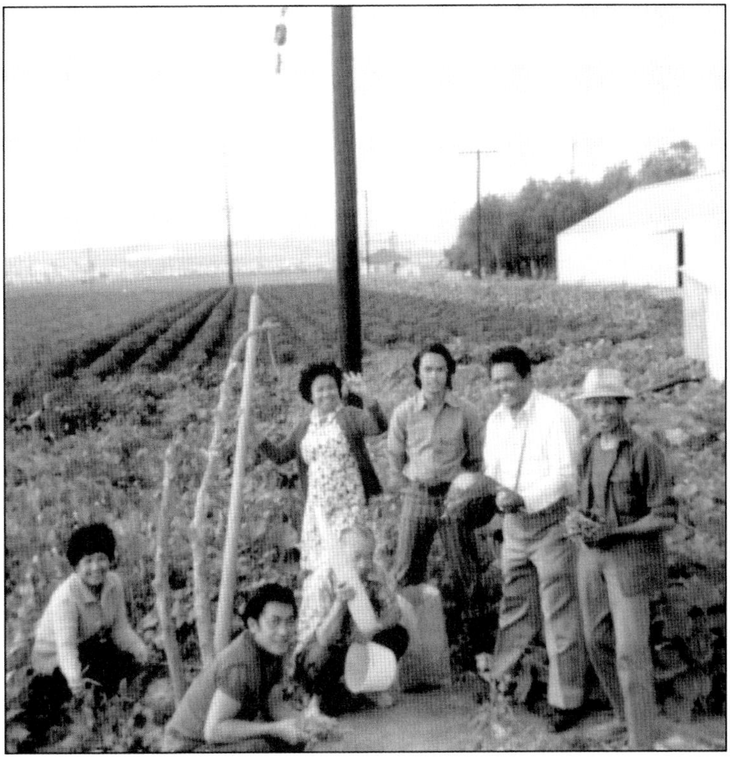

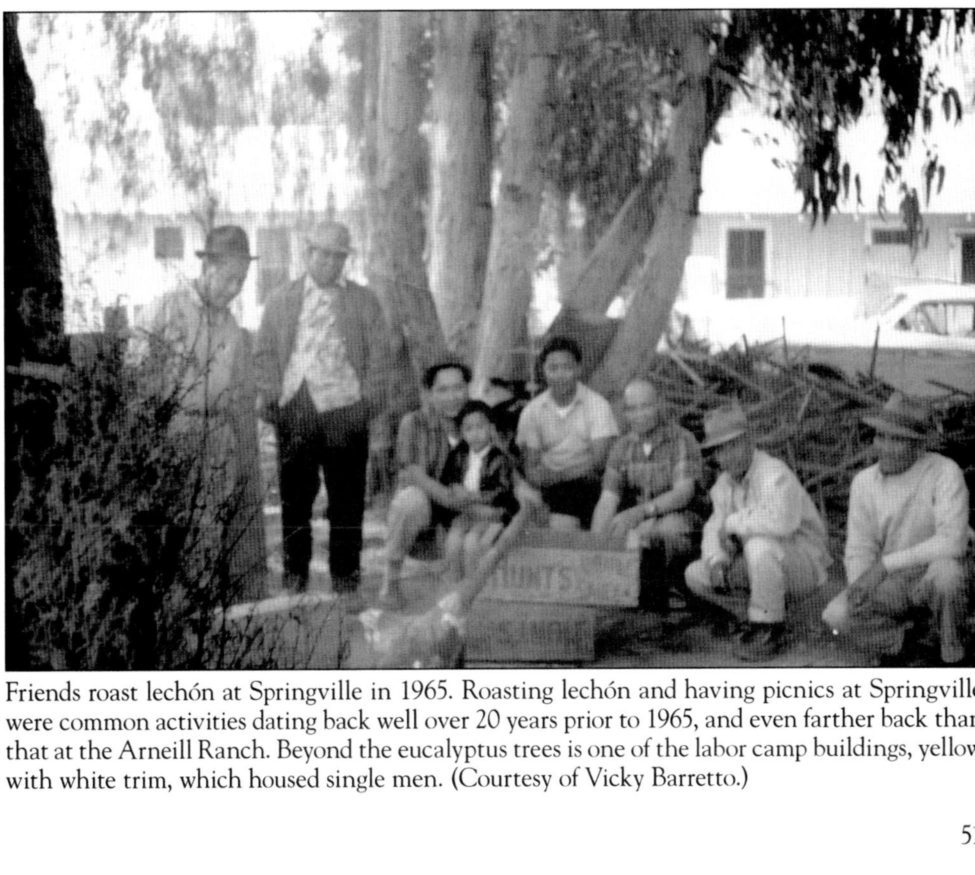

Friends roast lechón at Springville in 1965. Roasting lechón and having picnics at Springville were common activities dating back well over 20 years prior to 1965, and even farther back than that at the Arneill Ranch. Beyond the eucalyptus trees is one of the labor camp buildings, yellow with white trim, which housed single men. (Courtesy of Vicky Barretto.)

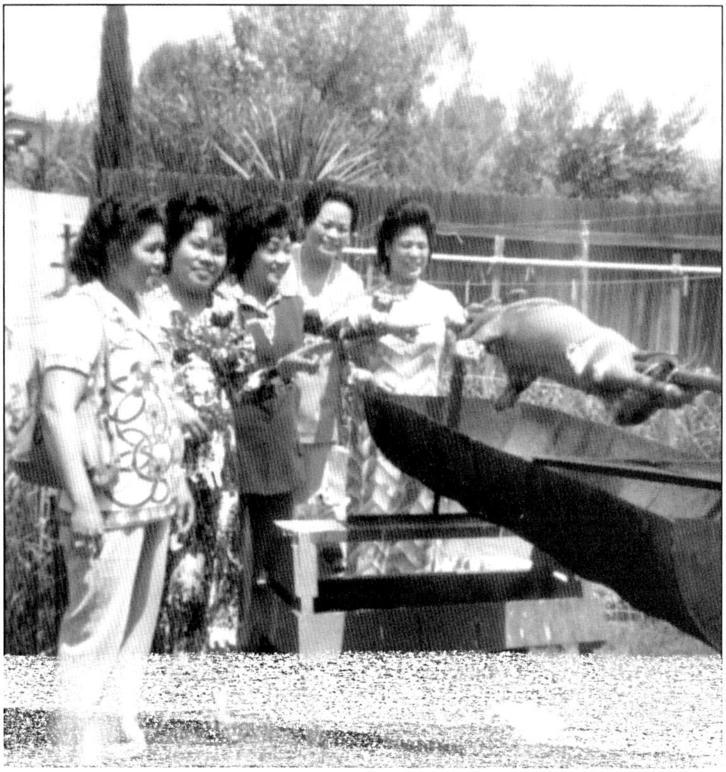

Friends gather to grill lechón in Vicky and Leopoldo Barretto's backyard at 941 Gill Avenue in Port Hueneme in 1966. It was common for families to get together and roast a pig or goat at their homes or at the local farms on weekends. (Courtesy of Vicky Barretto.)

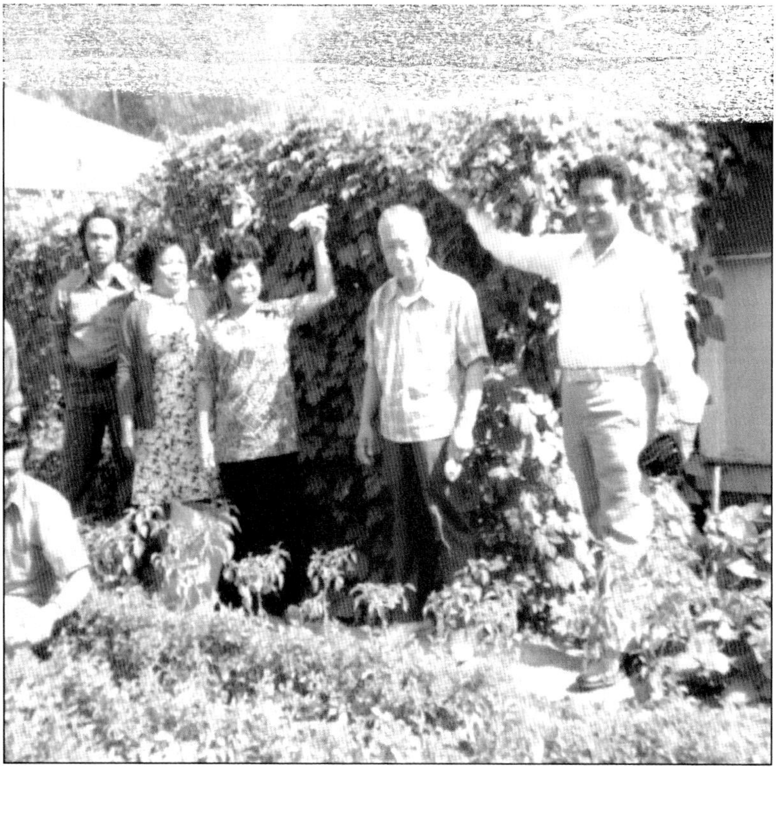

Friends from Palo Alto visit the Barrettos in 1966. This picture was taken in their backyard where a variety of Filipino vegetables were grown like *sili* (chili pepper), *ampalaya* (bitter melon), and *saluyot* (jute). (Courtesy of Vicky Barretto.)

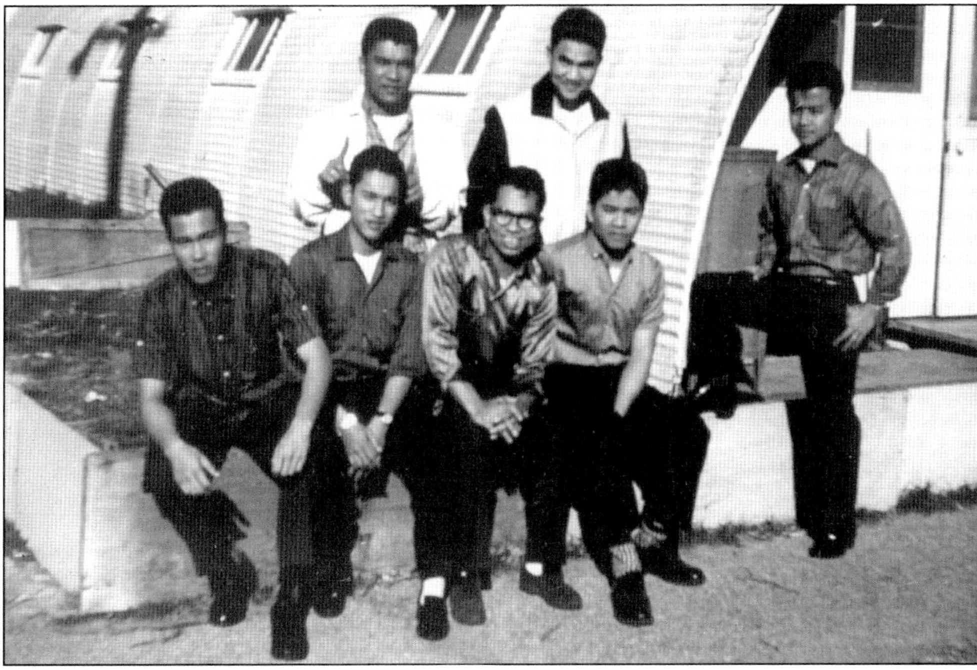

Navy servicemen are shown in front of Hamoja Housing barracks at Port Hueneme Naval Base. Hamoja Housing comprised of quonset buildings that were divided inside. Those pictured are, from left to right, Ernie Pilapil, Tony Grey, "Slim" Barcega, Efren Tilau, and Ernie Atilano. (Courtesy Tony V. Grey.)

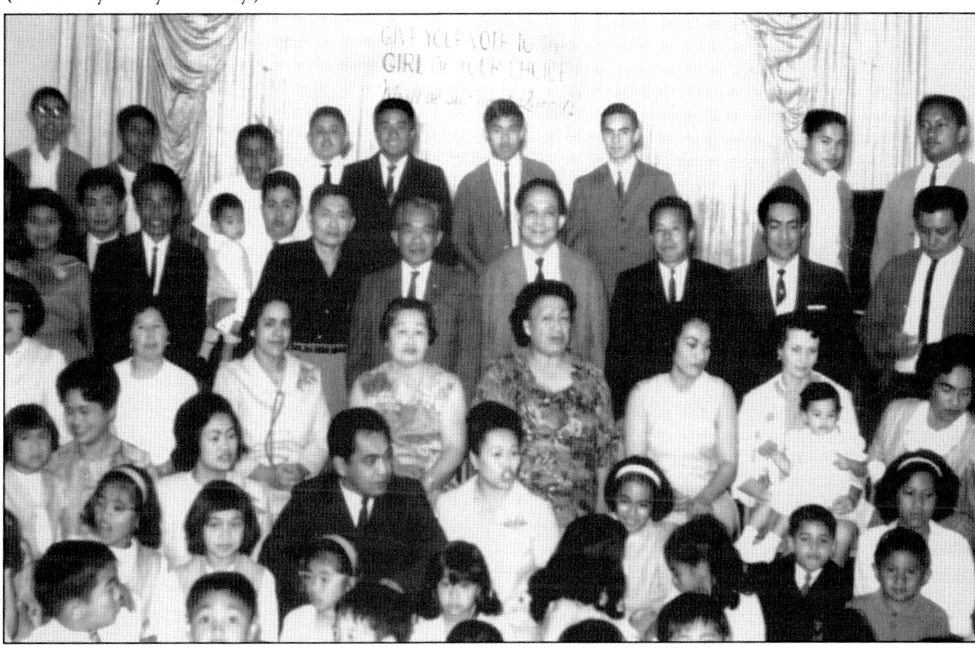

This group shot was taken at a Filipino party during the 1960s. Signs in the background read, "Give your vote to the girl of your choice. Who'll be our next queen?" Queen contests were fundraisers based on a girl's popularity, and each vote brought in a monetary donation. (Courtesy of Vincent Ines and Isidora Ines Vaca.)

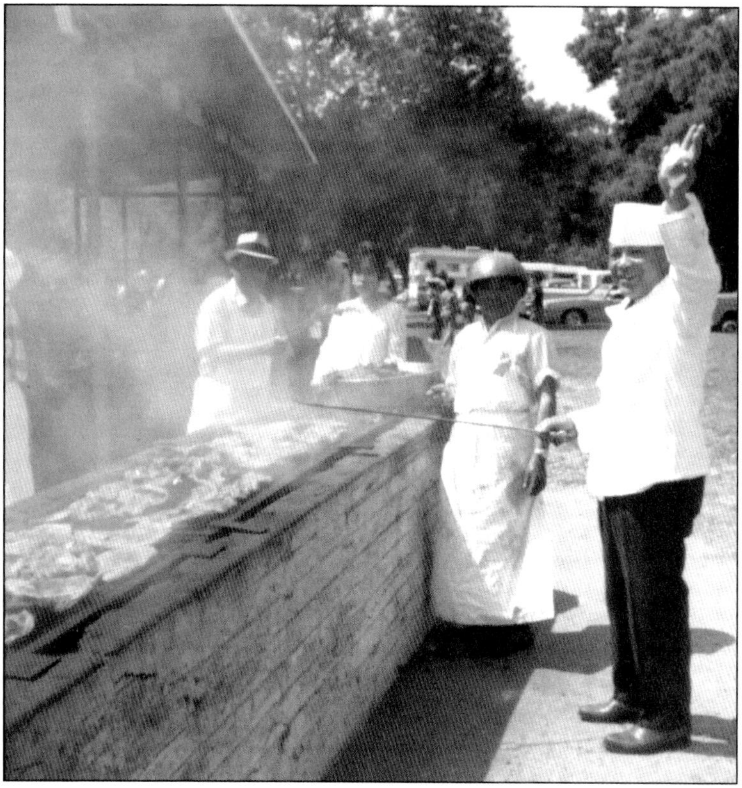

The Filipino Community of Ventura County Inc.'s (FCVCI) 1970 picnic took place at Arroyo Verde Park in Ventura. With Edith Castaneda watching, king of the grill is Silver Ines. (Courtesy of Julia Carrillo Macasieb.)

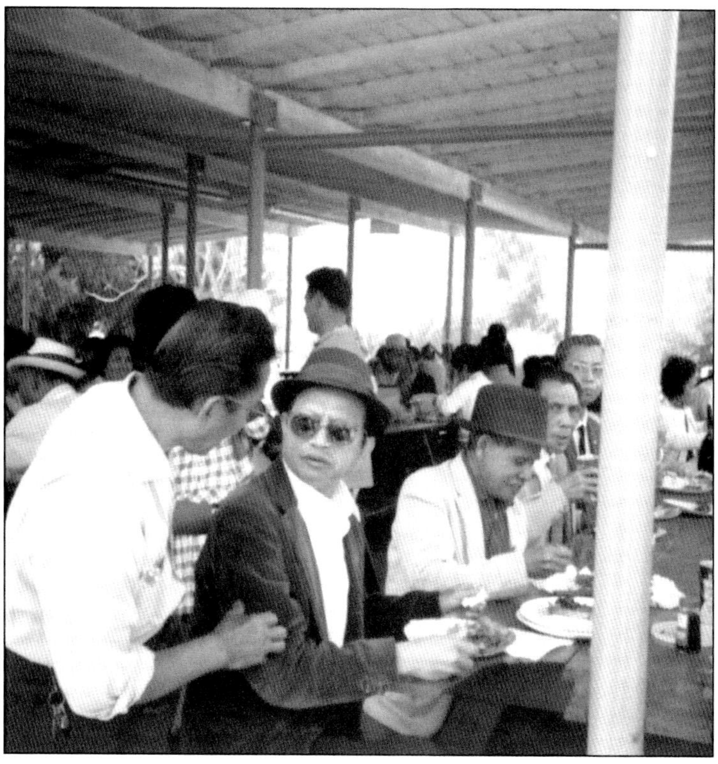

Pictured at Arroyo Verde Park in 1970 is Eddie Delmundo (in sunglasses), who is sitting next to Domingo Dela Rosa. (Courtesy of Julia Carrillo Macasieb.)

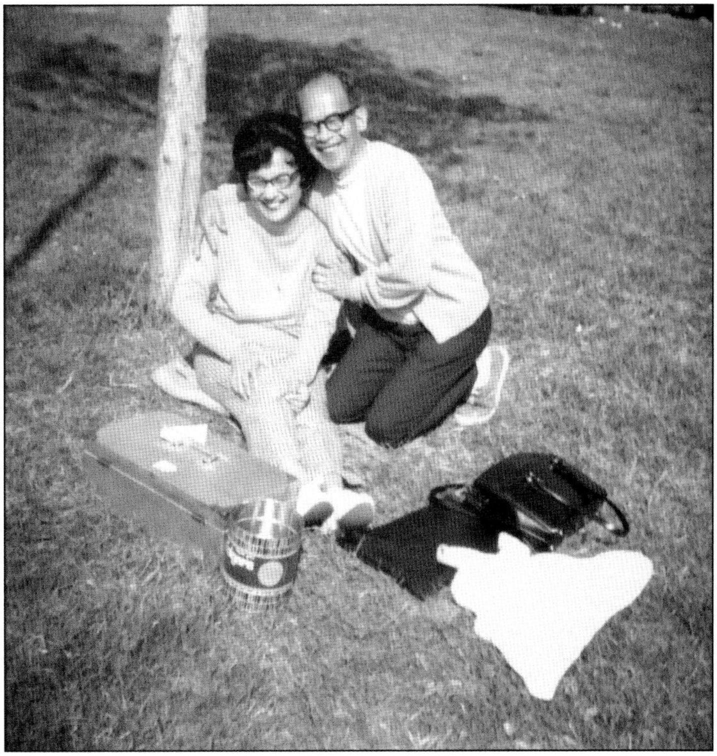

Patrocino "Pat" Carrillo and Julia Carrillo pose together at the FCVCI picnic at Arroyo Verde in 1970. Julia and Pat were married in 1954 and settled in Oxnard in 1958. They were married for 50 years. Julia has been involved with the Filipino community ever since she moved to Ventura County in 1958. She also served 37 years of civil service at Point Mugu. (Courtesy of Julia Carrillo Macasieb)

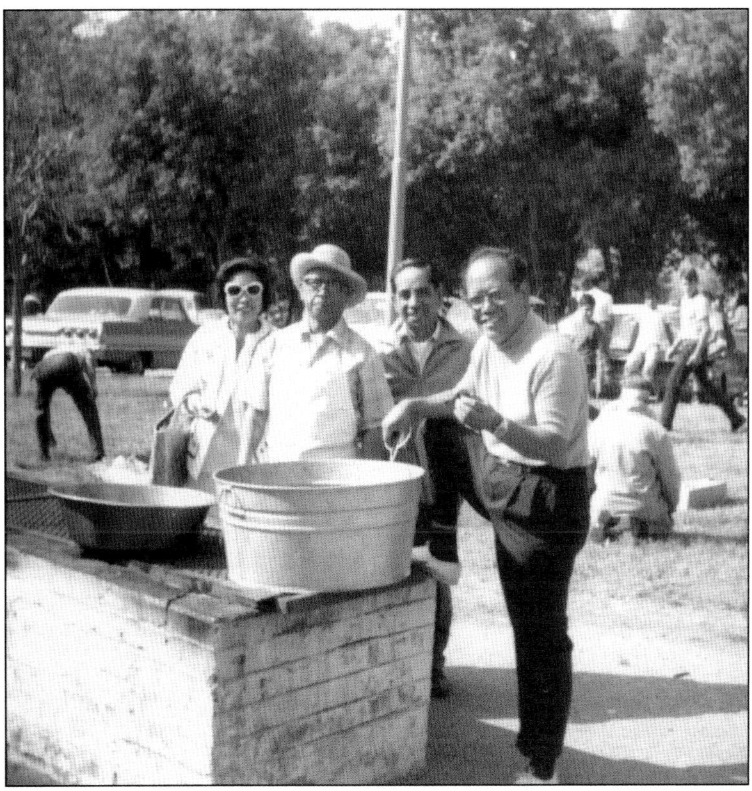

Friends and family enjoy the FCVCI picnic at Arroyo Verde in 1970. From left to right are Belen Castaneda, Frank Calucag, Augie Castaneda Sr., and Rudy Salazar. (Courtesy of Julia Carrillo Macasieb.)

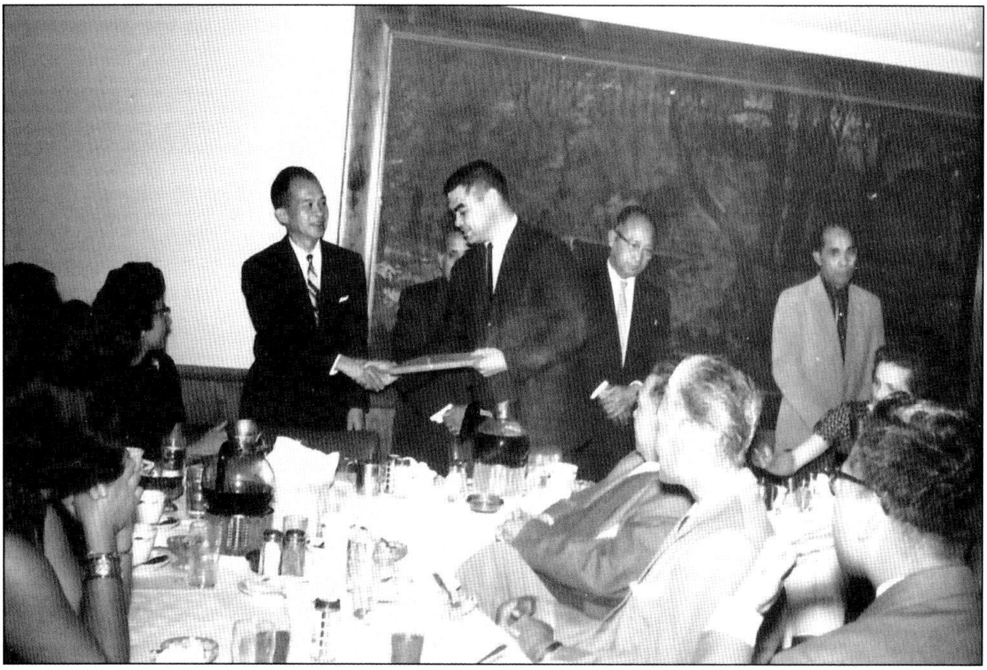

FCVCI president James "Jim" Omo presents Pat Carrillo an award at a Filipino Community of Ventura County Inc. event in the 1960s. Behind Omo is Domingo Dela Rosa, and to the right are Frank Calucag and Julian Simon. (Courtesy of Augie Castaneda Jr.)

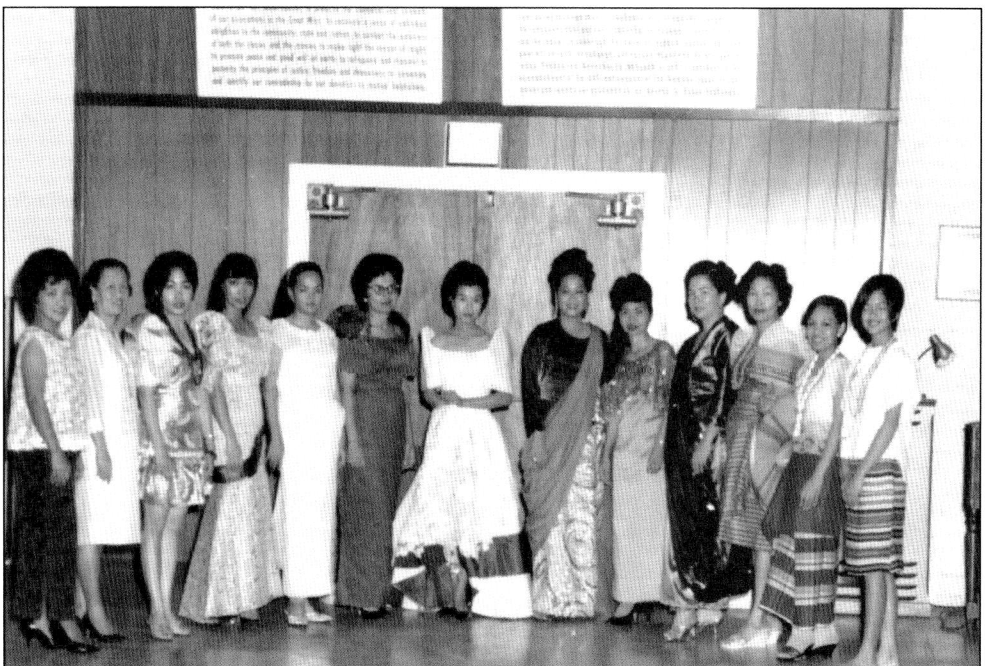

The Filipino community loved to put on fashion shows that highlighted cultural dresses from different regions of the Philippines. This one took place at the American Legion Hall in June 1969. (Courtesy of Julia Carrillo Macasieb.)

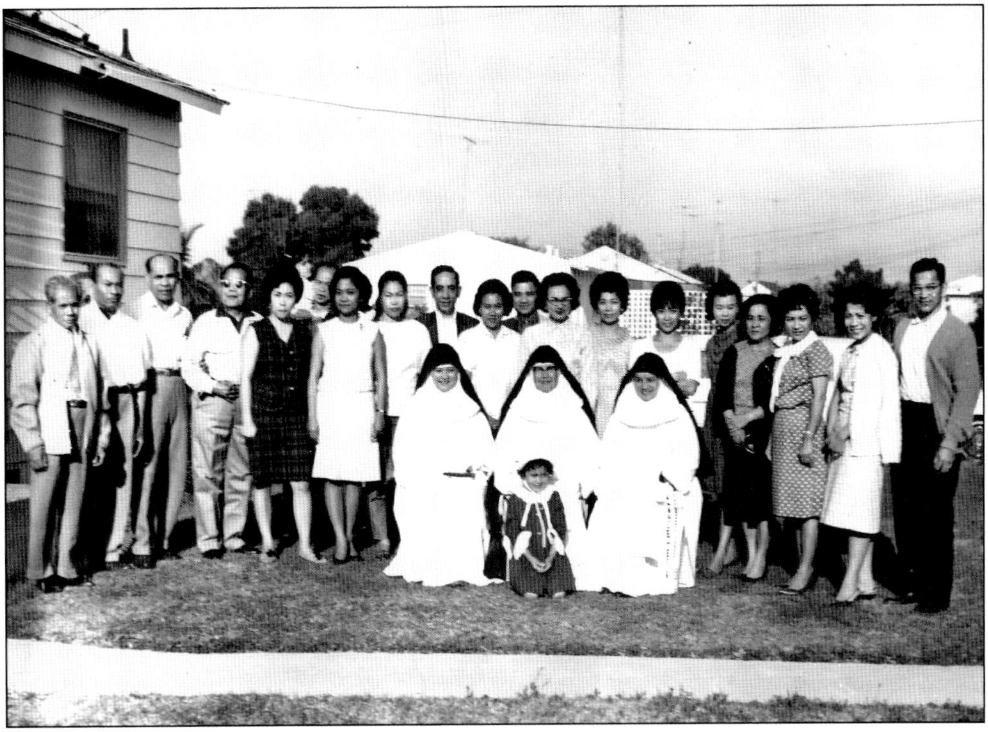

The Filipino American Community of Ventura County was first incorporated in 1955 and is currently the oldest of the 26 Filipino American organizations under the Filipino American Council today. The FCVCI held meetings at the house pictured here, which is located on the corner of Elm Street and C Street in Oxnard. Those standing are, from left to right, Domingo Dela Rosa, Albert Sindayan, Julian Simon, Aquilino "Akie" Bagay, Edith Santos, two unidentified, Belen Castaneda, Augie Castaneda Sr., two unidentified, Julia Carrillo, unidentified, Josie Castaneda, Gloria Serame, Mary Abrero, Vicky Barretto, Nina Majarucon, and Fel Majarucon. (Courtesy of Augie Castaneda Jr.)

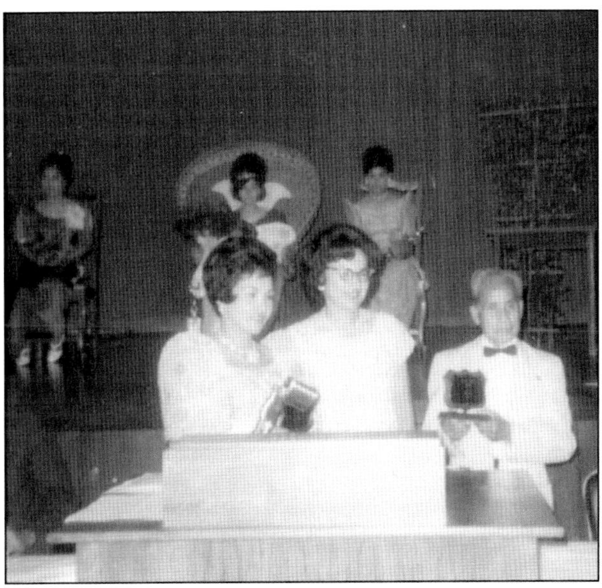

Julia Carrillo presents the Mother of the Year Award to Vicky Barretto and the Father of the Year Award to Domingo Dela Rosa during the FCVCI Program in July 1968 in Oxnard. The program also included a queen pageant coronation ceremony. (Courtesy of Vicky Barretto.)

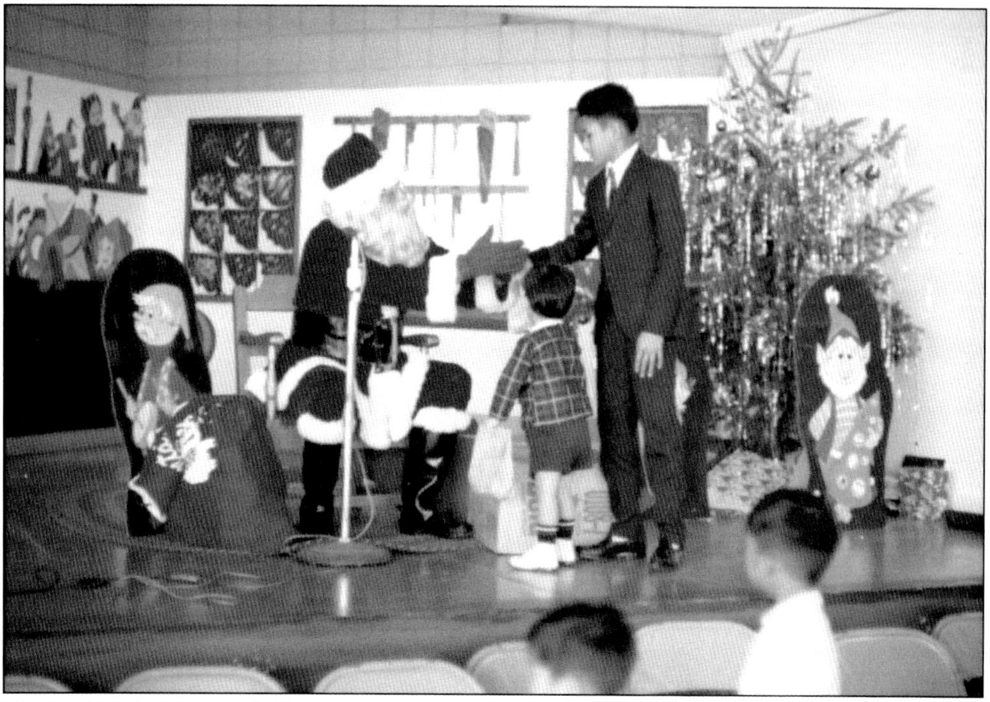

The FCVCI held annual Christmas programs for the children and families. All the Christmas programs included a special visit from Santa Claus. The photograph below depicts a sunny 1960s Christmas celebration behind the FCVCI Building, located at the corner of Elm and C Streets. (Courtesy of Julia Carrillo Macasieb.)

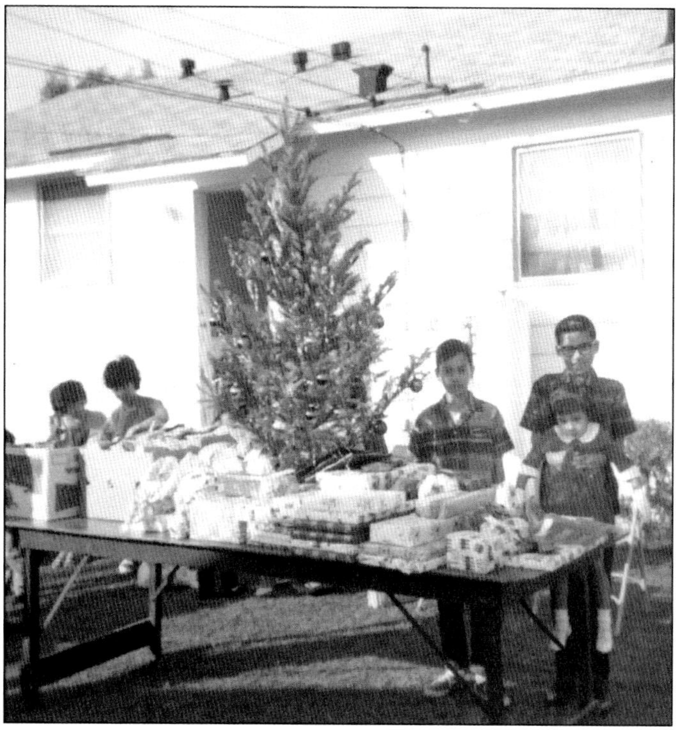

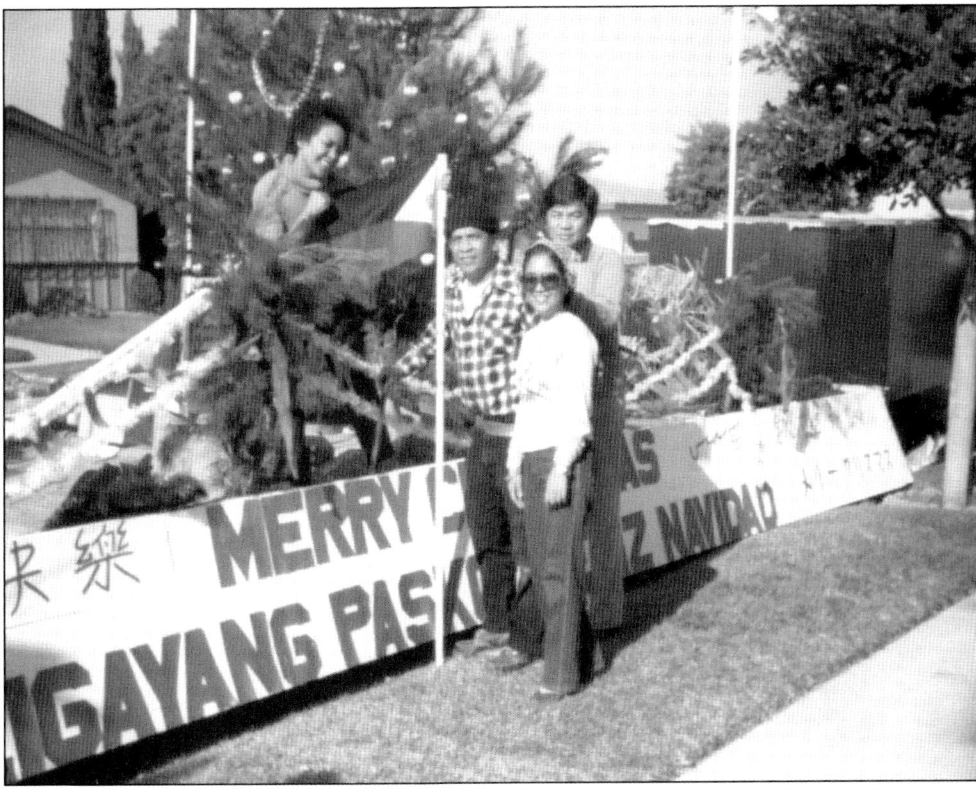

FCVCI volunteers, like those pictured above, helped construct the Christmas float for the Oxnard Christmas Parade in a member's backyard during the 1970s. Josie Bautista was part of the float design team. Below shows the float fully assembled, parked on the curb, and ready for the parade. *Malingayang Pasko* translates to "Merry Christmas" in Tagalog, the national language of the Philippines. (Courtesy of Josie and Al Bautista.)

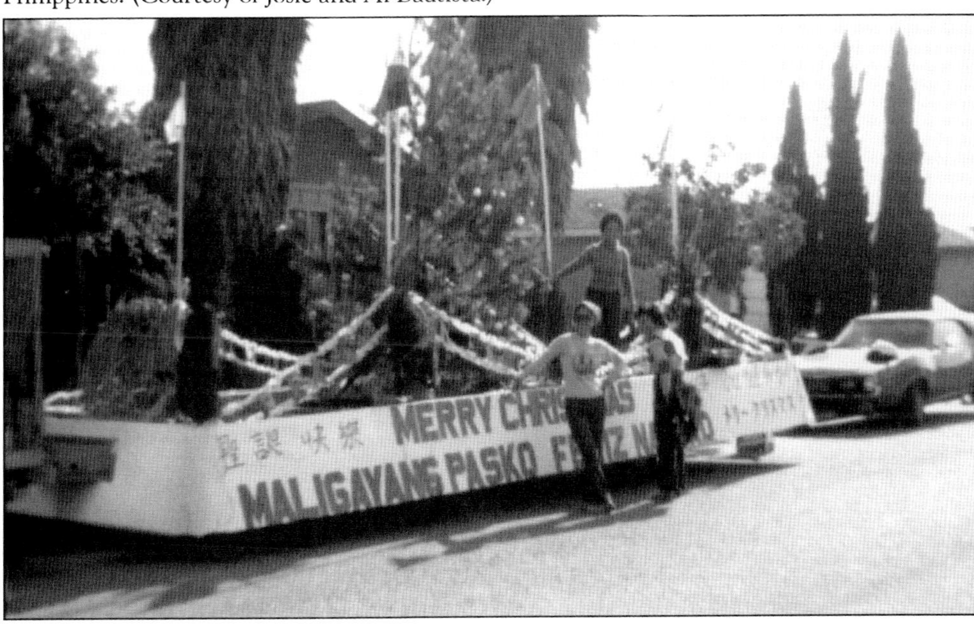

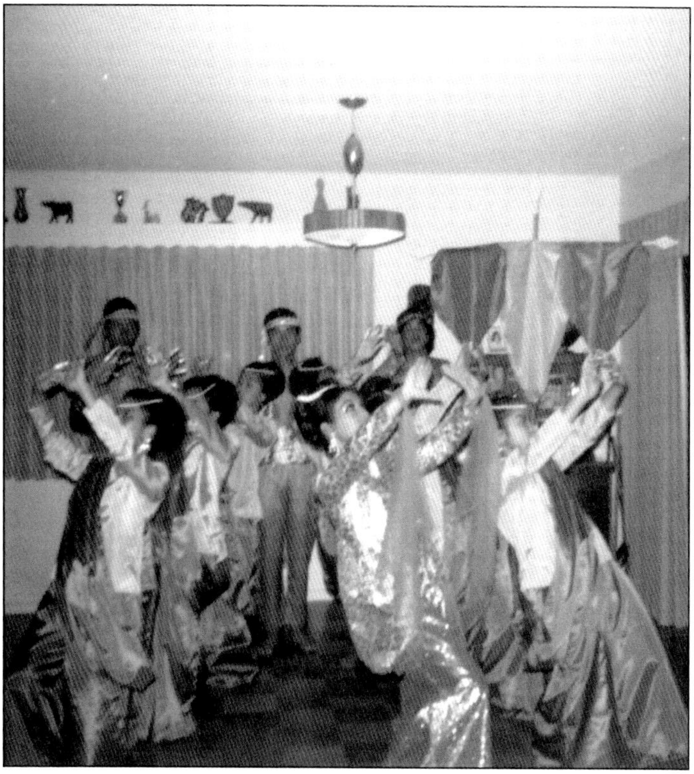

Young people practiced Filipino cultural dances at various members' homes in preparation for FCVCI events. This Filipino cultural practice took place at the residence of Pat and Julia Carrillo at 4510 South B Street in Oxnard in 1970. The photograph at left shows ladies wearing traditional *malongs* (dresses) performing a Filipino Muslim dance with the Muslim princess at the foreground. The *tinikling* dance, shown below, involves two people tapping and sliding two bamboo poles to a beat while two dancers step over and in between the poles. (Courtesy of Julia Carrillo Macasieb.)

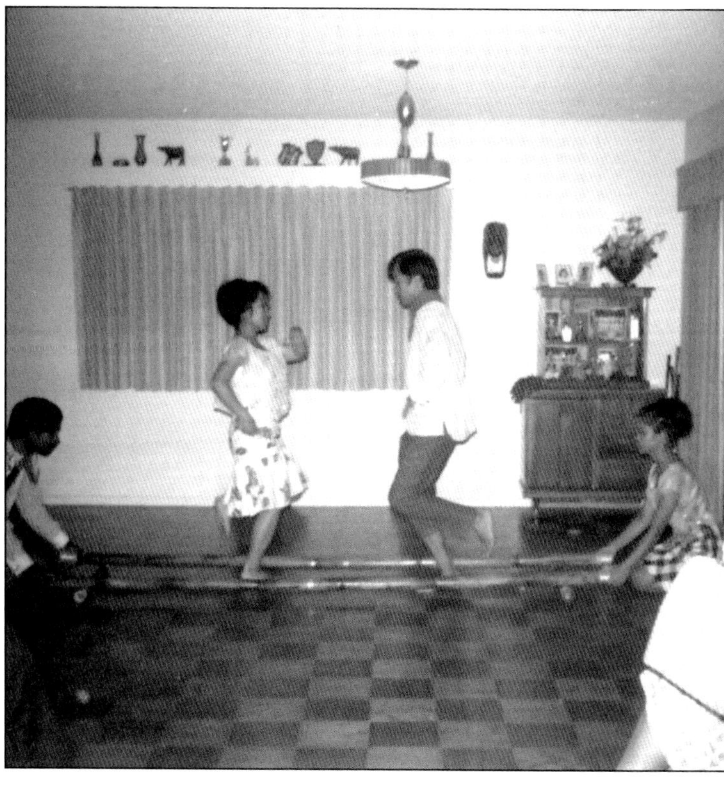

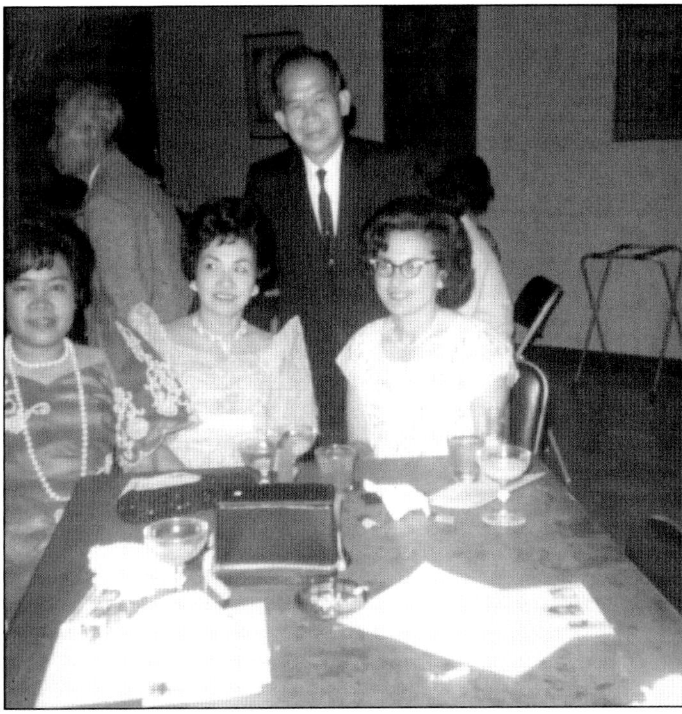

The photograph at right shows audience members enjoying the cultural festivities at the 1967 FCVCI Program. They are, from left to right, unidentified woman, Vicky Barretto, Julia Carrillo, and Pat Carrillo (standing). Below, young Filipinos perform different cultural dances on stage during the program. (Courtesy of Julia Carrillo Macasieb.)

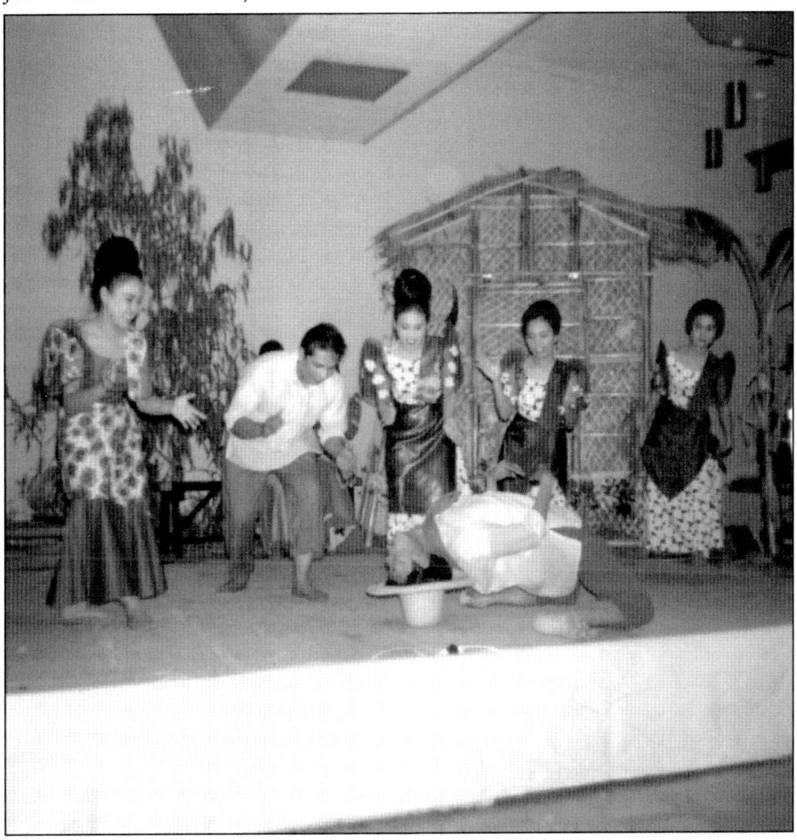

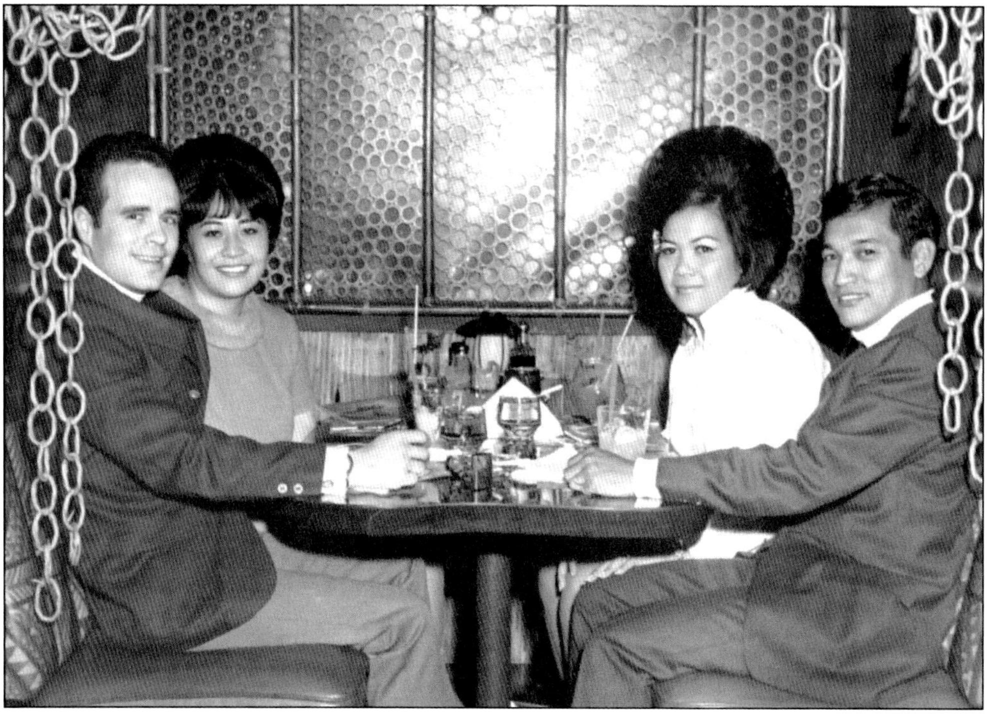

On April 4, 1969, Larry Stamper, Ann Stamper, Mary Grey, and Tony Grey enjoy an evening at Mr. C's Club in Long Beach. Larry was Tony's first American friend in the US Navy. (Courtesy of Tony V. Grey.)

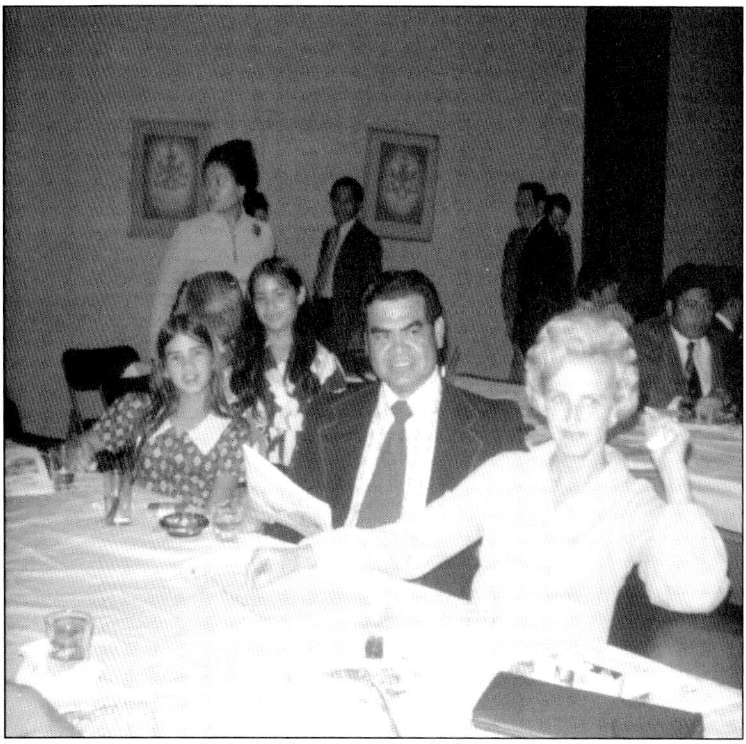

James Omo and his wife, Joyce, enjoy festivities at an FCVCI event in 1972. Jim Omo was the executive director of the Boys and Girls Club of Oxnard and later became the executive director at Hayward's Boys and Girls Club. One year he helped raise $27,000 for a new gymnasium for the Boys and Girls Club in Oxnard and recruited volunteer contractors and labor from all over the county. (Courtesy of Julia Carrillo Macasieb.)

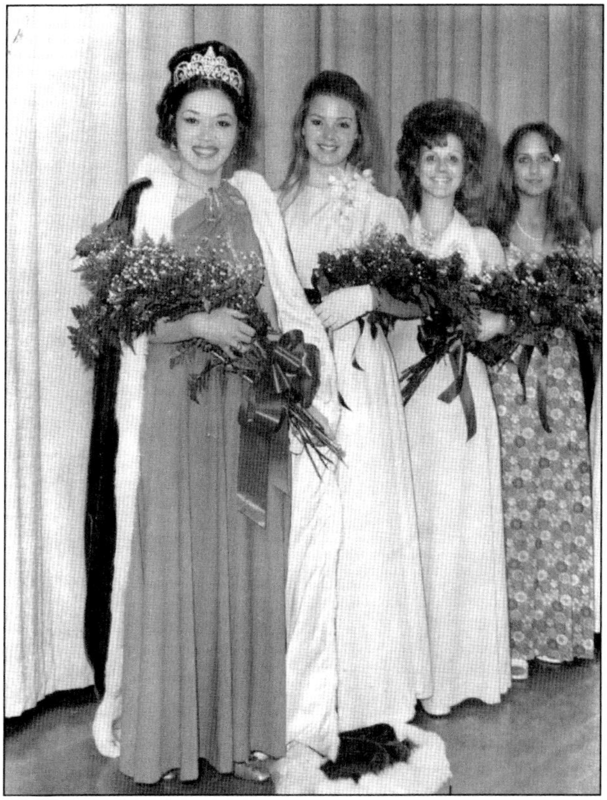

Darlene Abarca (far left) was selected Seabee queen 1974 from a field of 29 candidates, who were nominated by the Civil Engineer Corps (CEC) and judged in the categories of formal appearance, expression, poise, beauty, and character. Abarca called for more involvement by utilizing her position as an opportunity to do more in the community, such as charity drives, social events, hostess duties, hospital visits, and open houses. (Courtesy of the US Navy Seabee Archives.)

Reflections of a Queen

Story by JO2 John Walker

The day is quickly approaching when the Port Hueneme Seabees will select a queen to rule for 1975. The date set for the Seabee Ball is March 15 and the Seabee Queen will be crowned a few days preceding that date.

Darlene Elizabeth Abarcas, the 1974 Seabee Queen, looks back on her reign with mixed emotions. Darlene represented the commissary store in last year's judging.

Some of her official duties for 1974 included attending the Seabee Ball and greeting Construction Battalions Three and Four on their return to the U.S.

Some of her duties? "That was all I did," said Darlene. She continued, "When I won the contest, I felt like Cinderella. I felt that it would all end at midnight — and — in a way it did!

"Don't get me wrong. I think that being queen was a wonderful and beautiful experience. Everyone was super-nice to me. Everyone went out of their way to ensure that everything and every place was aware of my queen status. It was beautiful and great, that's all I can say about it.

"I hope, however, this year's queen will be given the opportunity for involvement in more base activities."

According to Miss Abarcas, one of her biggest surprises was finding herself involved in very few things after the Seabee Ball.

She said, "After the ball no other demands were placed on my time with the exception of the greeting of returning battalions.

"I know there were plans to have the queen and court at various functions throughout the year but the plans seemed to always fall through. Possibly the explanation lies in a reluctance to impose on our time.

"There is so much that the queen and court could do. We could help with charity drives, social events or act as semi-official hostesses for the base.

"Some of the specific things I can think of are visiting with hospital patients, representing our friends on base in the local parades and greeting people during open-houses.

"Our time shouldn't be limited to just official functions. We could be utilized by wives' and men's clubs for promotion of sanctioned charities.

"The lack of requests for participation in activities was rather a let-down after the build-up prior to the ball."

Darlene thought that one of the really positive things about the contest and ball was the efforts of the people on the committees for those events.

"Everyone was positively beautiful. They all went out of their way to make us feel at ease. About the judges, I can't say enough. They realized that this wasn't a beauty contest and they judged us as just people.

"They didn't allow prejudice and were absolutely the most un-biased, fair group of people I have met. They did a great job."

The queen said that you have your ups and downs in your reign. It is possible to be disheartened and enthusiastic at the same time.

She said, "If I could say one thing about the job, it would be that it was a wonderful experience. I would not want to be queen again though, the first time was so beautiful that a second reign would only be anti-climatic.

"One thing I want to say is thank you. It was people who nominated me, selected me and supported me. Without them I wouldn't have gotten anywhere. Thank you, everyone."

A smile appeared on Darlene's face. "You know," she said, "if ever I have a daughter, I would want her to be Seabee Queen."

A note of ending, prior to press time this interview was shown to officials at CBC.

"This is interesting," they said, "she is right, of course, in everything that she said. Her recommendations for utilization of the queen and court are sound and we can assure everyone that in the future the job of queen or princess will have a definite meaning in base activities."

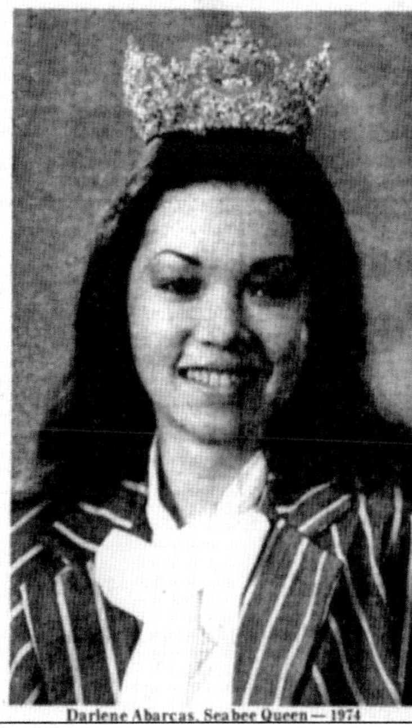

Darlene Abarcas, Seabee Queen — 1974

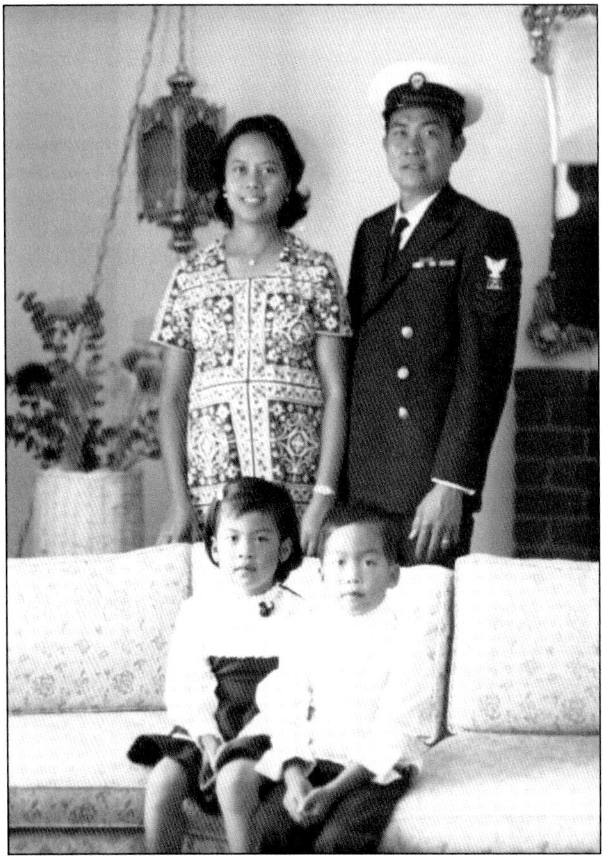

The Obispo family in 1977 enjoys their brand-new home at 5001 San Juan Avenue in Oxnard. Seated are Joan and Antony with Nellie and John Obispo standing behind them. In this image, Nellie is pregnant with Dorothy. (Courtesy of Nellie and John Obispo.)

John Obispo says good-bye to his daughter Joan Obispo (20 months old) before his deployment to Diego Garcia, site of a joint military facility of the United Kingdom and the United States. They are standing in front of Vicky and Leo Barretto's house at 941 Gill Avenue in Port Hueneme. (Courtesy of Nellie and John Obispo.)

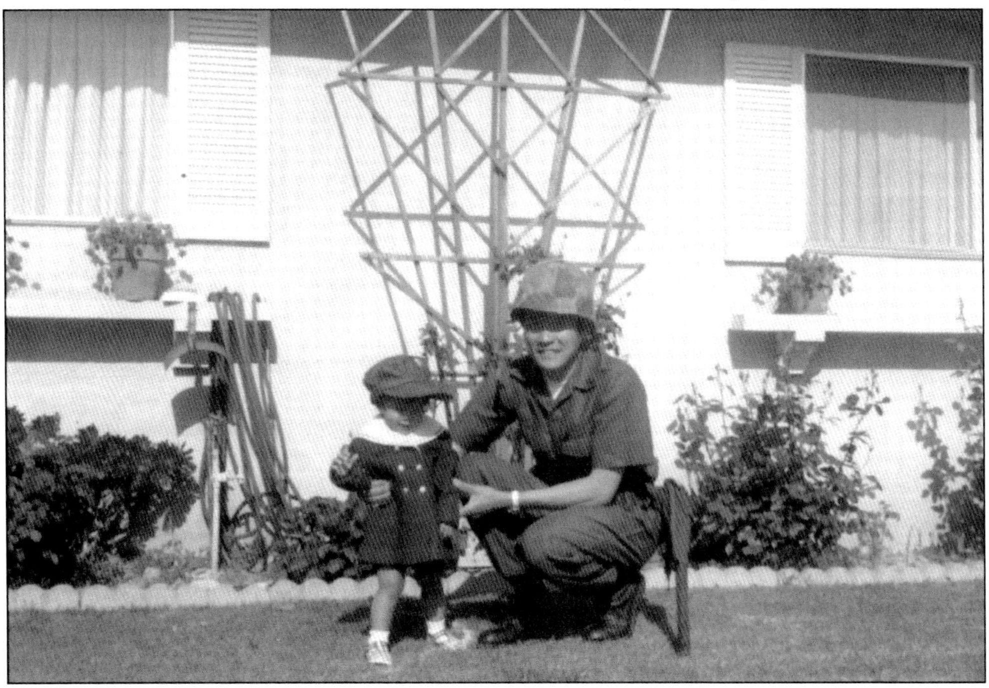

Dante Honorico and his family immigrated to the United States in 1975 and settled in Oxnard. In this photograph, the family celebrates Honorico's graduation from the Ventura County Police and Sheriff Academy on December 16, 1976. Pictured are Honorico, his wife Ellen, and daughters Abigail and Genevieve. (Courtesy of Ellen and Dante Honorico.)

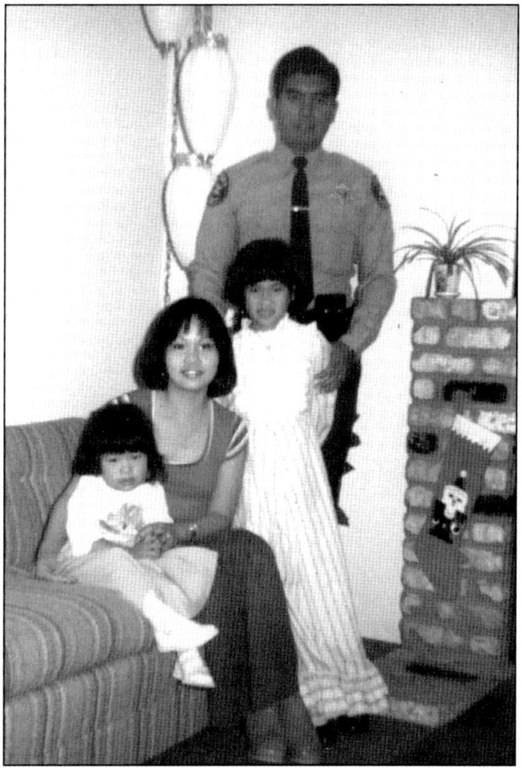

The Castaneda family enjoys Bubbling Springs Park in Port Hueneme in 1975. Those pictured are, from left to right, (first row) Augie Castaneda Sr., Virgie Castaneda, Josie Castaneda; (second row) Millie Castaneda, Belen Castaneda, Augie Castaneda Jr., Albert Castaneda, and Edith Castaneda. All three Castaneda men participated in the military. Augie Sr. served in the Philippine Scouts in World War II, Augie Jr. was in the US Air Force, and Albert was in the US Navy. (Courtesy of Augie Castaneda Jr.)

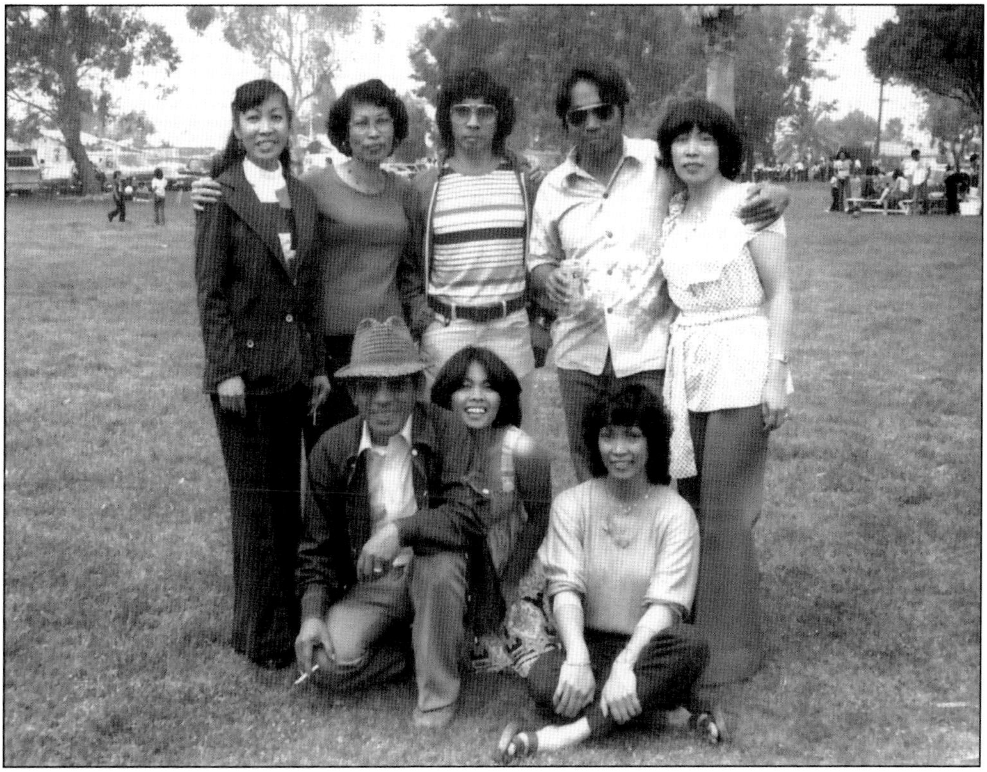

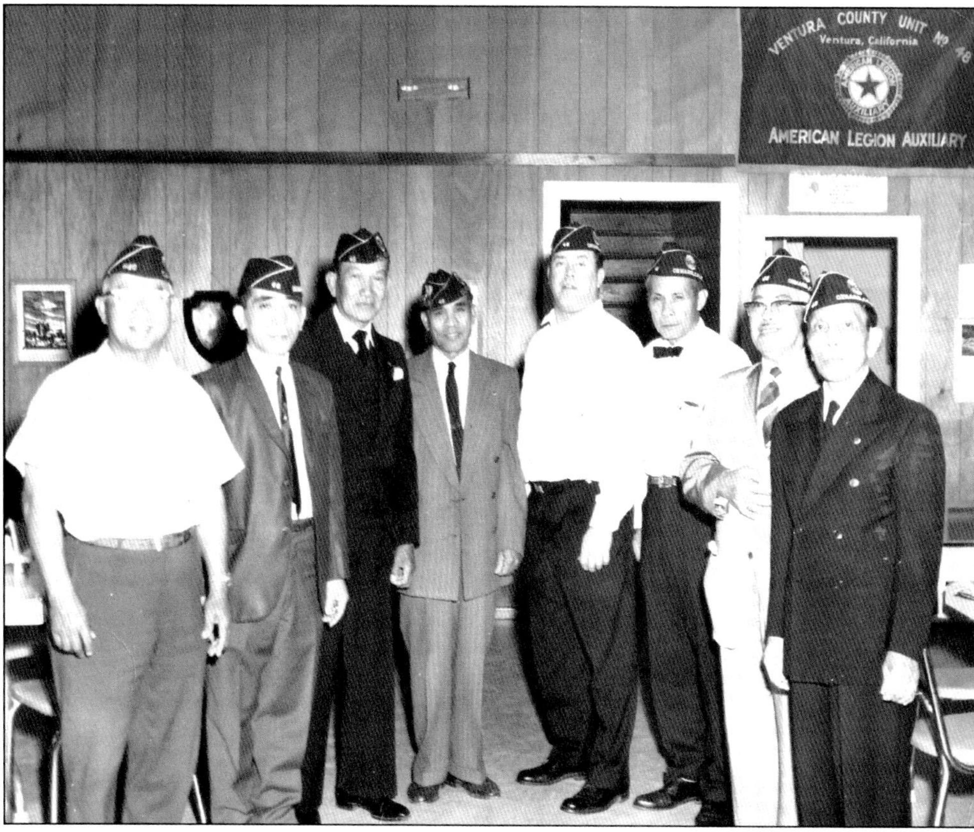

The Ventura County American Legion No. 48 is a veteran service organization promoting mentorship, youth programs, advocacy, and devotion to fellow veterans. Pictured from left to right are Frank Calucag, Augie Castaneda Sr., unidentified, Julian Simon, unidentified, Jose Soriano, and two unidentified. (Courtesy of Augie Castaneda Jr.)

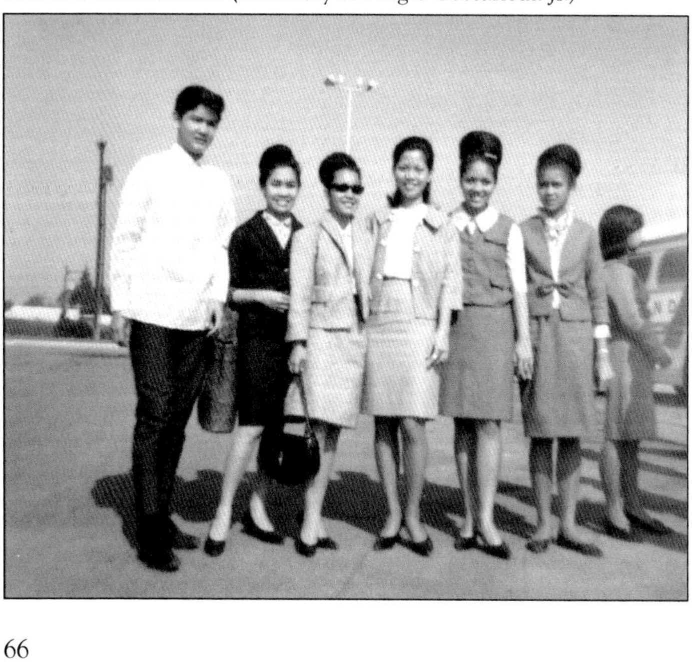

Filipino Leyte Dancers from the Philippine Islands performed for the FCVCI in the 1960s. FCVCI has also hosted other organizations from the Philippine Islands, such as the bankers from the Philippine National Bank. (Courtesy of Julia Carrillo Macasieb.)

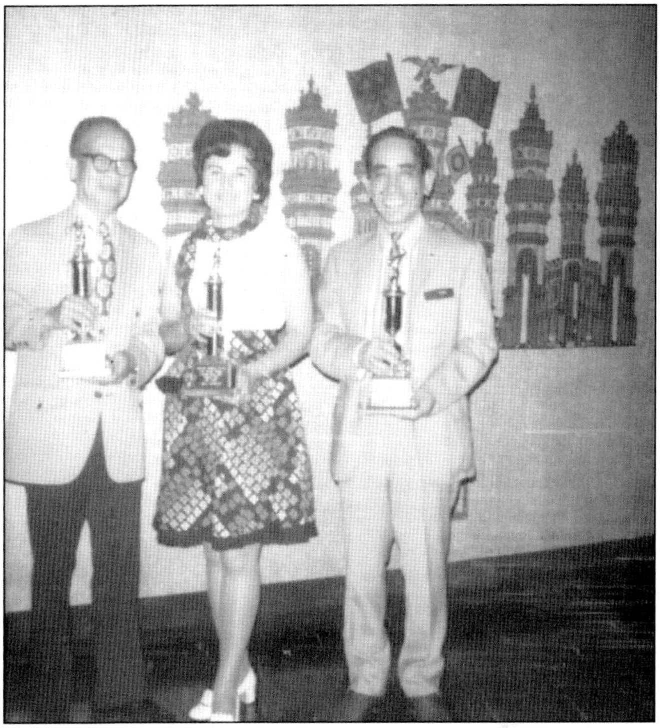

Pictured are three members of the FCVCI Mixed-Winter Bowling League in 1972. Team members include Pat Carrillo, Julia Carrillo, Augie Castaneda Sr., and Al Bautista (not pictured). The league played at the Wagon Wheel Bowl at 2801 Wagon Wheel Road in Oxnard. (Courtesy of Julia Carrillo Macasieb.)

The 1973 US Navy Mobile Construction Battalion 3 (MCB3) bowling champs, based in Port Hueneme, are pictured here during their deployment to Roosevelt Road, Puerto Rico. (Courtesy of Socorro and Vic Mercado.)

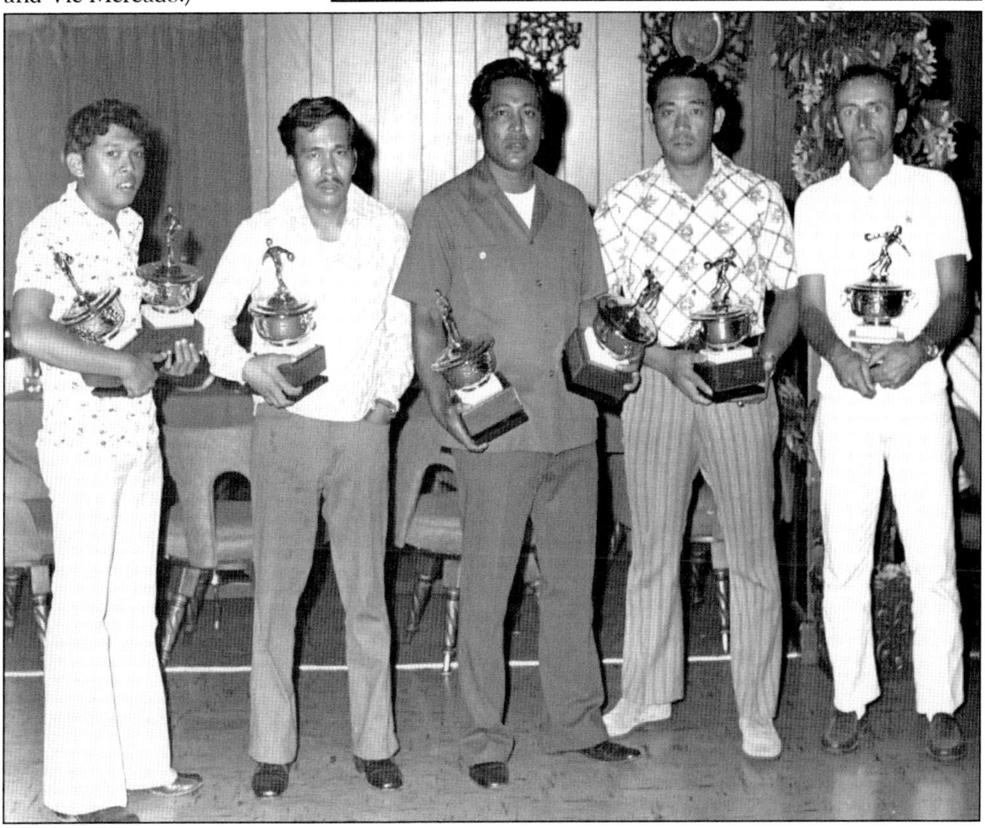

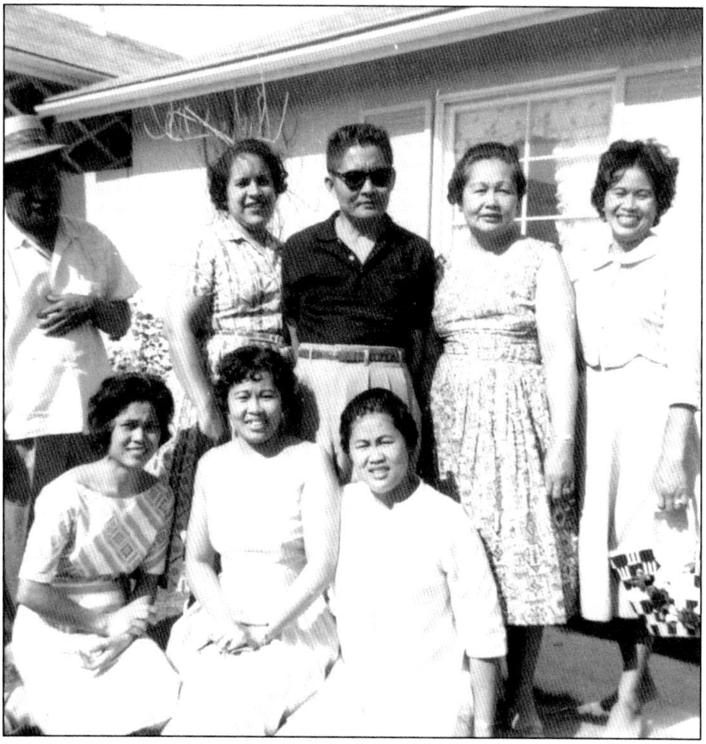

The Ines family is shown outside their home in the 1960s. Valinte Ines was naturalized and became a US citizen in 1951. Ever since then, Valinte was always compelled to carry a small piece of paper with his naturalization number for fear of being questioned by authorities. Those pictured are, from left to right, (first row) Leling Ines, Ana Ines, and Grace Ines; (second row) Jerry Rossi, Mary Ines, Valinte Ines, Amalia Ines (Valinte's sister), and Laura Ines Rossi. (Courtesy of Vincent Ines and Isidora Ines Vaca.)

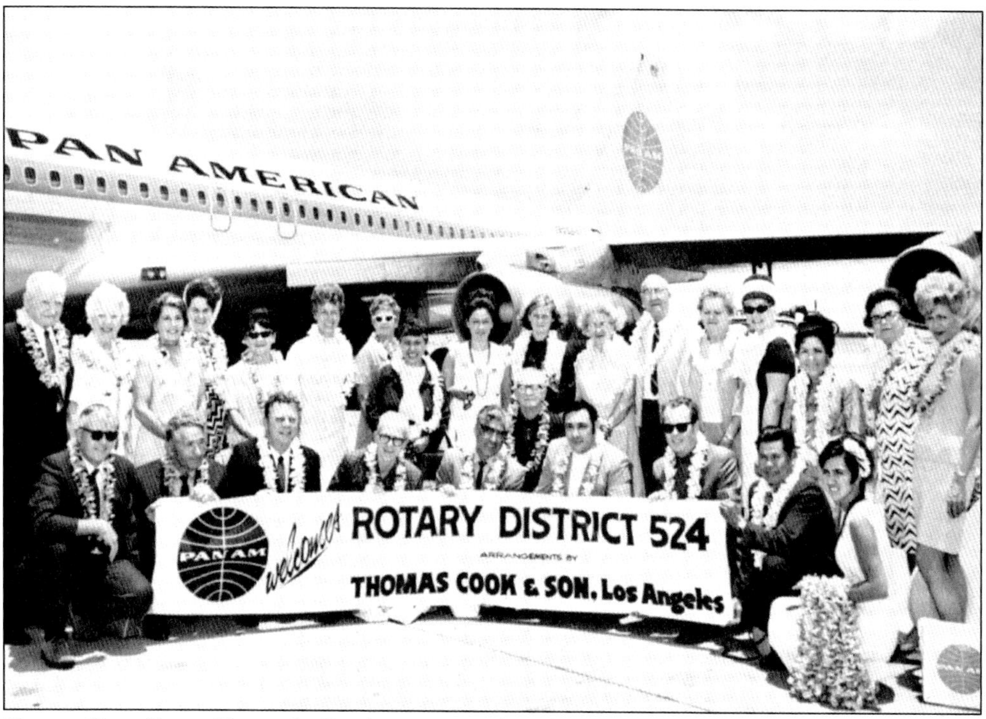

George Omo Sr. and his wife, Sarah, rotarians from Rotary District 524, won a trip to Hawaii on Pan Am in the 1960s. Filipinos were involved in service organizations in addition to Filipino community organizations. (Courtesy of Lillian Omo Roman.)

Four

MILITARY LIFE

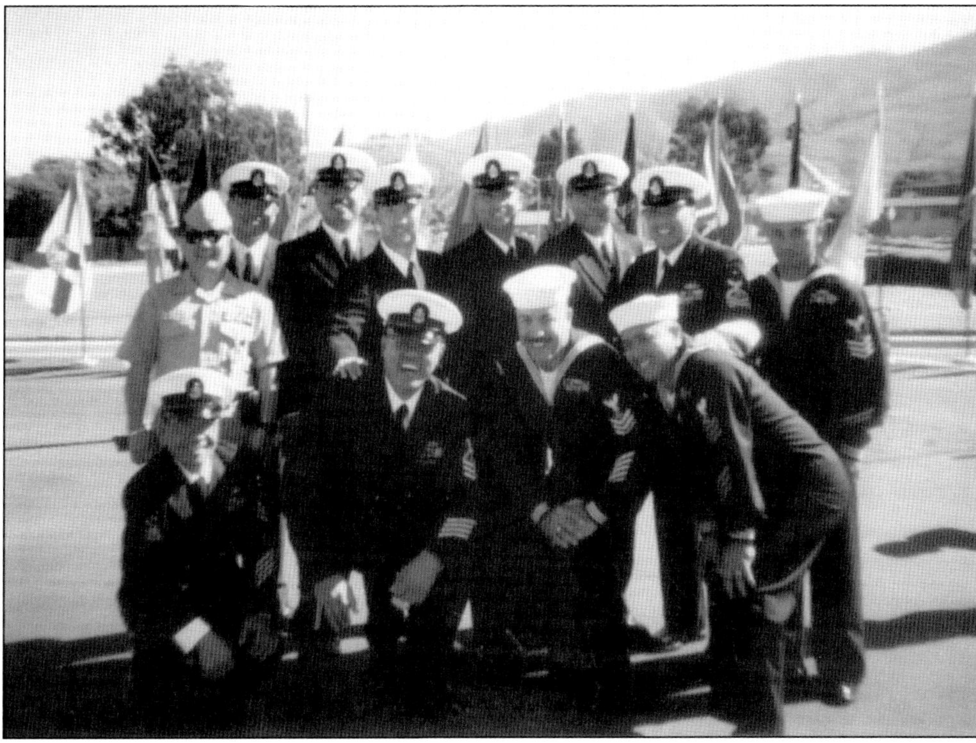

Heeding the call to the military life is an honor that is unique, challenging, and rewarding. Filipinos fought side by side with other American soldiers over the decades, including World War II, with the Philippine Scouts and the 1st and 2nd Filipino Infantry Regiments. After World War II, there was a surge of military enlistments, especially in the three bases in Ventura County. During World War II, Port Hueneme was an Advance Base Depot (1942) until it was renamed the Naval Construction Battalion Center in 1945. In 1946, Point Mugu served as a Naval Air Missile Test Center until it was renamed the Naval Air Station to provide support for the center in 1949. The Oxnard Air Force Base (1940–1945 and 1951–1970) was a fighter-training airfield during World War II and is located in Camarillo. Military families endure separations and relocations as part of their unique burden to ensure security of the United States. Military wives ensure a sense of security and normalcy for their children at home and for their husbands abroad. Their charge is to maintain households so that daily life continues, especially during lengthy deployments and wartime service. Many Filipino men served bravely and are decorated servicemen, serving in World War II, Korea, Vietnam, the Gulf Wars, and continue to serve today. They are honored by their family members and members of their communities. (Courtesy of Peter Villanueva.)

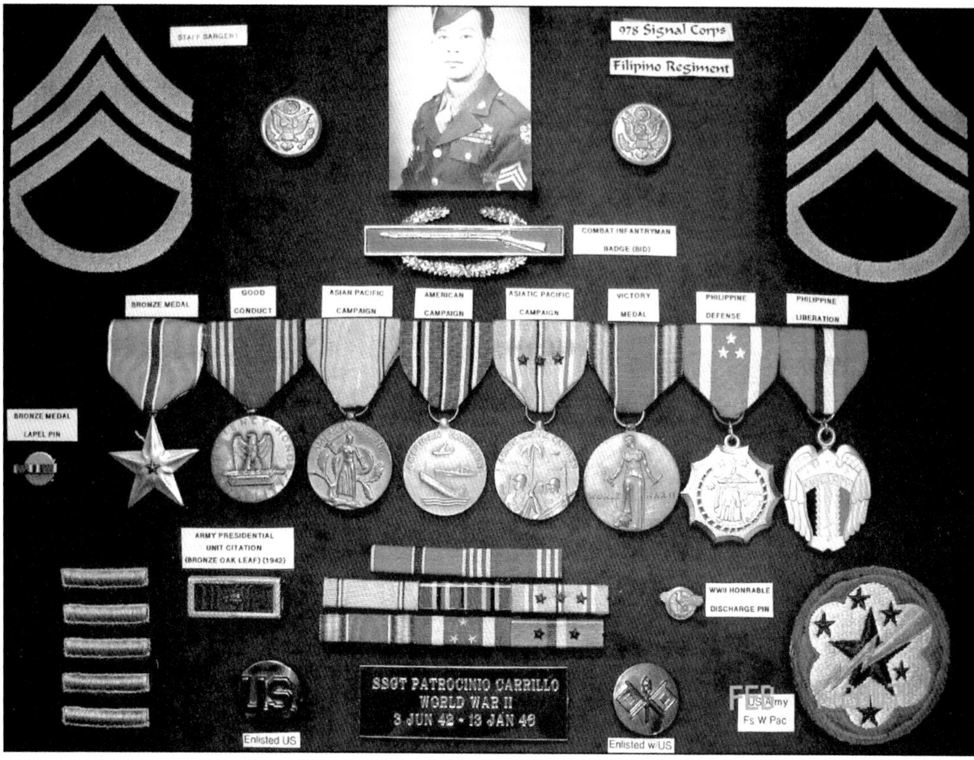

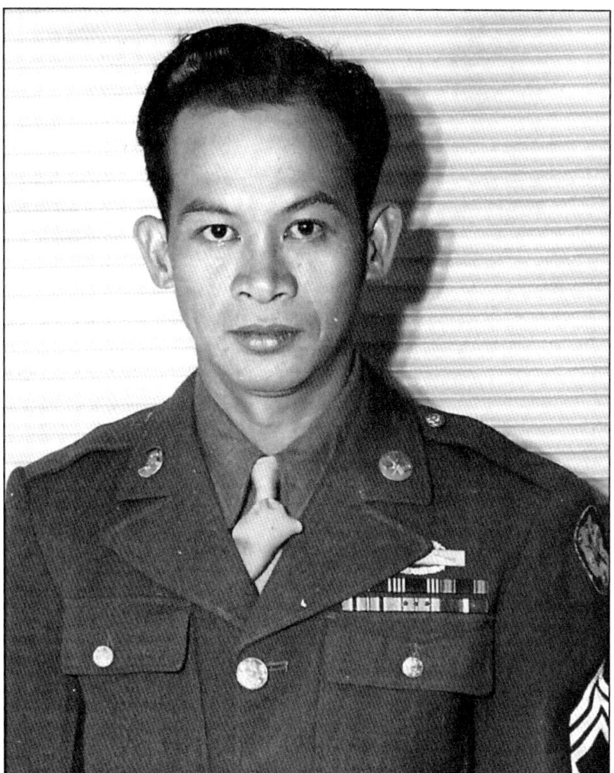

In 1943, Patrocino "Pat" Sobido Carrillo was in the US Army 978th Signal Service Company in the Philippines during World War II. Staff Sergeant Carrillo arrived in Brisbane, Australia, and was personally briefed by General MacArthur to be his eyes and ears. From Brisbane, he flew to Darwin, Australia, and boarded a US Navy submarine for Sablayan, Mindoro, Philippines. Carrillo and six Army soldiers were met by guerillas and immediately embedded. In danger at all times, he was part of the intelligence team transmitting encoded messages to headquarters in Brisbane on Japanese movements and resources. He received the Philippine Liberation Ribbon with two Bronze Stars, the Asian Pacific Campaign Medal, the World War II Victory Medal, and the American Campaign Medal. (Courtesy of Julia Carrillo Macasieb.)

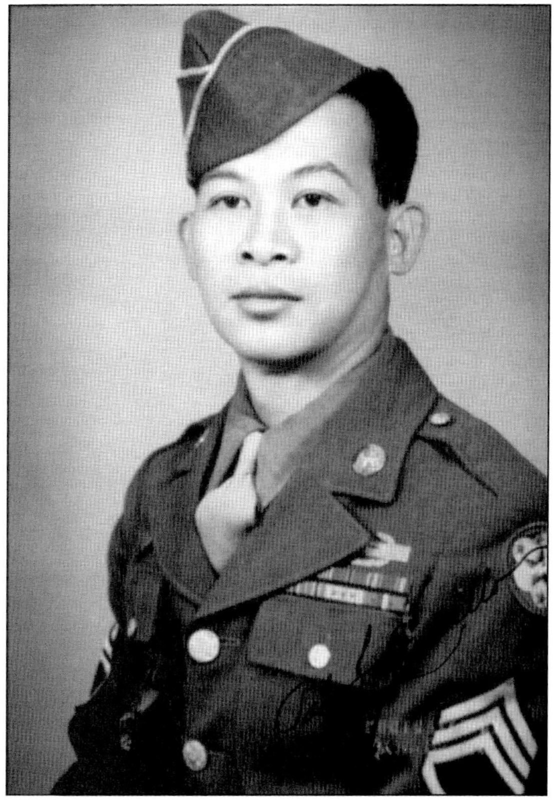

In 2003, S.Sgt. Pat Carrillo was grand marshal at the Camarillo Christmas Parade. He lived in Ventura County for 45 years, was a life member of the Filipino American Association of Camarillo, and the Filipino Community of Ventura County. Pat was married to Julia Carrillo for 50 years and has three children. (Courtesy of Julia Carrillo Macasieb.)

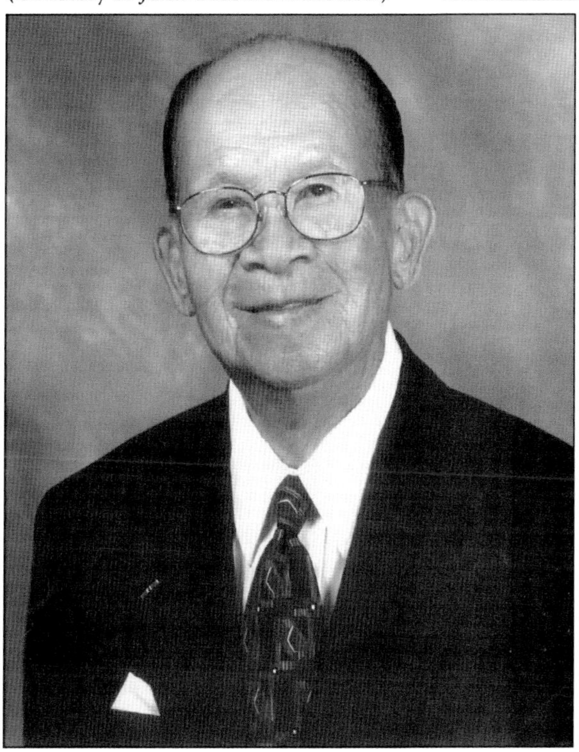

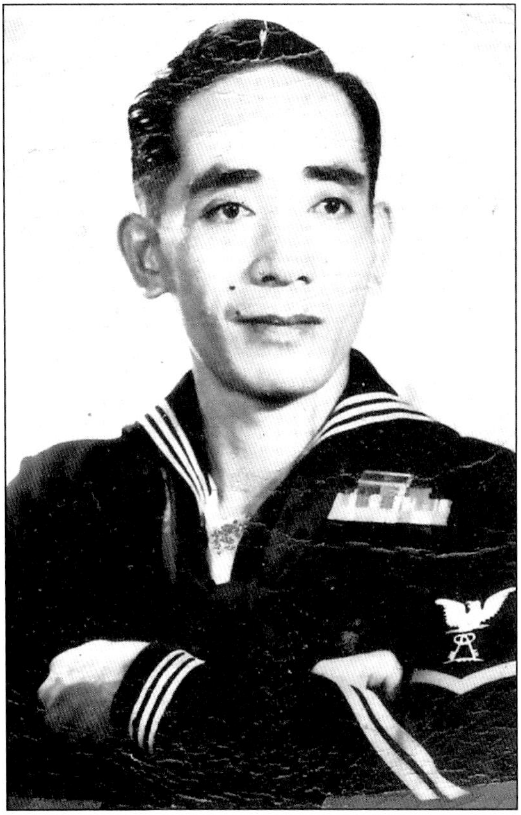

Agustin Castaneda Sr. was born in Cavite, Philippines, and served in the Philippine Scouts, later transferring to the US Navy. Castaneda, a second-class seaman at the time, was at Pearl Harbor when the Japanese attacked and witnessed the loss of fellow crewmen, a trauma that haunted him for years. His unit was sent to Corregidor, Philippines, and fell to the Japanese. He was a prisoner of war and was held in captivity for 13 months until he was finally released in April 1943. (Courtesy of Augie Castaneda Jr.)

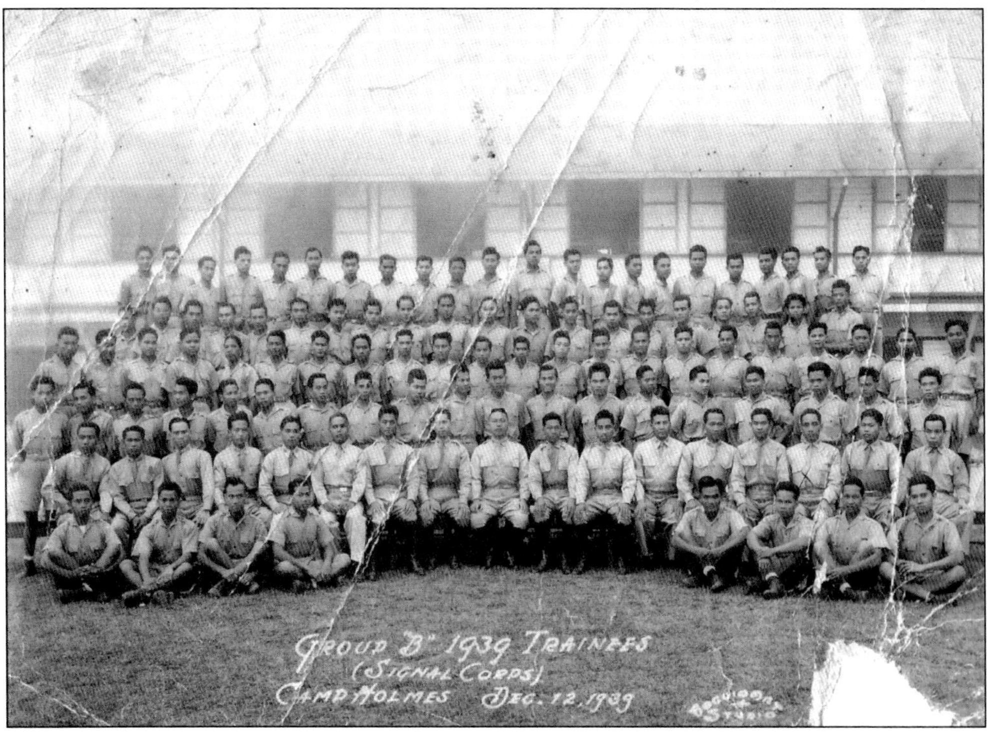

Meritorious Service Awardee

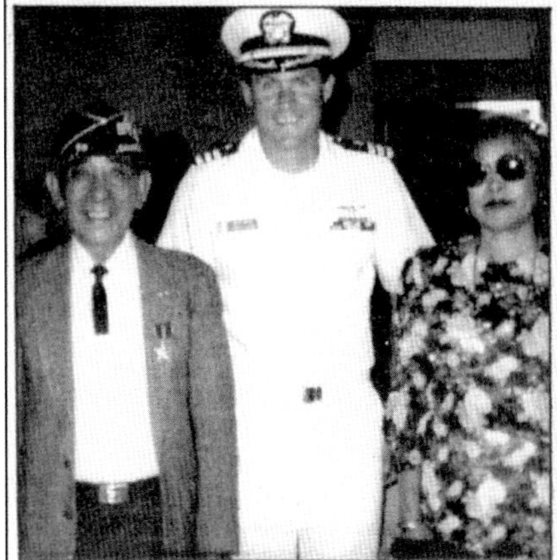

Agustine Castaneda (left) received a medal of merit from the United States Congress for his service during World War II. The awarding ceremonies took place at Pt. Mugo last June 16, 1992 during the installation of officers of the American Legion. The award was given under the auspices of Congress for joint services in Bataan, Philippines. With Castaneda in photo are VFA-305 Pt. Mugo Cmdr. Hayef (center) and Mrs. Belen Castaneda.

In 1992, Augie Castaneda Sr. was awarded a Medal of Merit and a Bronze Star at the age of 75. Augie Sr. retired in 1962, after having served 20 years in the US Navy. He worked another 16 years in the civil service at the US Navy Construction Battalion Center and retired in 1978. (Courtesy of Augie Castaneda Jr.)

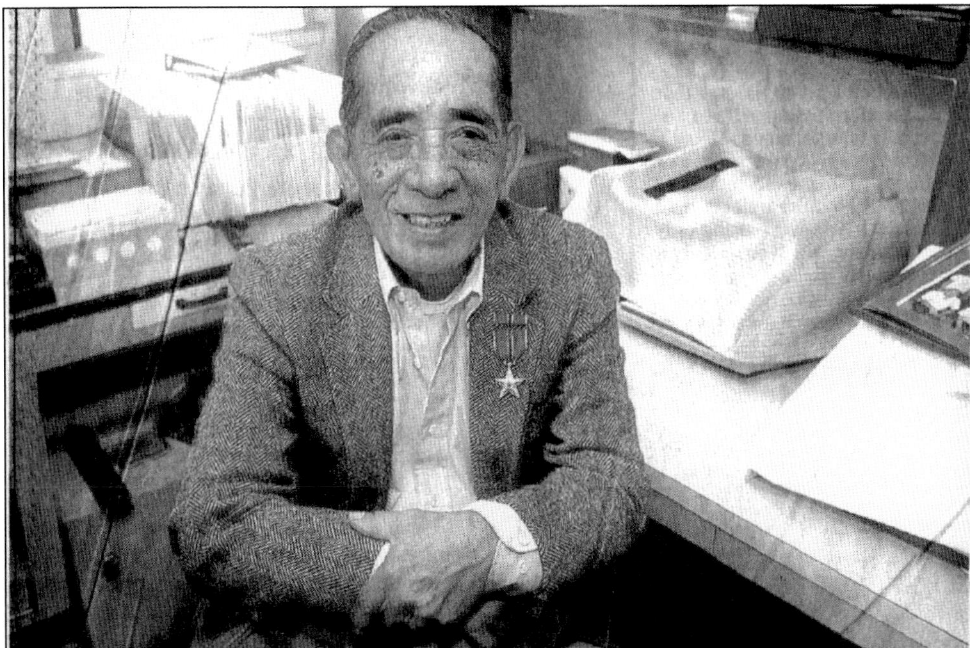

TOM GAPEN/PRESS-COURIER

Augustin Castaneda wears the Bronze Star Medal he recently received. He was a prisoner of war during World War II.

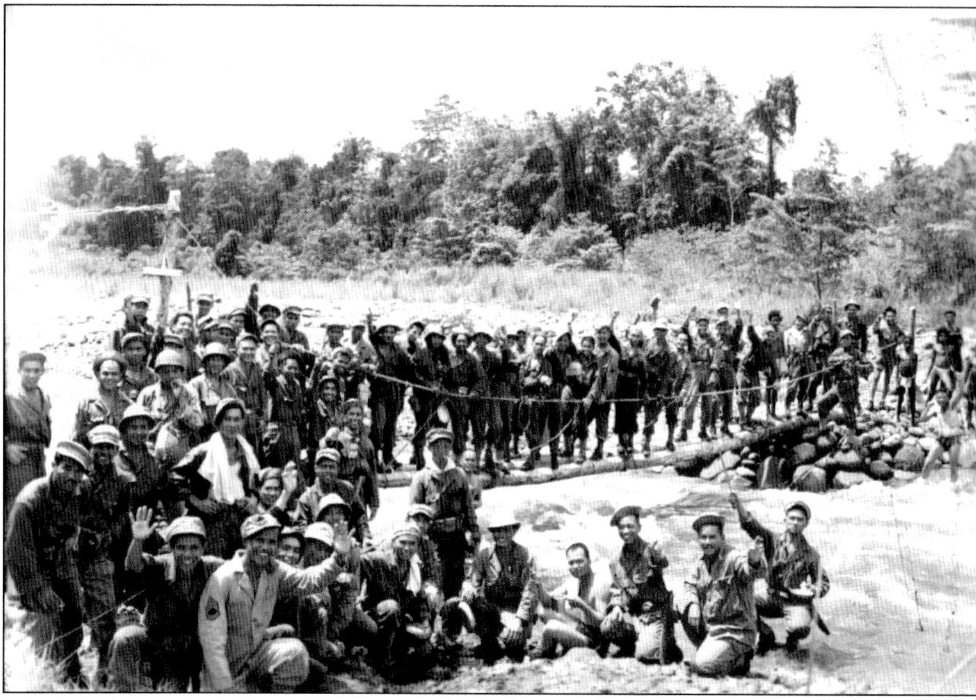

The 1st Filipino Regiment in New Guinea building a bridge during World War II. The back of the photograph is dedicated to Pacita Montayre, Fedreico Jr.'s aunt, from a soldier named Johnny. It was written in 1944 as a keepsake for her. (Courtesy of Nora and Federico Talaugon Jr.)

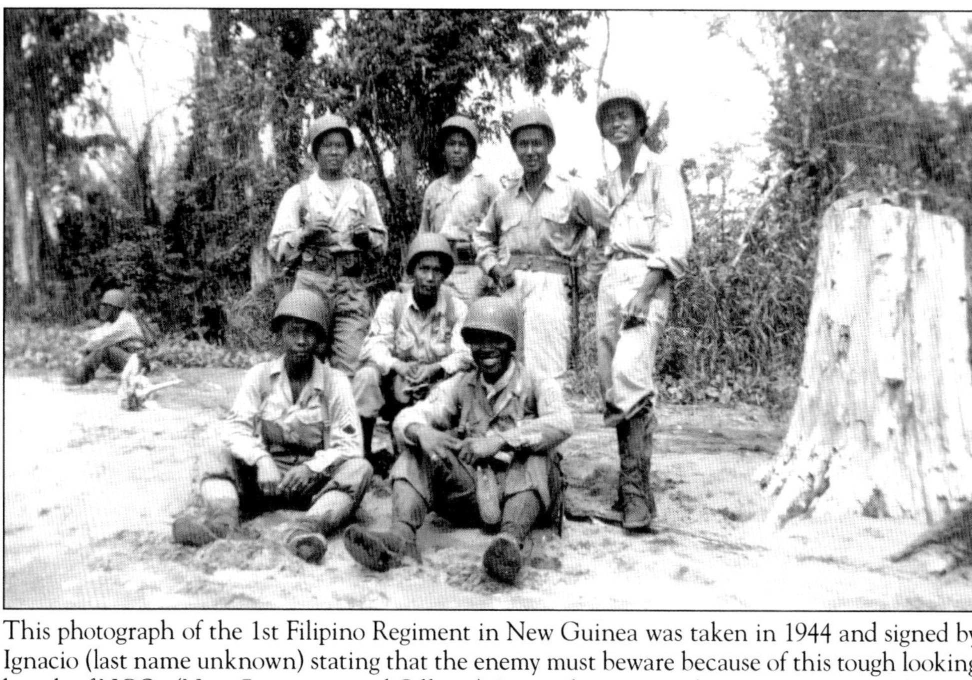

This photograph of the 1st Filipino Regiment in New Guinea was taken in 1944 and signed by Ignacio (last name unknown) stating that the enemy must beware because of this tough looking bunch of NCOs (Non-Commissioned Officers). It is unknown to whom Ignacio was addressing his note. (Courtesy of Nora and Federico Talaugon Jr.)

Tawa Montayre and Marcy Jacobe pose with a soldier named Rauol during a visit to Camp Beale in Marysville, California, just north of Sacramento. Camp Beale was one of the boot camps the US Army used to train the 1st Filipino Infantry Regiment during World War II. (Courtesy of Tawa Desaucido.)

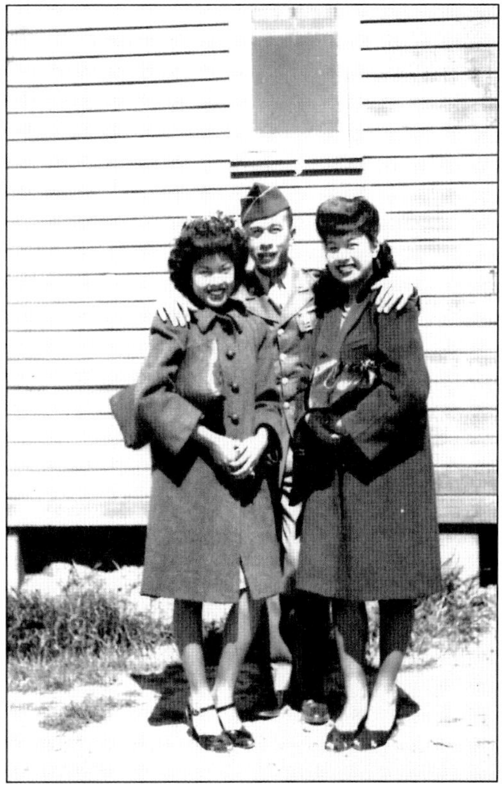

Filipinos stationed in the Dutch East Indies, also referred to as the Netherland East Indies, are pictured in 1945. The back of the photograph notes one problem: "Not enough gals." (Courtesy of Tawa Desaucido.)

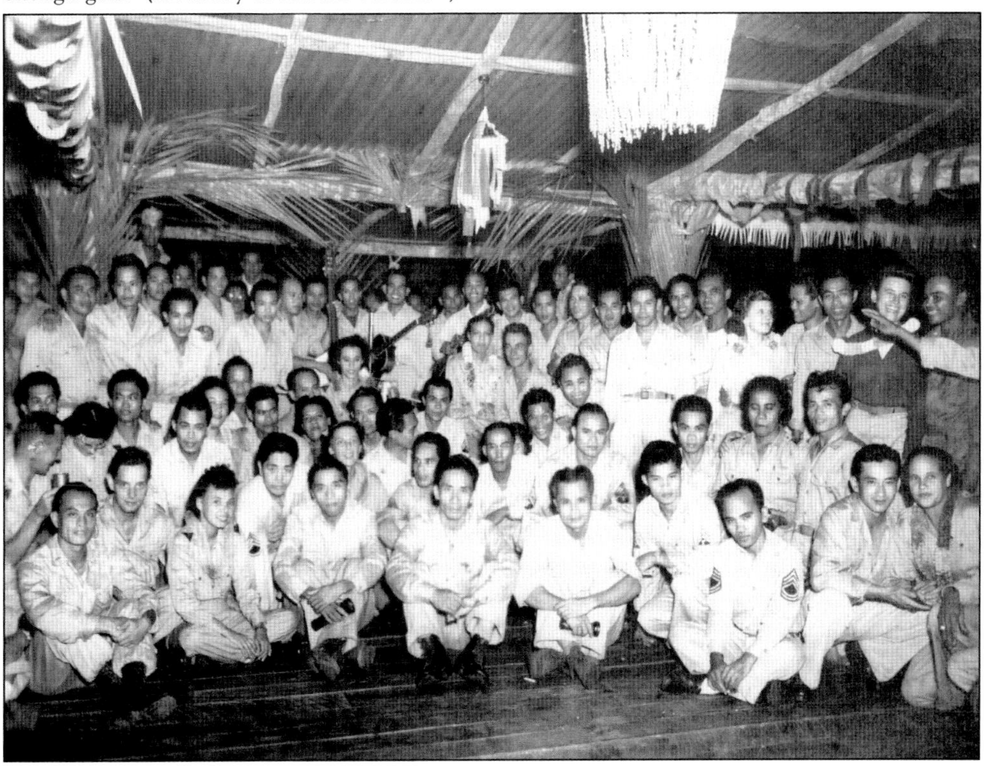

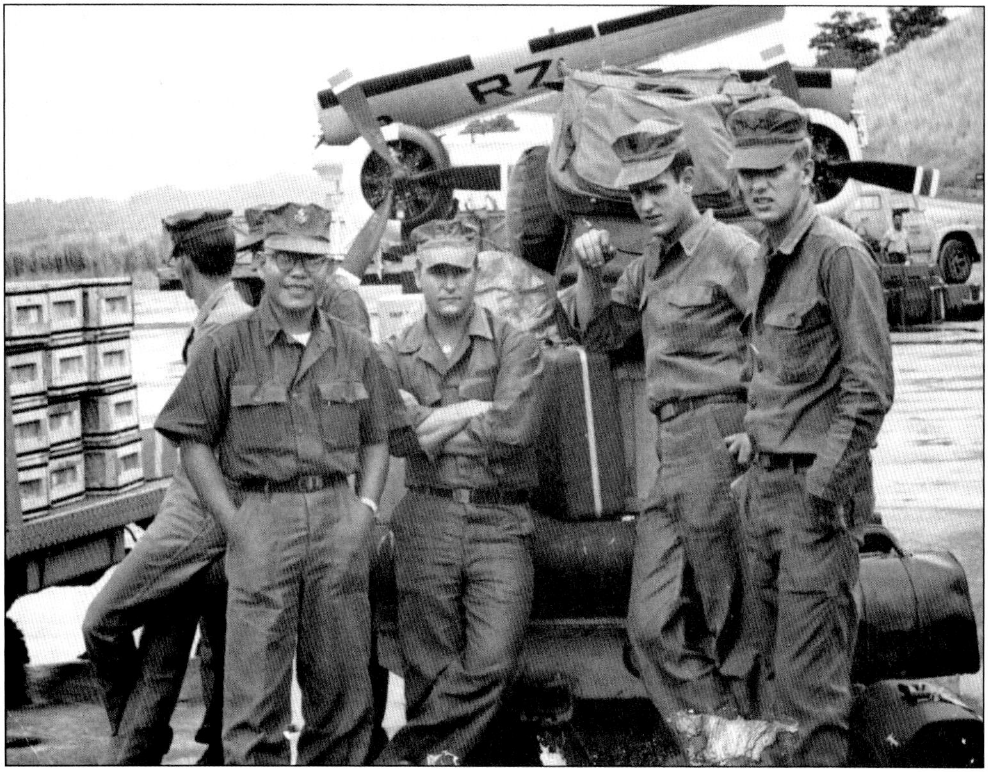

Florentino "Toots" Vinzon served as a US Navy Engineering Seabee since 1957. He joined the Navy in the Philippines as a steward but upon arriving in San Diego for boot camp, he applied for a rate change and selected engineering construction battalion. At the time, he was the only one out of 300 new Filipino recruits who selected construction battalion. (Courtesy of Fe and Florentino "Toots" Vinzon.)

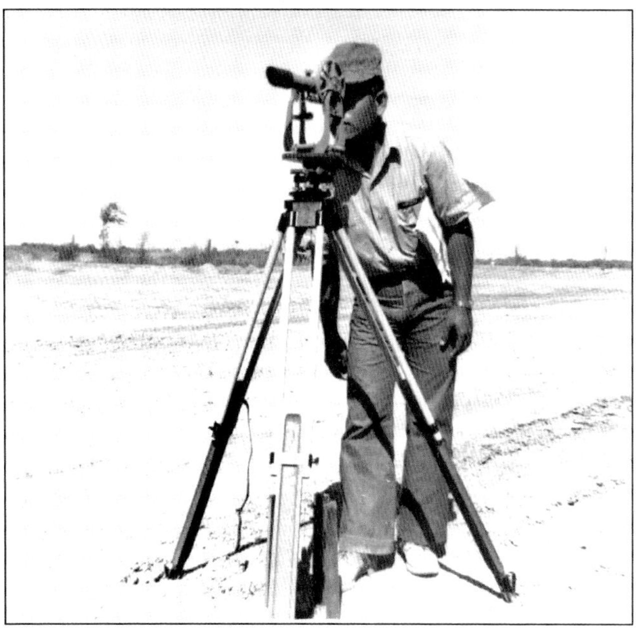

In 1963, Toots Vinzon lead a team of five Seabee civil engineers who were part of the US Marines landing party at the beaches of Chu Lai, Vietnam. His engineering department was charged with surveying, designing, and preparing the beaches for runway construction. (Courtesy of Fe and Toots Vinzon.)

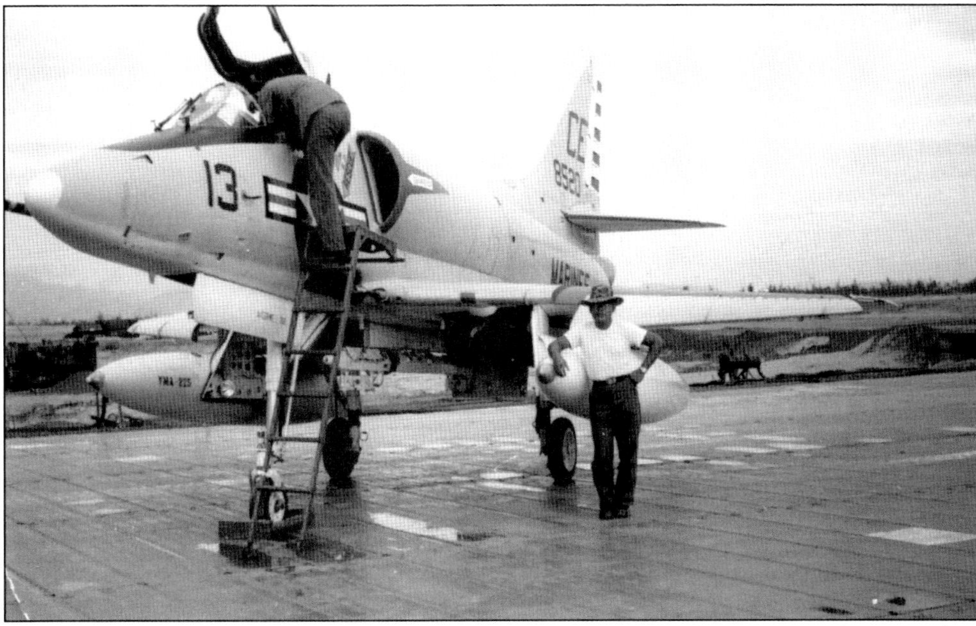

Toots Vinzon surveys the beaches of Chu Lai to design the layout of the runway and prepare plans until the rest of his battalion MCB10 arrived with supplies. The Seabees performed the impossible by creating a 4,000-foot-long runway in 21 days. The runway was equipped with arresting gear for US Marine and Navy planes. (Courtesy of Fe and Toots Vinzon.)

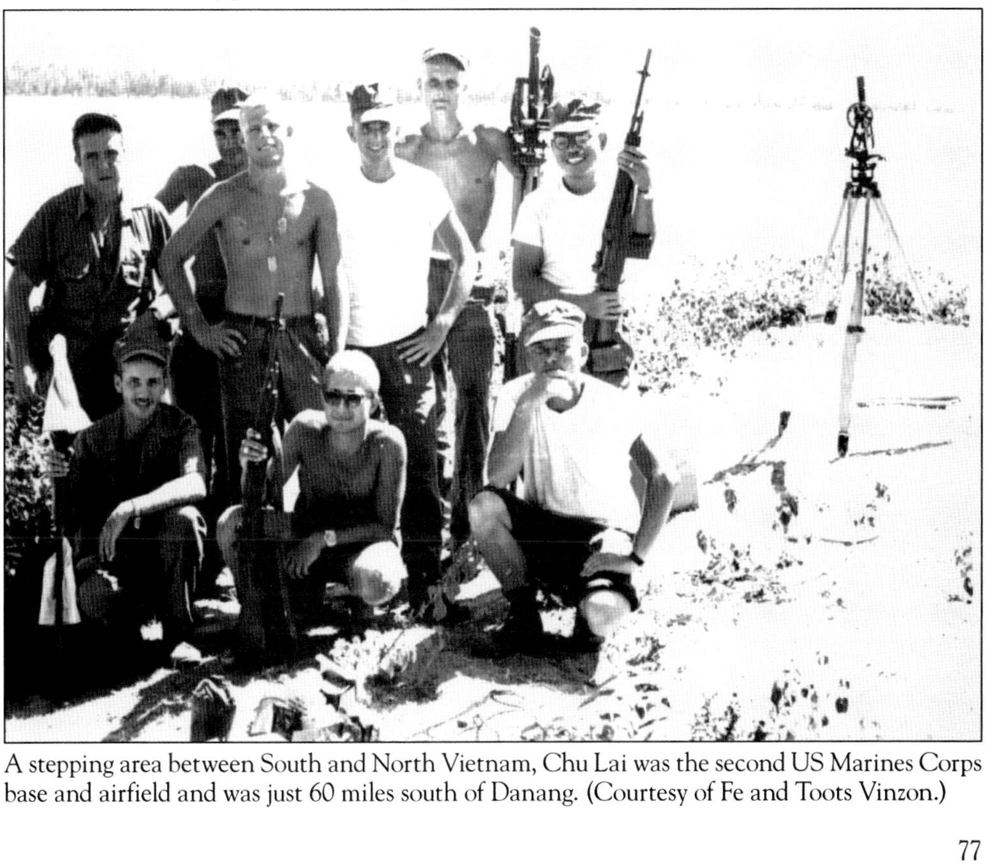

A stepping area between South and North Vietnam, Chu Lai was the second US Marines Corps base and airfield and was just 60 miles south of Danang. (Courtesy of Fe and Toots Vinzon.)

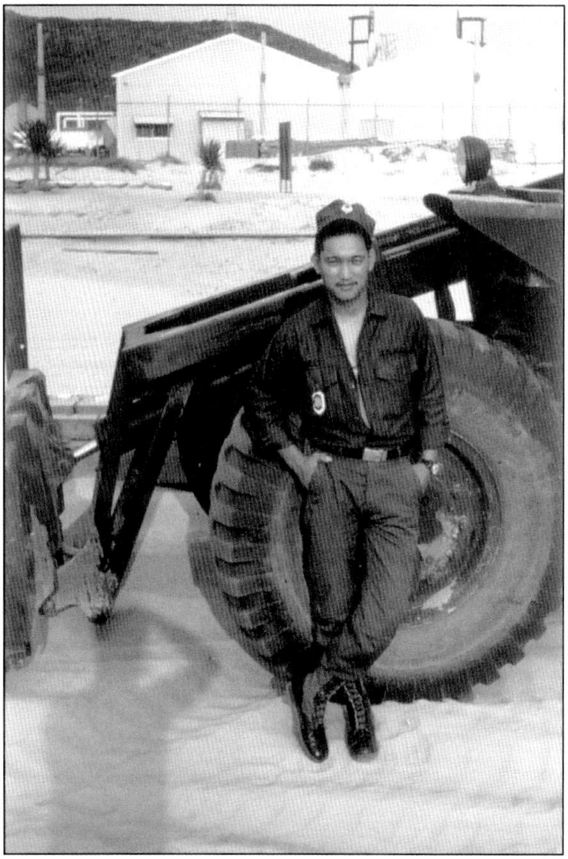

Tony Grey was assigned an in-country tour at the Naval Support Facility at Cam Ranh Bay in Vietnam from 1968 to 1969. Grey stands in front of a rough terrain forklift (RTR) in front of Warehouse D. (Courtesy of Tony V. Grey.)

Below, Navy Fleet Sailors, also called "Black Shoes," are assigned to shore duty at the Naval Support Facility at Can Ranh Bay, Vietnam. (Courtesy of Tony V. Grey.)

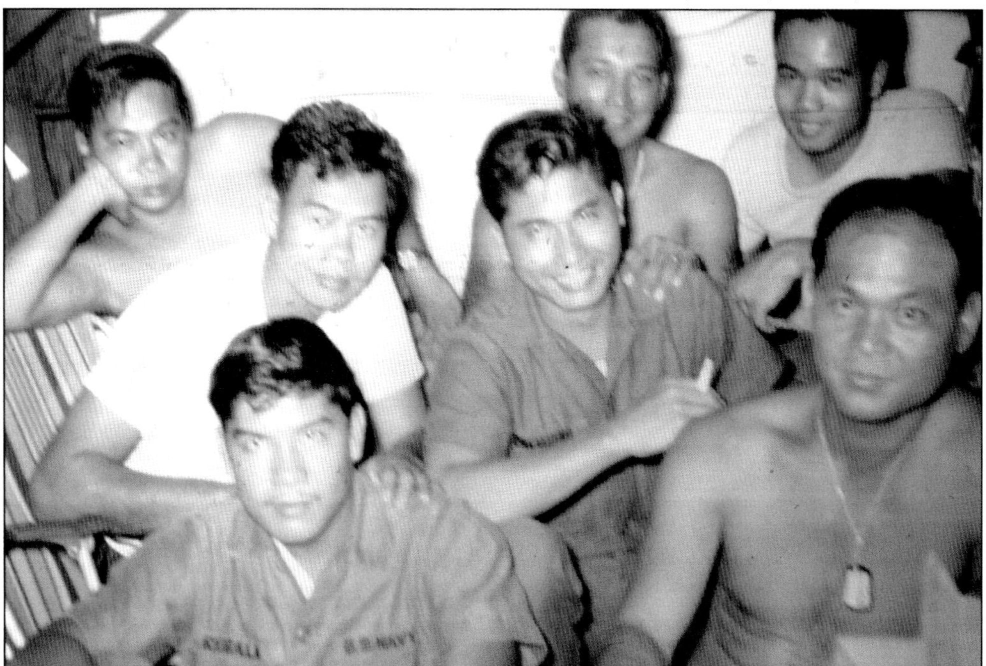

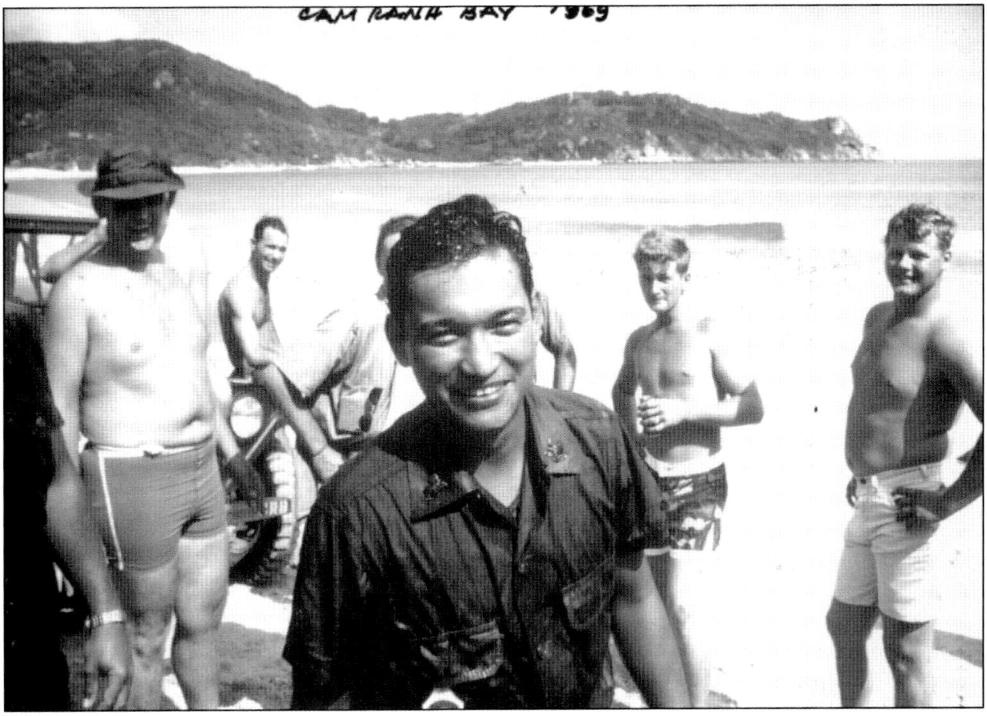

In his uniform, Tony Grey is pictured soaking wet after a Navy crew initiation at Cam Ranh Bay, Vietnam, in 1969. Grey arrived as a squad leader for the Navy's Security Battalion in 1968 and became an assistant platoon commander by the time he left Vietnam in 1969. (Courtesy of Tony V. Grey.)

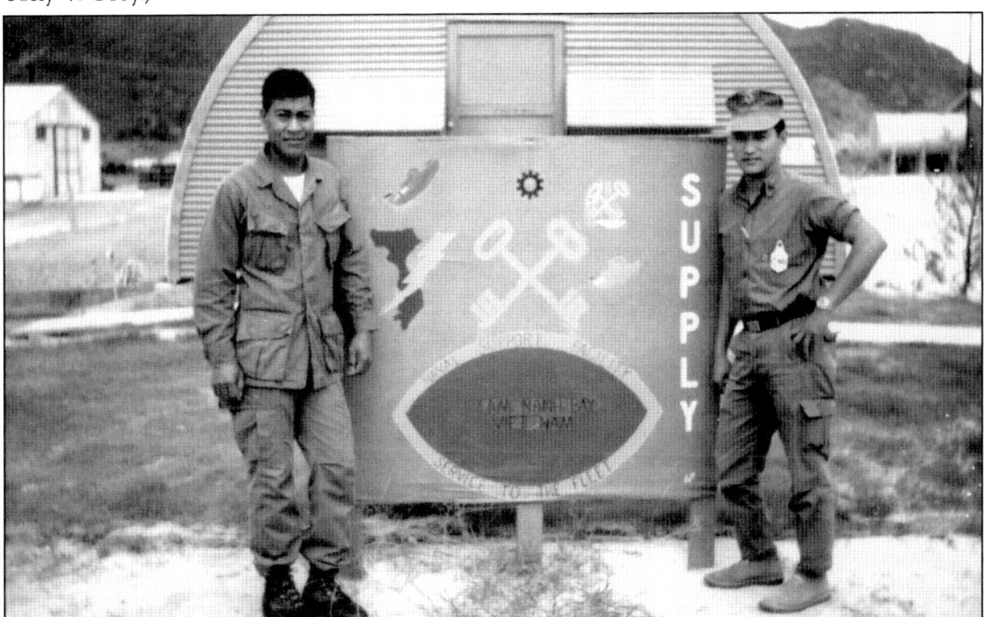

The Naval Support Facility sign reads, "Service to the fleet." The Naval Support Facility provided supplies and heavy equipment for all construction battalion projects at Cam Ranh Bay, Vietnam. Pictured here is SD2 Valencia on the left and Grey on the right. (Courtesy of Tony V. Grey.)

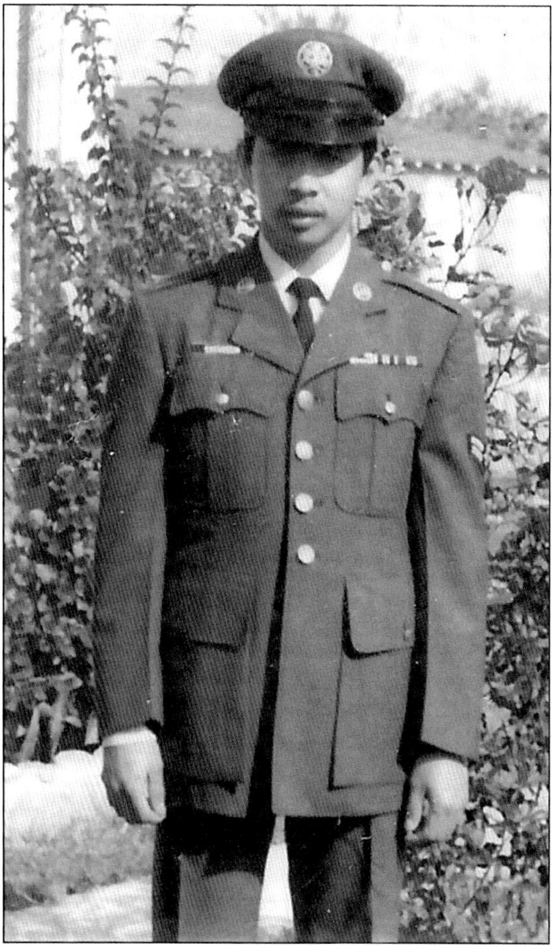

Augie Castaneda Jr. joined the Air Force in 1967 and was sent to Lackland Air Force Base in San Antonio, Texas, for boot camp. He was stationed in Kansas and later assigned worldwide duty and received special training at Fort Campbell in Kentucky. (Courtesy of Augie Castaneda Jr.)

This photograph of Augie Castaneda Jr., shown in the first row and second from the left, was taken during training at Lackland Air Force Base in San Antonio, Texas. (Courtesy of Augie Castaneda Jr.)

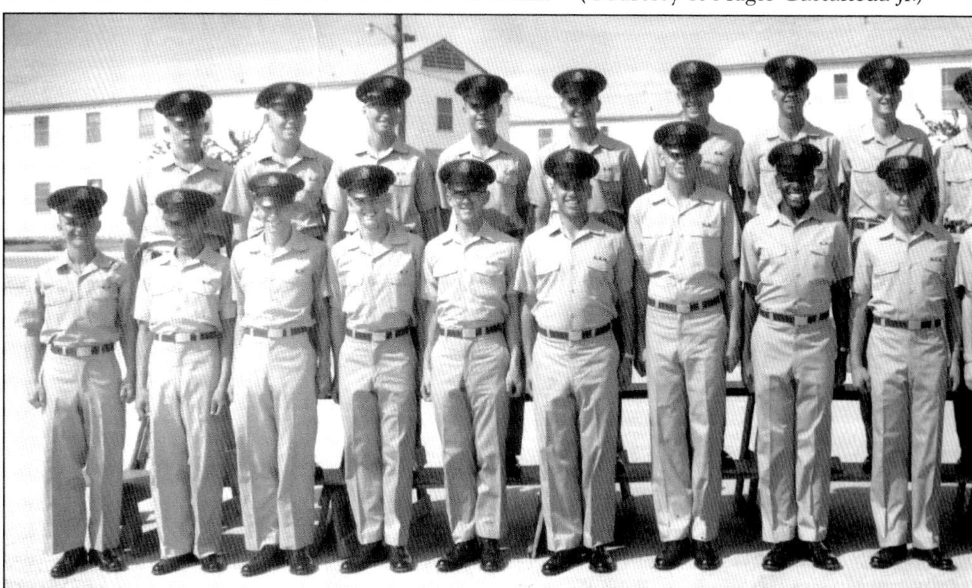

Ingemar "Mac" Macasieb was born in 1928 at Fort Stotsenburg (Clark Air Force Base) in the Philippines. Mac's father Fausto Macasieb, US Army, was a POW and survivor of the Bataan Death March. Mac went on three tours of Vietnam: Chu Lai (1964–1967), Danang, and Saigon (1970–1971). He has been with the following battalions: MCB11, MCB9, MCB10, 31st NCR, and MCB4. He became a chief in 1970 and retired in 1976 as chief builder. (Courtesy of Ingemar Macasieb.)

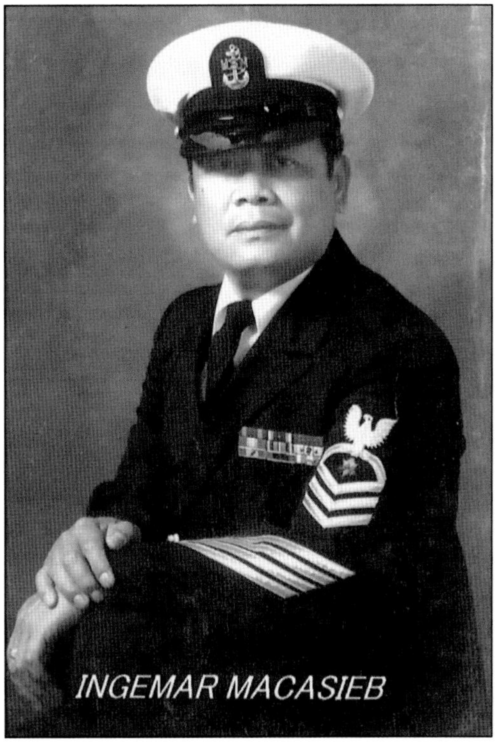

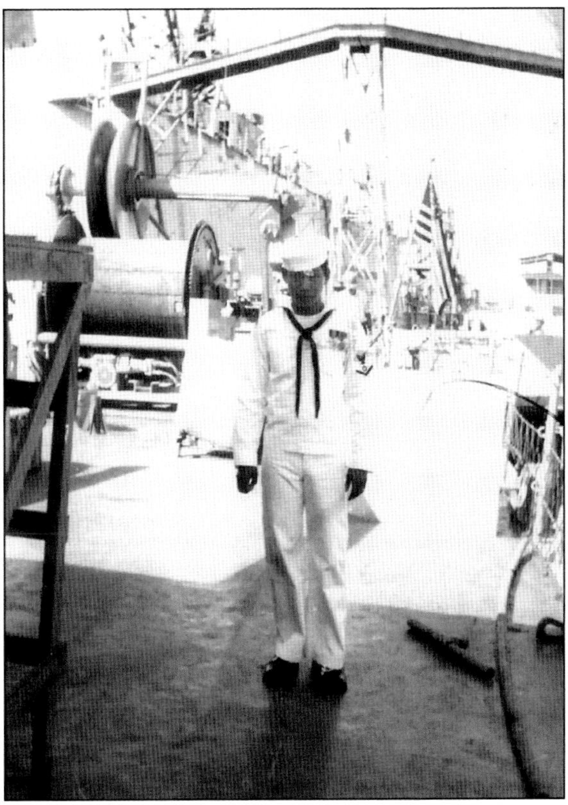

Albert Castaneda joined the Navy in 1965 and was a boilers engineer stationed on a destroyer off the coast of Vietnam in the late 1960s. Albert served four years in the Navy. (Courtesy of Augie Castaneda Jr.)

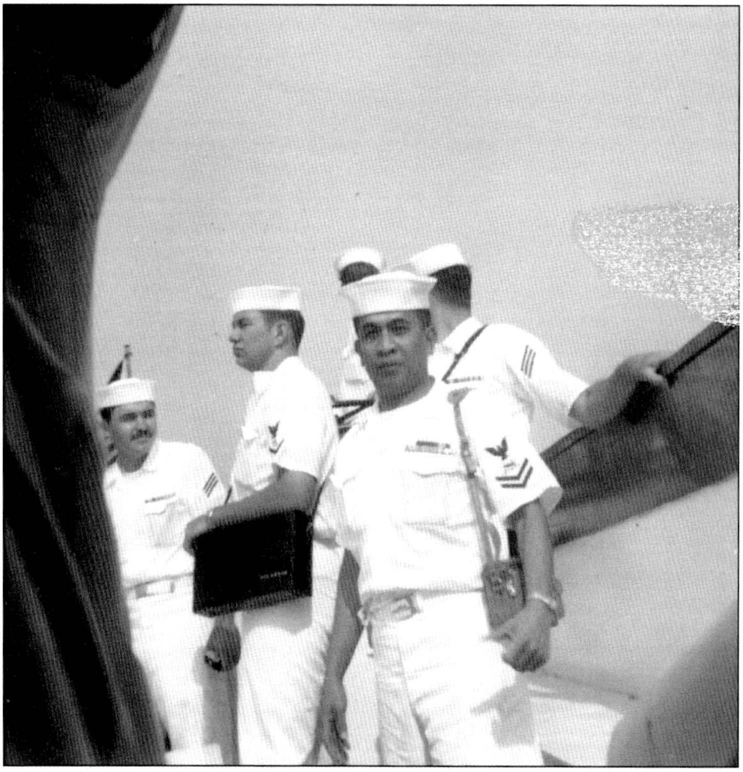

Al Bautista was stationed on the USS *Tolovana*, an oil tanker, off the coast of Vietnam in 1965. He served 20 years in the Navy, after which he took nursing courses and worked as an operating room technician at St. John's Hospital in Oxnard for several years prior to retiring. (Courtesy of Josie and Al Bautista.)

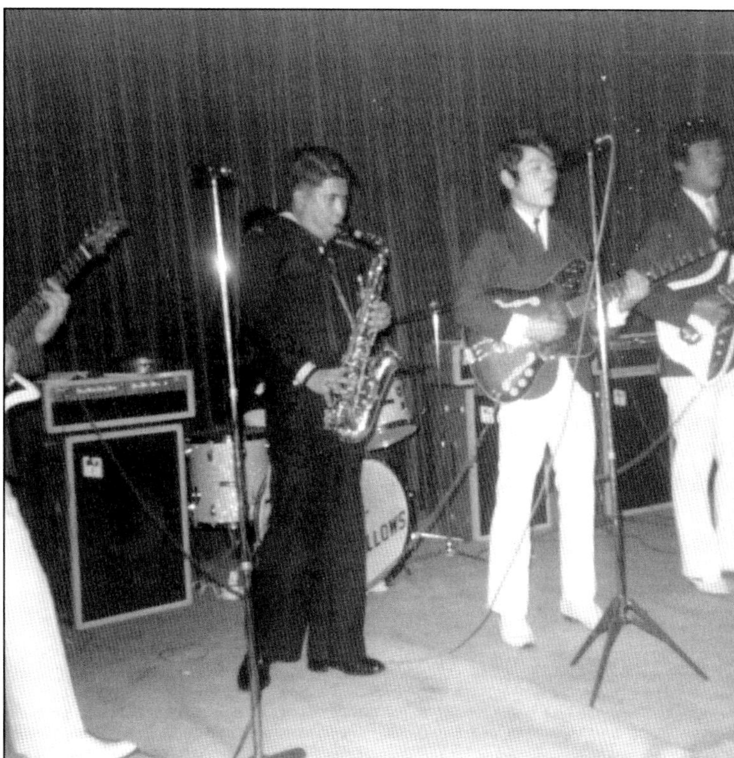

Al Bautista always traveled with his saxophone, especially during deployment. Al loves playing with other musicians on board the navy ships, and although he was not part of a band, he always loves playing for others. In this picture, Al jams with the band, Japanese musicians he just met in Yukosuka, Japan. (Courtesy of Josie and Al Bautista.)

Jimmy Ines was presented with the Navy Achievement Award in 1979 at Point Mugu. Ines served 22 years in the Navy and retired in October 1981 at Point Mugu. Many servicemen stationed at Point Mugu and Port Hueneme decided to stay in Ventura County after retirement because of the great coastal weather. (Courtesy of Cathy and Jim Ines.)

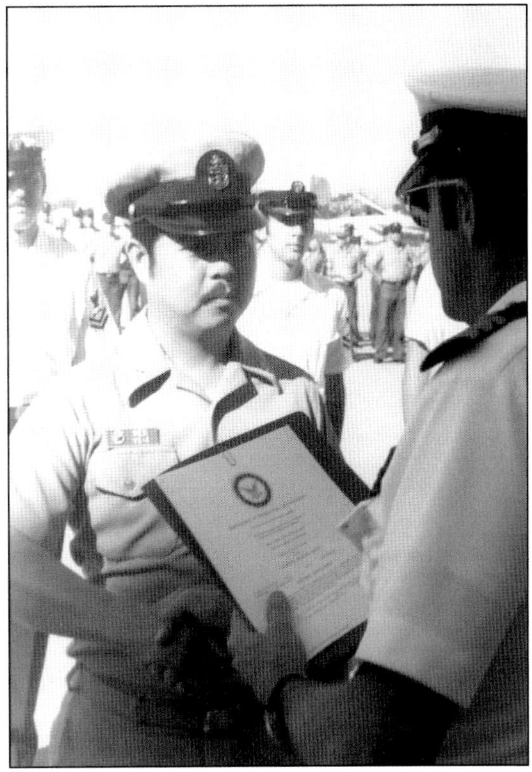

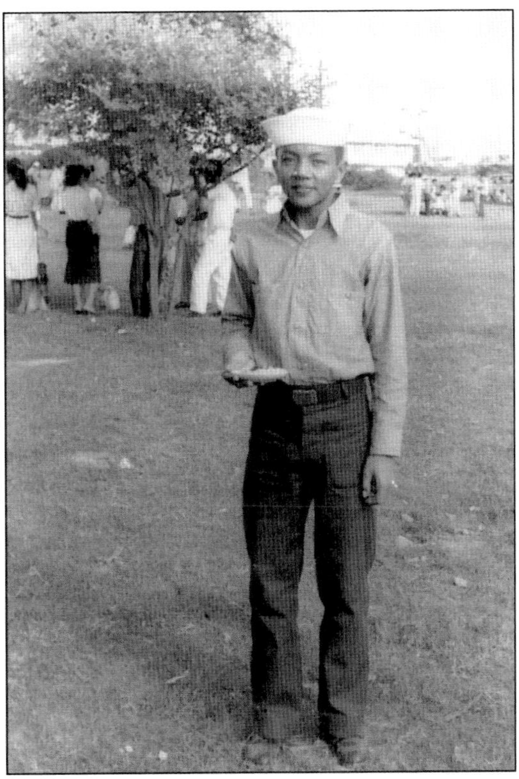

Eduardo Austria joined the Navy at 19 years old in Cavite, Philippines, in 1960. After 22 years of service in the Navy, he retired in 1982. (Courtesy of Irene and Eduardo Austria.)

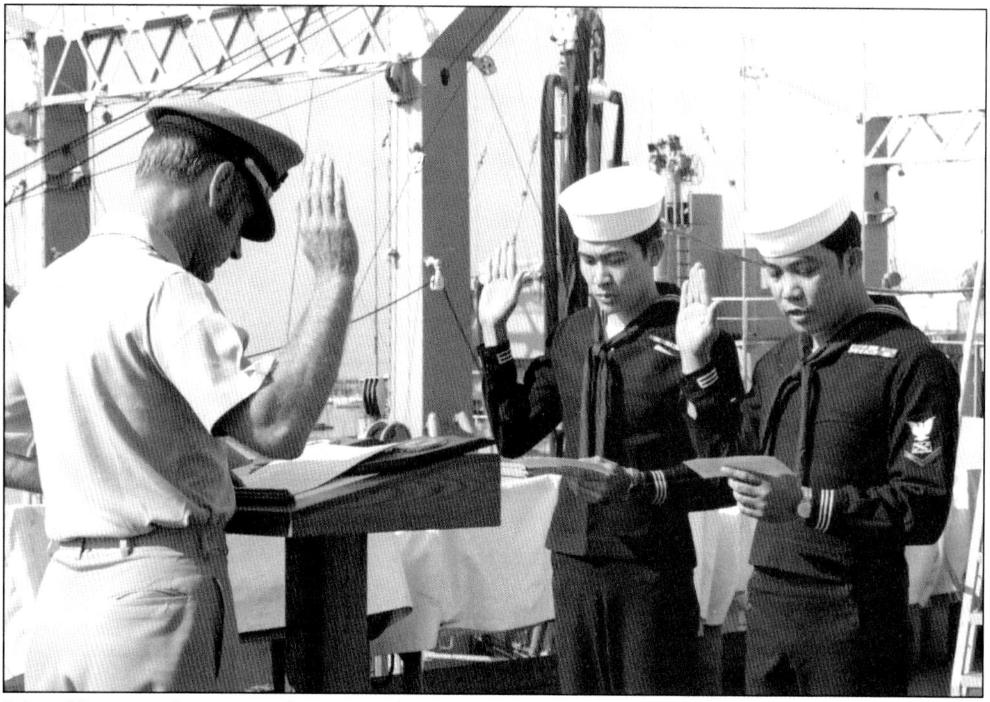

John Obispo is shown reenlisting in the Navy in 1971 on board the USS *Hector*. (Courtesy of Nellie and John Opispo.)

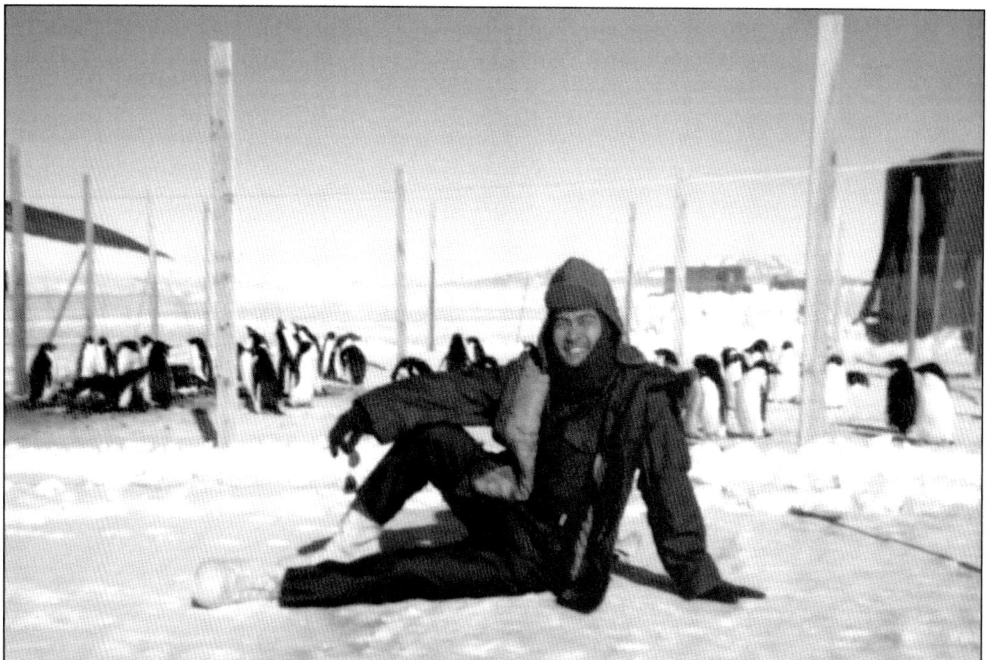

Navy deployments can take soldiers as far away as Antarctica. John Obispo poses with penguins in the background. John missed three Christmases (1975, 1976, and 1977) during his deployments to Antarctica. (Courtesy of Nellie and John Opispo.)

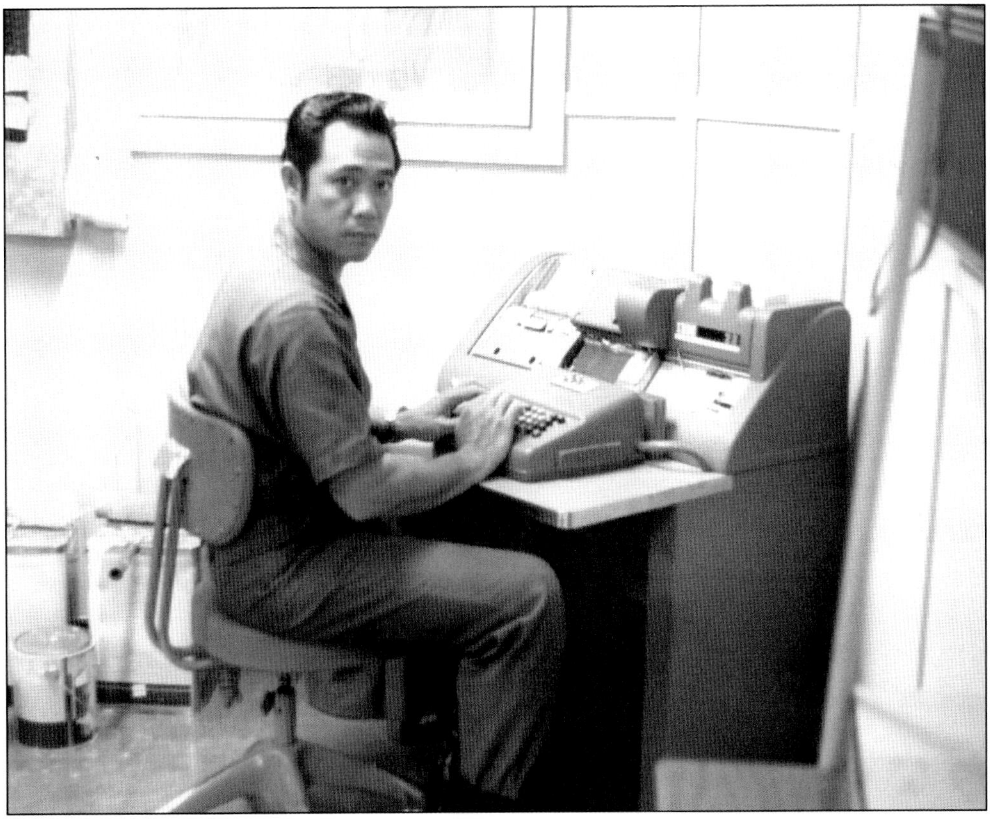

Vic Mercado is typing requisitions on IMB cards on an IBM computer machine in 1972. Mercado joined the Navy in 1953 and retired after 24 years of service. (Courtesy of Vic R. and Coring G. Mercado.)

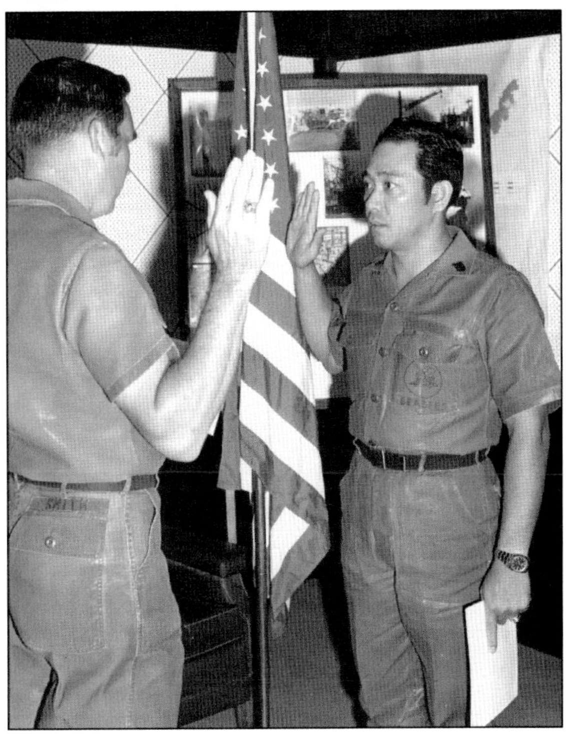

Vic Mercado reenlists in 1970 at Port Hueneme. He retired as master chief in 1977 and earned a master's degree in organizational management from La Verne University. (Courtesy of Vic R. and Coring G. Mercado.)

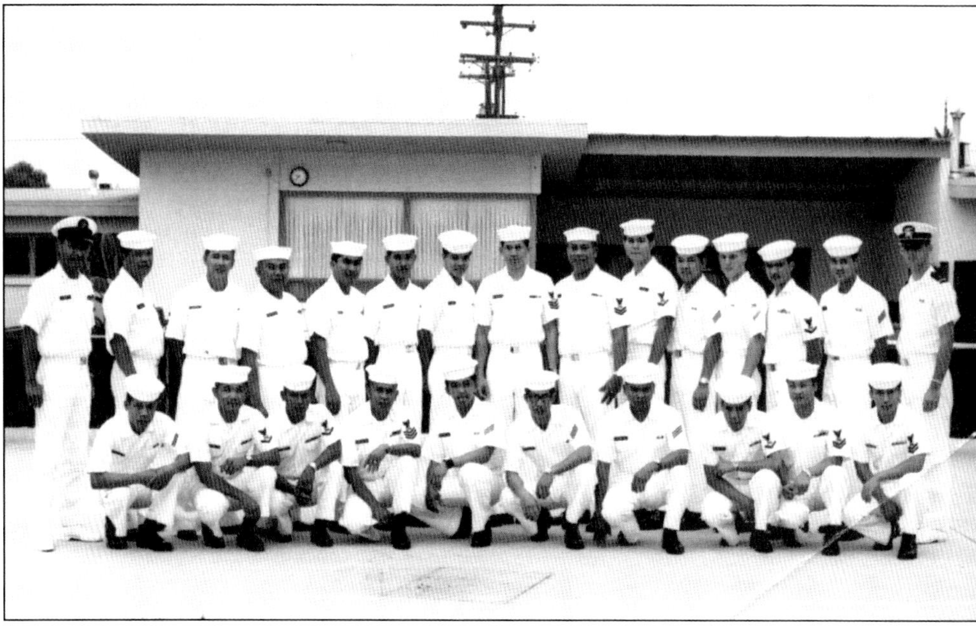

The US Navy Food Services Division is pictured at Point Mugu in 1969. Al Bautista is identified in the first row and fourth from the left. (Courtesy of Josie and Al Bautista.)

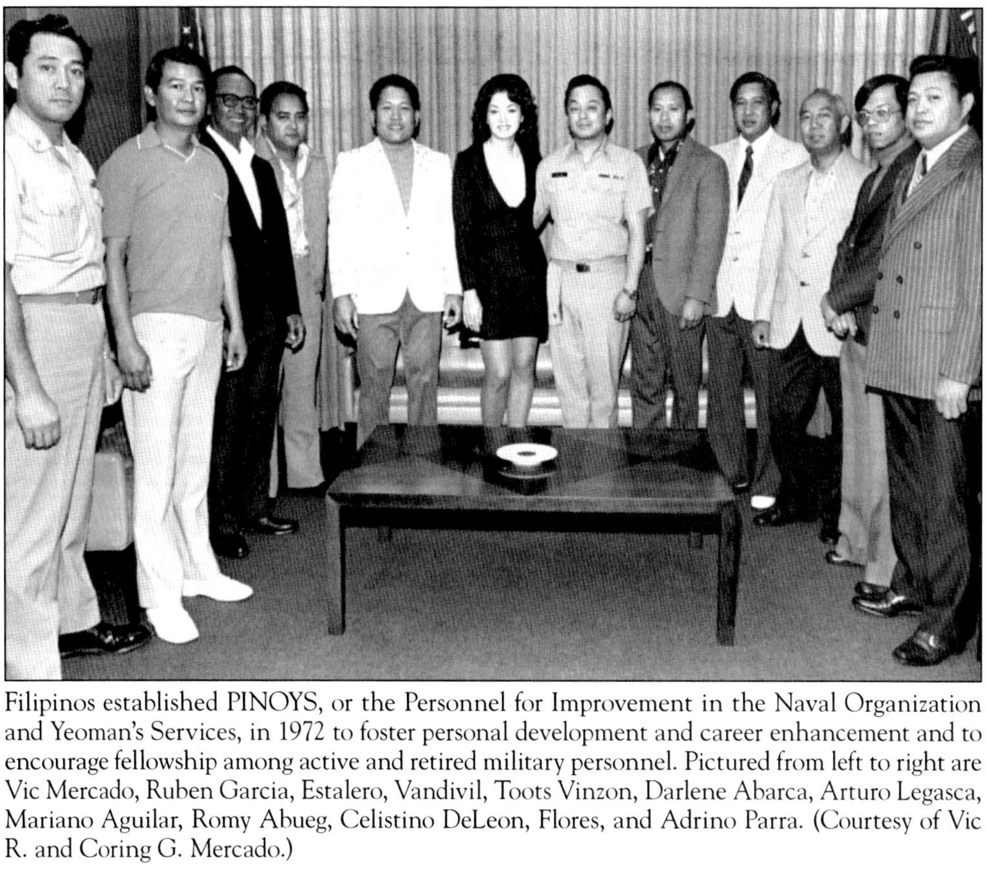

Filipinos established PINOYS, or the Personnel for Improvement in the Naval Organization and Yeoman's Services, in 1972 to foster personal development and career enhancement and to encourage fellowship among active and retired military personnel. Pictured from left to right are Vic Mercado, Ruben Garcia, Estalero, Vandivil, Toots Vinzon, Darlene Abarca, Arturo Legasca, Mariano Aguilar, Romy Abueg, Celistino DeLeon, Flores, and Adrino Parra. (Courtesy of Vic R. and Coring G. Mercado.)

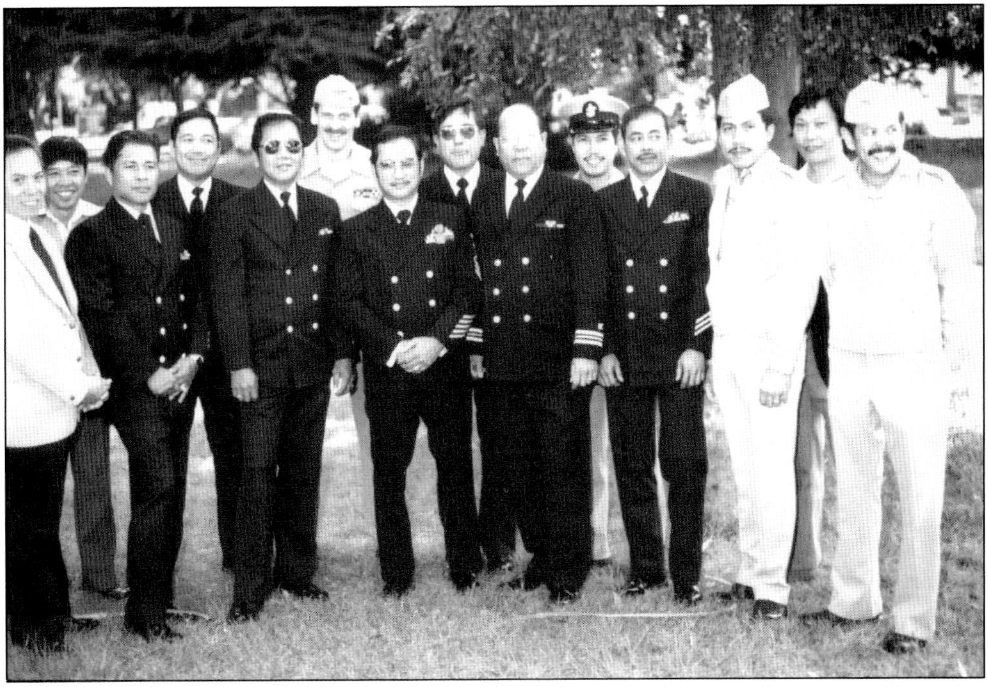

This picture of chief petty officers, senior chief petty officers, and master chief petty officers was taken during Tony Grey's retirement in 1982 at Port Hueneme. Pictured from left to right are Capt. Dr. Sito Serate, Bert Lim, Art Balayan, Fred Umayam, Doug Newcomer, Tony Grey, Father Palafox (Senior Navy Catholic Chaplain), Ernie Frial, Sam Apiado, Art Quilantang, Fred Pascua, Rick Fayloga, and Sonny Santos. (Courtesy of Tony V. Grey.)

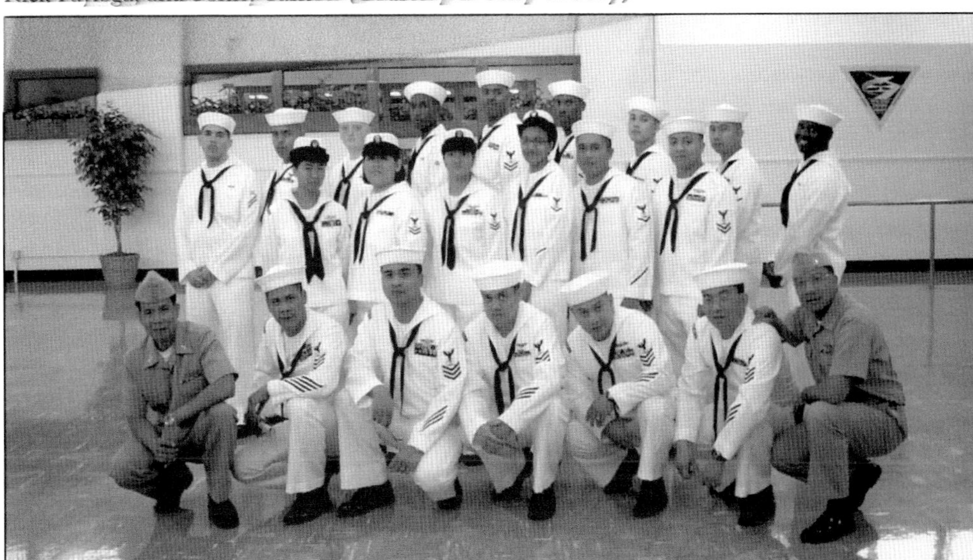

Pictured at the Naval Base Ventura County Port Hueneme Galley in 2004 are, from left to right, (first row) Mario Agsaulio, Alejandro Sarreal, Porfirio Rearos, Ramos, Joel Tividad, Arnulfo Cresines, Roberto Asuncion; (second row) unidentified, Angela Velo, Carmencita Jesse, two unidentified people, and Fontanilla. Aldarico Bermudez is second from right in the third row. (Courtesy of Rosalina and Alejandro Sarreal.)

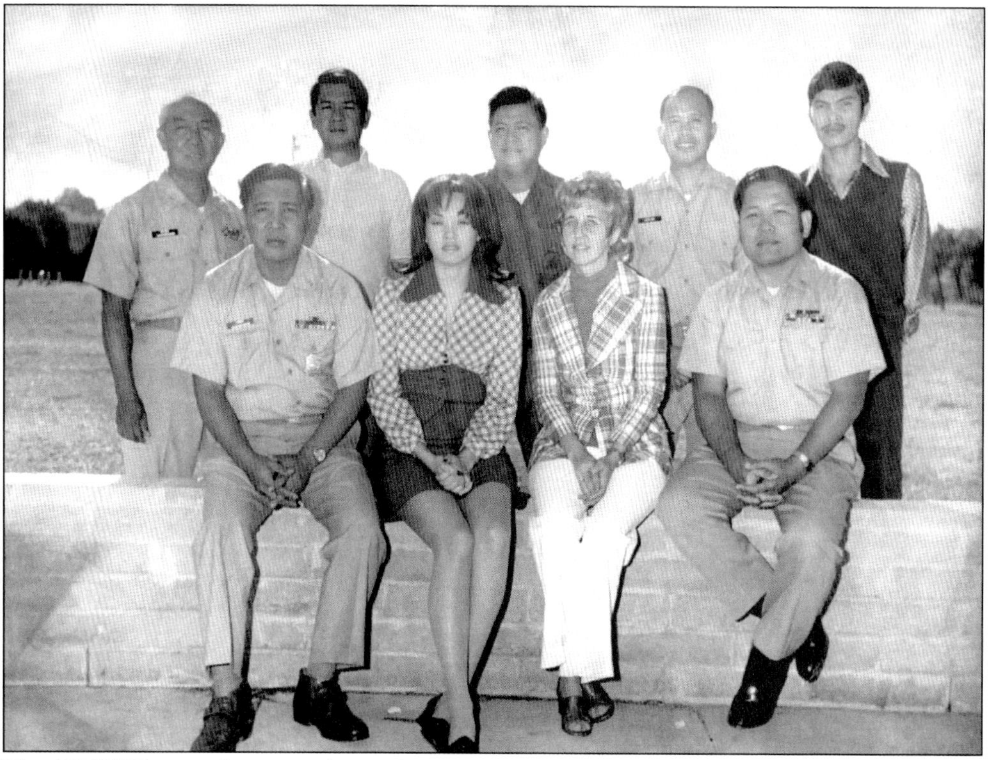

This PINOYS group shot was taken at Port Hueneme Navy Base in the 1970s. Pictured from left to right are Romy Abueg, Darlene Abarca, Margie, and Toots Vinzon; (second row) Celistino DeLeon, Rueben Garcia, unidentified, Mariano Aguilar, and unidentified. (Courtesy of Fe and Toots Vinzon.)

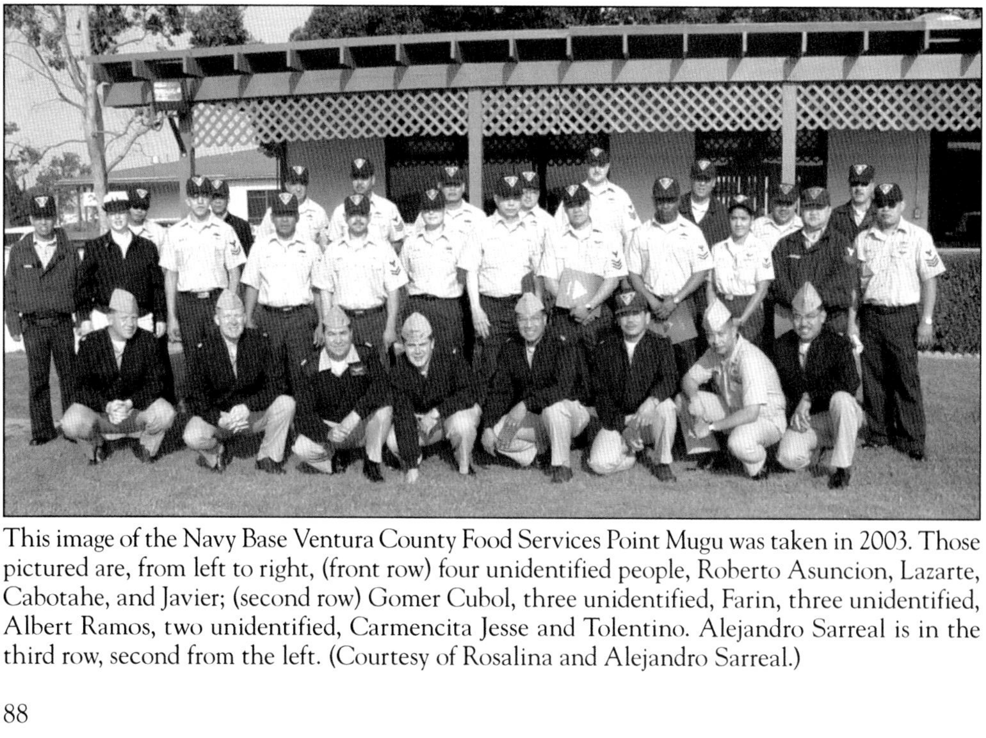

This image of the Navy Base Ventura County Food Services Point Mugu was taken in 2003. Those pictured are, from left to right, (front row) four unidentified people, Roberto Asuncion, Lazarte, Cabotahe, and Javier; (second row) Gomer Cubol, three unidentified, Farin, three unidentified, Albert Ramos, two unidentified, Carmencita Jesse and Tolentino. Alejandro Sarreal is in the third row, second from the left. (Courtesy of Rosalina and Alejandro Sarreal.)

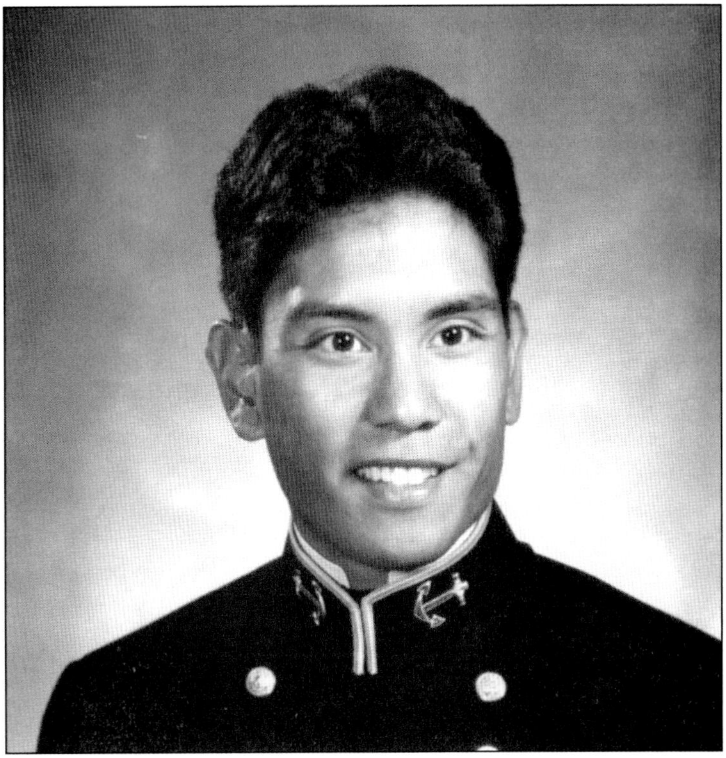

In 1984, Noel Vinzon graduated from the US Naval Academy in Annapolis. He was salutatorian of the class of 1980 at Channel Islands High School in Oxnard. He is the oldest of six children. (Courtesy of Fe and Toots Vinzon.)

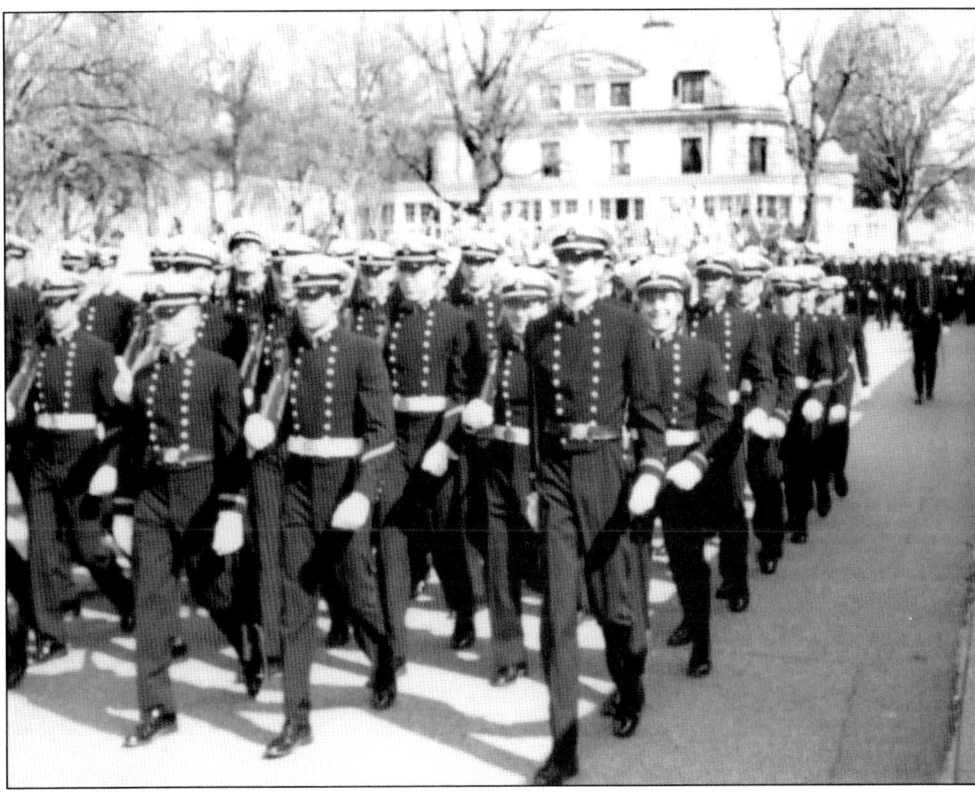

Noel Vinzon marches in a parade at the US Naval Academy in 1981. Noel is in the second row on the far right. (Courtesy of Fe and Toots Vinzon.)

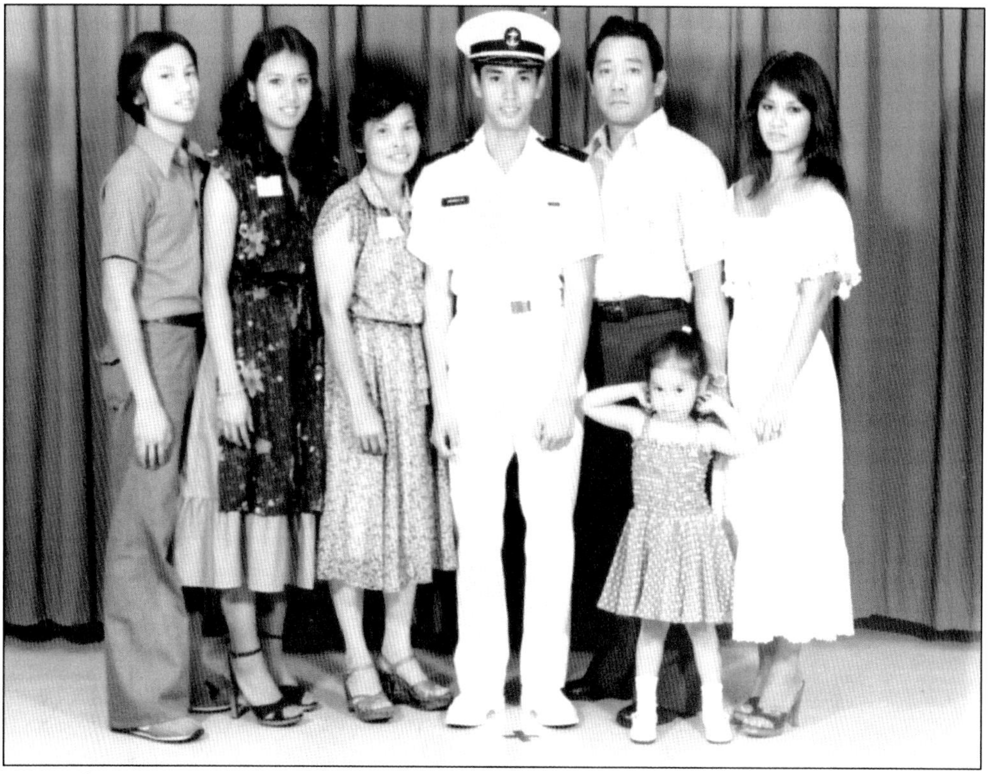

During his first year at the US Naval Academy in Annapolis, Maryland, Victorino G. Mercado is pictured with his family at the open house on parents' day in 1979. From left to right are Erwin Mercado, Elsie Mercado, Coring Mercado, Victorino G. Mercado, Vic Mercado, Kristine Mercado (front), and Helen Mercado. (Courtesy of Vic R. and Coring G. Mercado.)

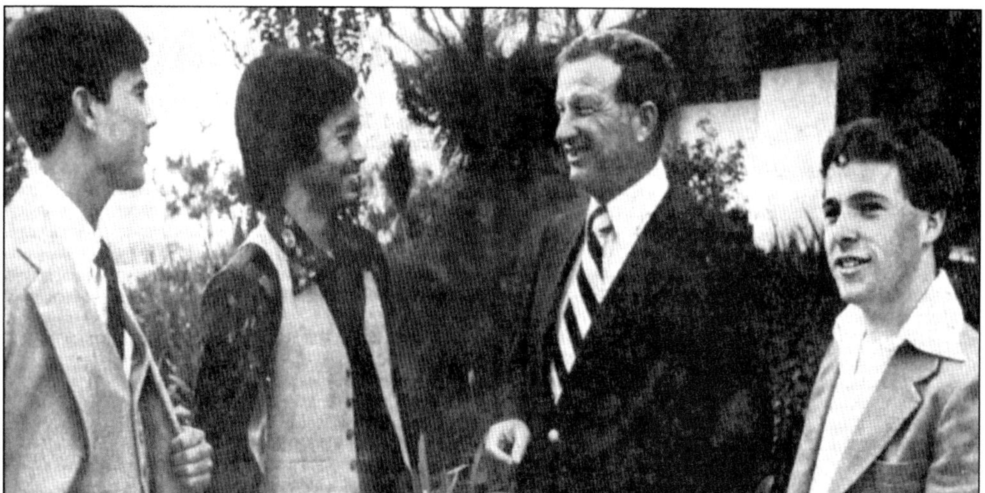

Congressman Lagomarsino is shown with three appointees with plans of attending elite military academies in the fall of 1979. Victorino G. Mercado graduated from the US Naval Academy in 1983 with a bachelor's degree in mathematics and computer science and later earned his master's degree in systems technology in joint command, control, and communications from the Naval Postgraduate School in Monterey, California. (Courtesy of Vic R. and Coring G. Mercado.)

Capt. Victorino G. Mercado served as weapons officer and combat systems officer on the USS *Antietam* (CG 54) and was part of the Carl Vinson Battle Group during Operation Southern Watch, which enforced the no-fly zone in southern Iraq. He was executive officer on the USS *Curtis Wilbur* (DDG 54) in Japan. Next he commanded the USS *Decatur* (DDG 73) with the John C. Stennis Battle Group for Operation Enduring Freedom in Afghanistan and enforced United Nations sanctions on Iraq. On his last tour, he was commander for Destroyer Squadron 21 and sea combat commander for the John C. Stennis Carrier Strike Group. (Courtesy of Vic R. and Coring G. Mercado.)

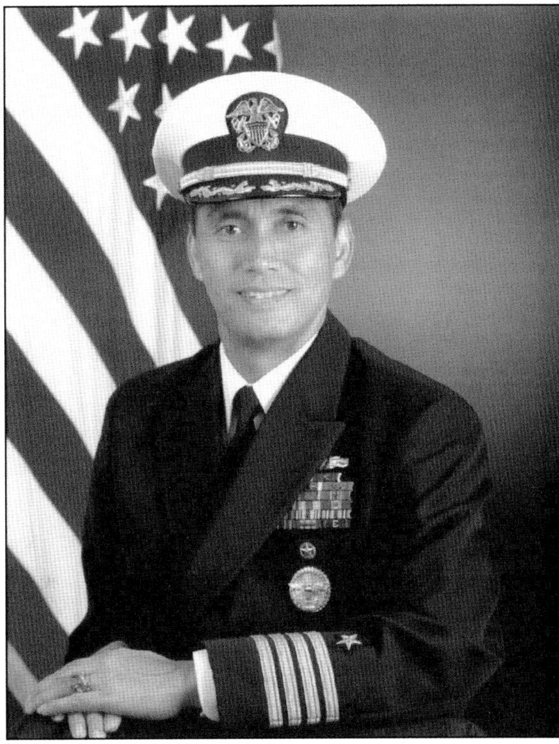

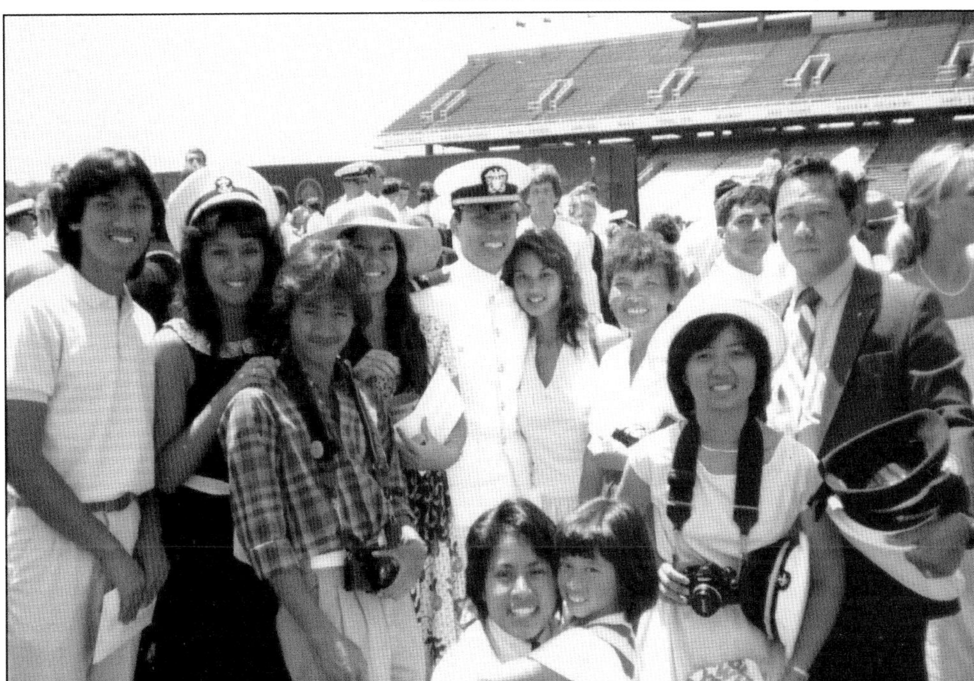

Victorino G. Mercado is pictured with his family on graduation day from the US Naval Academy in 1983. Mercado was a missile/fire control officer and then combat information center officer on the USS *Leftwich* (DD984) for his first assignment. (Courtesy of Vic R. and Coring G. Mercado.)

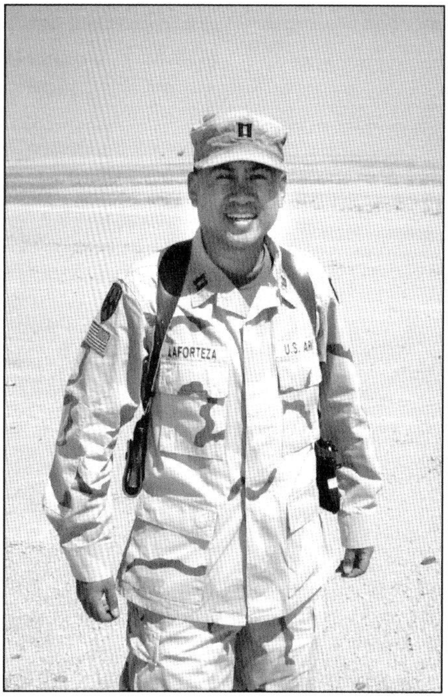

Judge Bernie LaForteza is also a major in the Army Reserve's 22nd Legal Support Organization in Grand Prairie, Texas. Judge Advocate General's (JAG) Corps officer LaForteza has held assignments as a legal assistance attorney, operational law attorney, administrative law attorney, civil law attorney, and trial counsel. In 2004, he was deployed at Camp Arifjan, Kuwait, for Operation Iraqi Freedom where he was an Army prosecutor and an administrative law attorney for the 377th Theater Support Command, Forward. He earned the Meritorious Service Medal for his service in the Southwest Asia theater of operations. (Courtesy of Marie and Bernie LaForteza.)

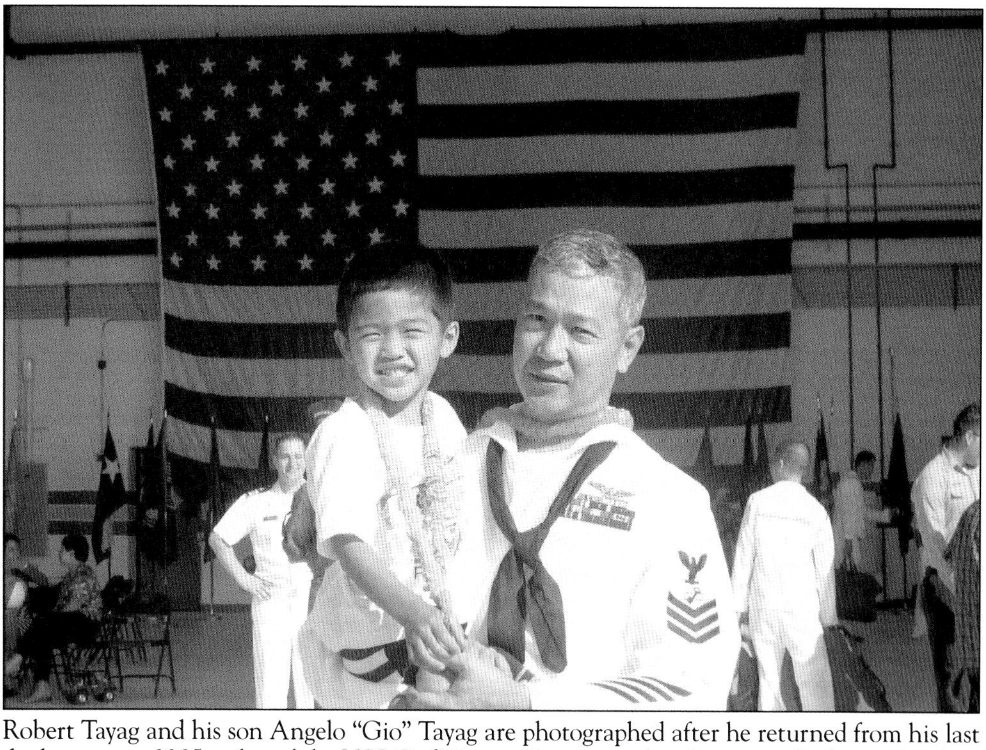

Robert Tayag and his son Angelo "Gio" Tayag are photographed after he returned from his last deployment in 2005 on board the USS *Carl Vinson*. Tayag served in Operation Enduring Freedom on board the USS *Kitty Hawk* in the gulf after September 11, 2001. He joined the US Navy in 1986 and retired after 20 years of service. He currently works for Ventura County Public Works in the Water & Sanitation Department. (Courtesy of Lynette and Robert Tayag.)

Five

Community Engagement and Creating Traditions

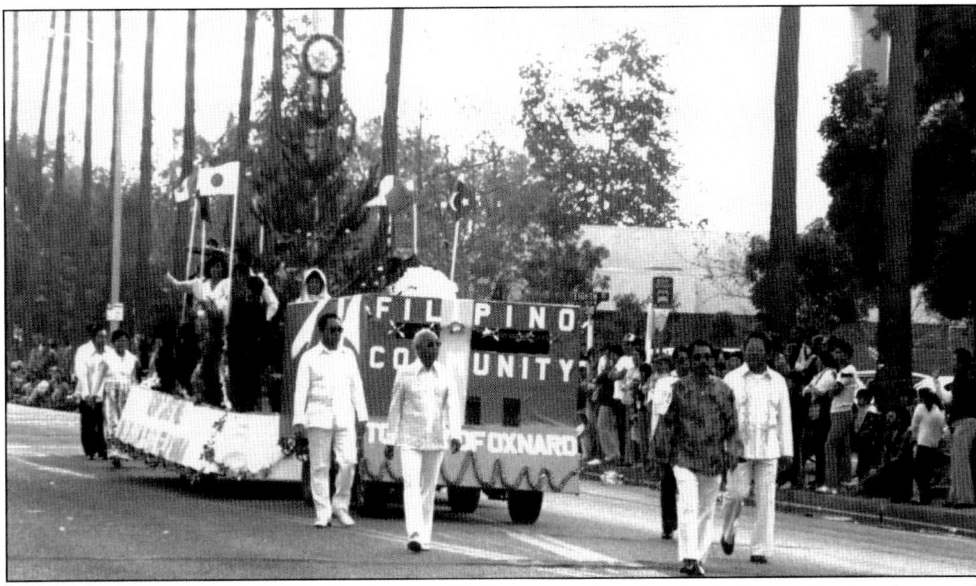

The advent of the 1970s saw the third wave of Filipino immigration, including professionals, as well as a cultural shift in the community from one organization (FCVCI) to many. The new organizations are aligned mostly regionally, though some are aligned professionally, such as the Filipino Nurses Association or PINOYS. The FCVCI has become the oldest out of the 26 organizations that fall under the Filipino American Council. The Salute to the Graduates Program was established in 1979, which started the tradition of honoring graduates by hosting Baccalaureate Masses and awarding annual scholarships to students in the Filipino community of Ventura County. Throughout the 1980s and beyond, other annual events and new traditions have taken root like Simbang Gabi, Fiesta Filipinas, and the Maria Clara Debutante Ball. Filipinos are engaging and getting involved politically, organizing neighborhood forums, addressing community issues, and establishing media presence on the web and in print with *Kapitbahay*, a Filipino newspaper about their community. Filipinos are faced with new challenges and recurring challenges, like getting elected to public offices in local government. The Philippine centennial in Oxnard was celebrated in 1998, which had over 6,000 people in attendance, a 30-car motorcade, and a picnic in Plaza Park. This celebration demonstrated what a force the Filipino community can be when its enthusiasm, energy, and mobilization is harnessed. (Courtesy of Fe and Toots Vinzon.)

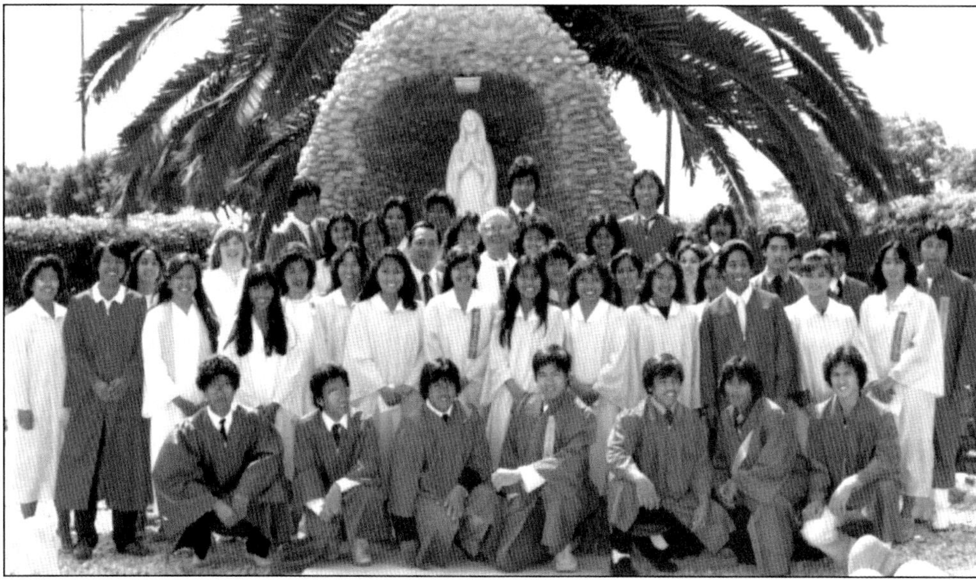

Graduates of the class of 1982 take their class picture together at Mary Star of the Sea Church in Port Hueneme. The Salute to the Graduates Program started in 1979, headed by the United Pacific Islanders group, to honor young men and women graduating from high schools all over the county. The Filipino Community of Ventura County Inc. took over the responsibilities of this annual event, which includes planning festivities, the Baccalaureate Mass, salute program, and fundraising for scholarship awards. Many of the graduate participants and award recipients have gone on to attend college and become well-educated professionals in Ventura County and beyond. (Courtesy of Vic R. and Coring G. Mercado.)

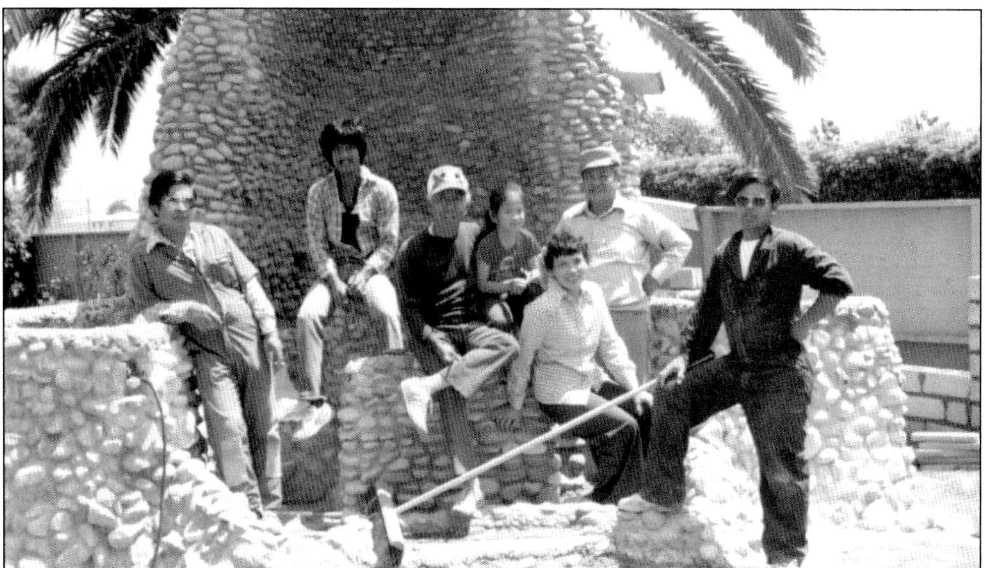

Volunteers worked every weekend for several months to build the new grotto at Mary Star of the Sea in Port Hueneme. Community volunteers donated materials and their time, and Vic Mercado led fundraising efforts, while Coring Mercado prepared lunches. Pictured from left to right are Ben Adriano, Randy Parras, Cel DeLeon, Kristine Mercado, Coring Mercado, Tony Morena, and an unidentified volunteer. (Courtesy of Vic R. and Coring G. Mercado.)

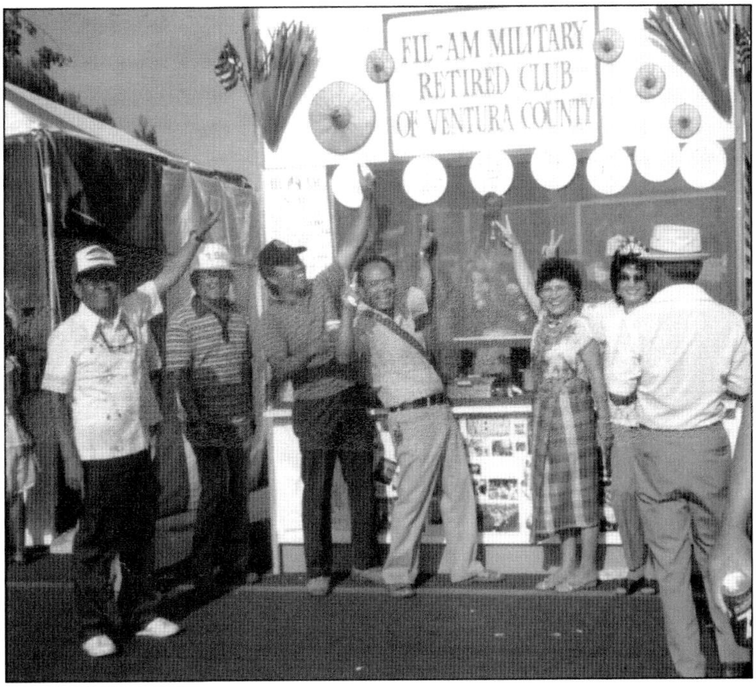

Members of the Filipino American Military Retired Club of Ventura County show their pride in front of their booth at a festival in Oxnard in July 1986. Originally named "Mabuhay Club," Romulo S. Villa founded the military retired club in 1973, and the Mabuhay Ladies Auxiliary was established shortly after in 1975. (Courtesy of Josie and Al Bautista.)

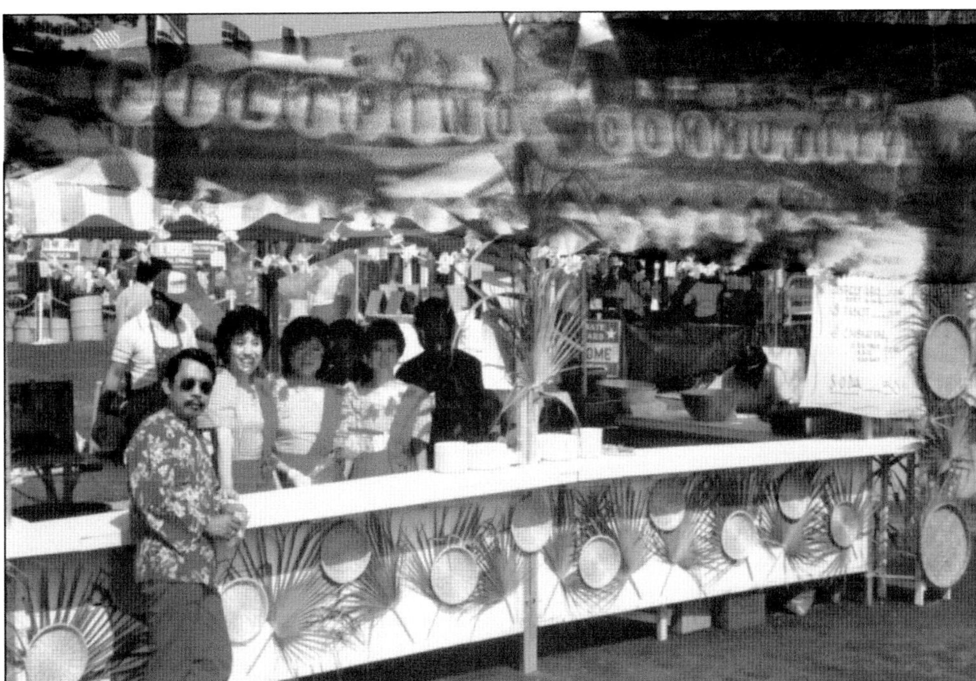

Volunteers man the Filipino Community of Ventura County Inc. food booth in the 1980s in Oxnard. (Courtesy of Josie and Al Bautista.)

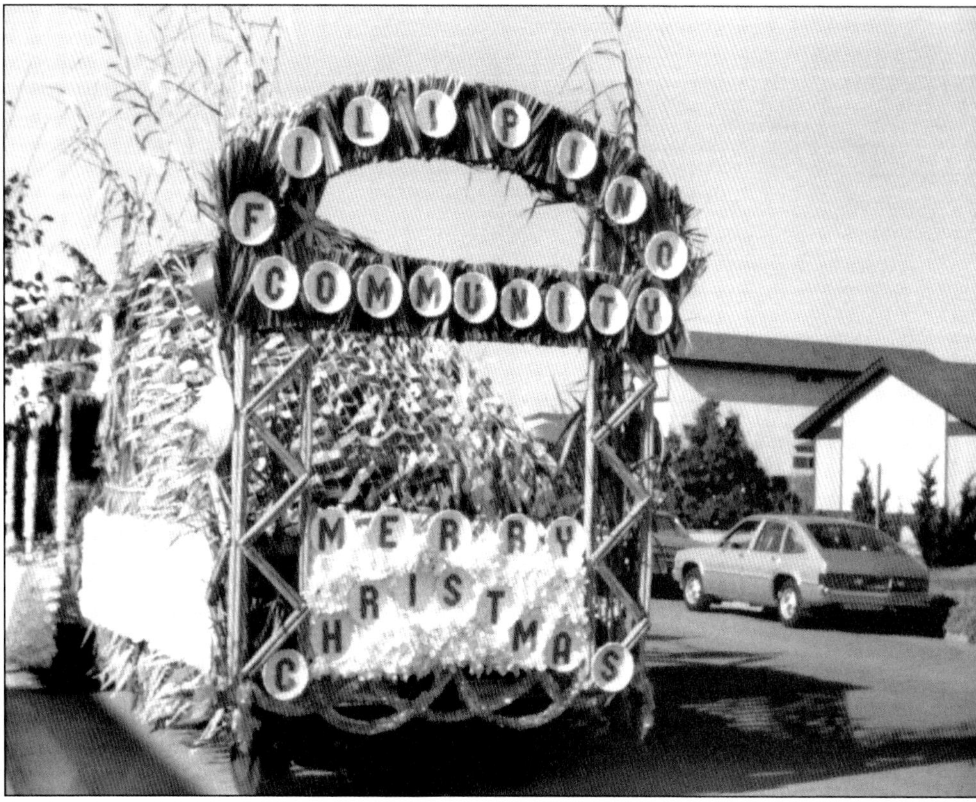

At the Oxnard Christmas Parade in the 1980s, The Filipino Community of Ventura County Inc. float is escorted by, from left to right, Del Villaruel, Toots Vinzon, Al Bautista, Art Legasca (behind), and Vic Mercado. (Courtesy of Fe and Toots Vinzon.)

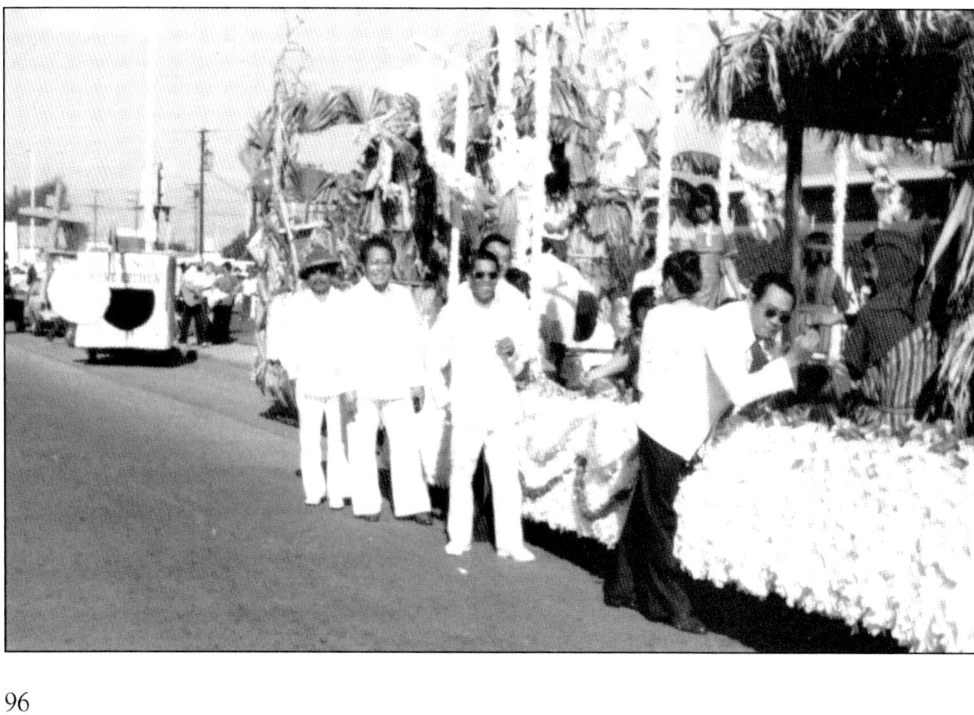

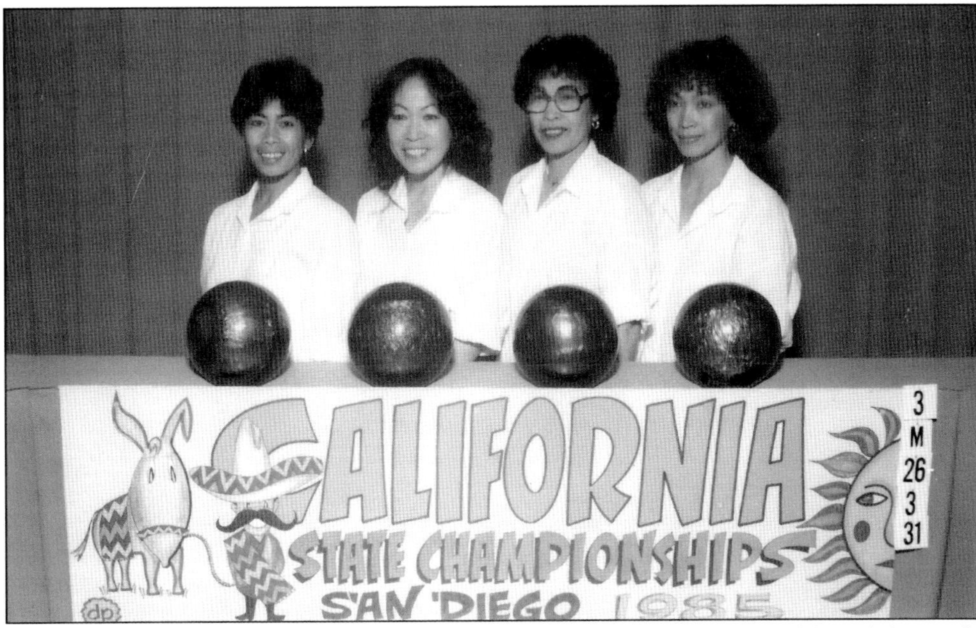

Bowling at the 1985 California State Championships in San Diego, pictured from left to right are Virgie Castaneda, Josie Castaneda, Belen Castaneda, and Edith Castaneda. The Castanedas were part of a local league, and the league competed all over the county and qualified to represent Ventura at the state championship games. Team members practiced at Tournament Bowl on Saviers Boulevard in Oxnard. (Courtesy of Augie Castaneda Jr.)

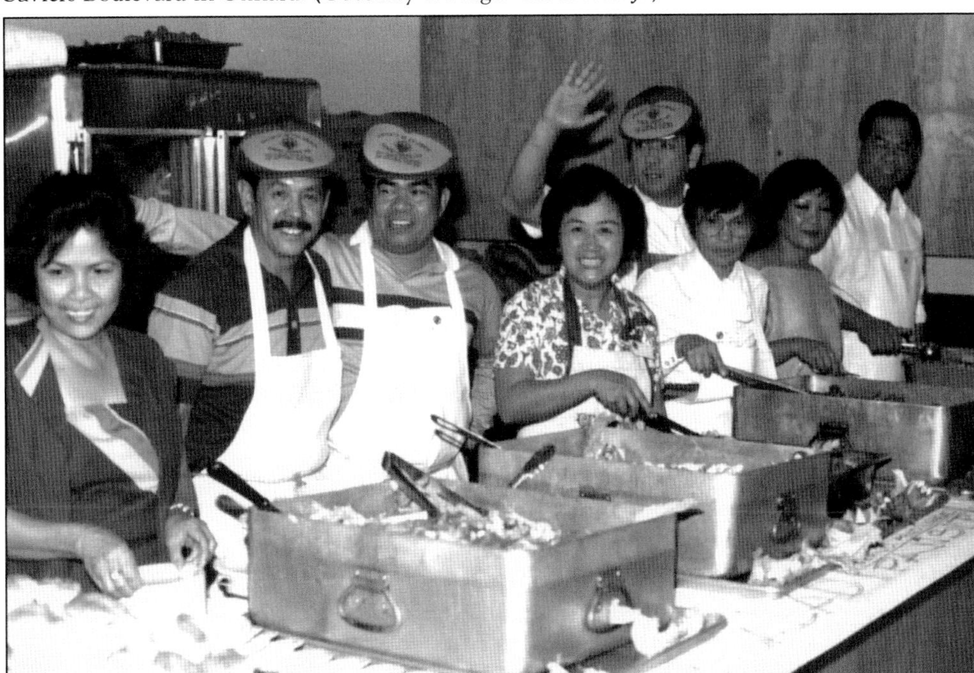

Friends prepare food for family night at the Knights of Columbus Hall in the 1980s. Those pictured are, from left to right, Fe Vinzon, Sonny Santos, Ernie Cruz, Loretta DeLeon, Coring Mercado, Vic Mercado, Mary Grey, and Alex Calayan. (Courtesy of Vic R. and Coring G. Mercado.)

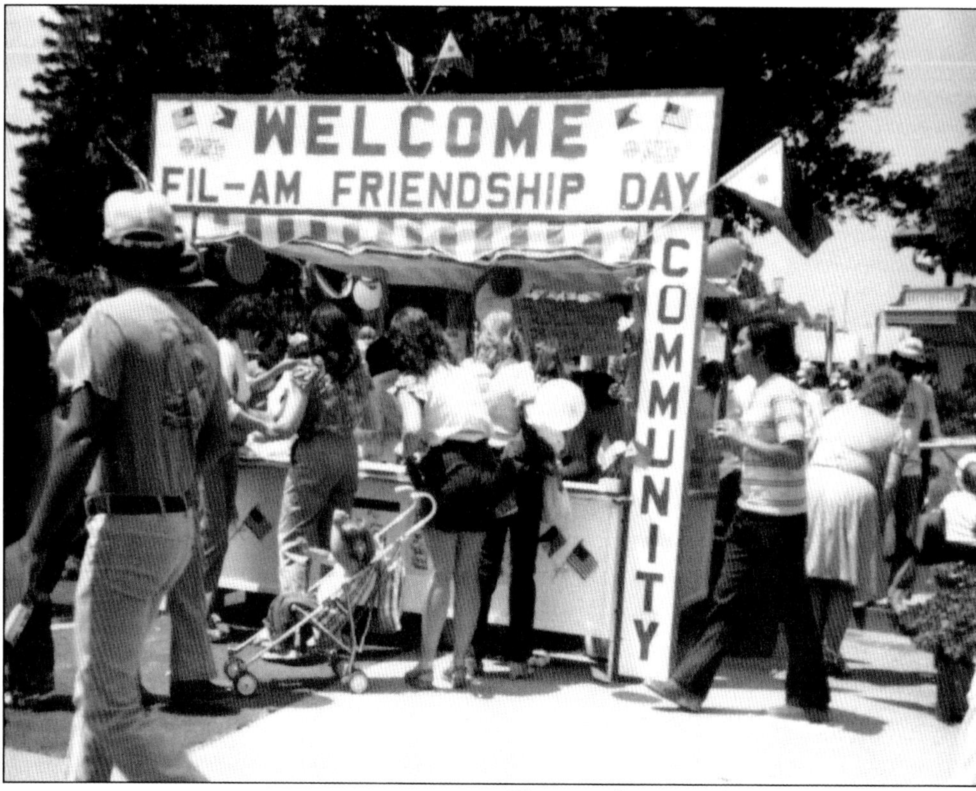

This snapshot was taken at Filipino-American Friendship Day at Plaza Park in Oxnard in the 1980s. Filipino-American Friendship Day is celebrated on the Fourth of July and commemorates the Filipino and American joint efforts to liberate the Philippines from Japanese occupation during World War II. (Courtesy of Josie and Al Bautista.)

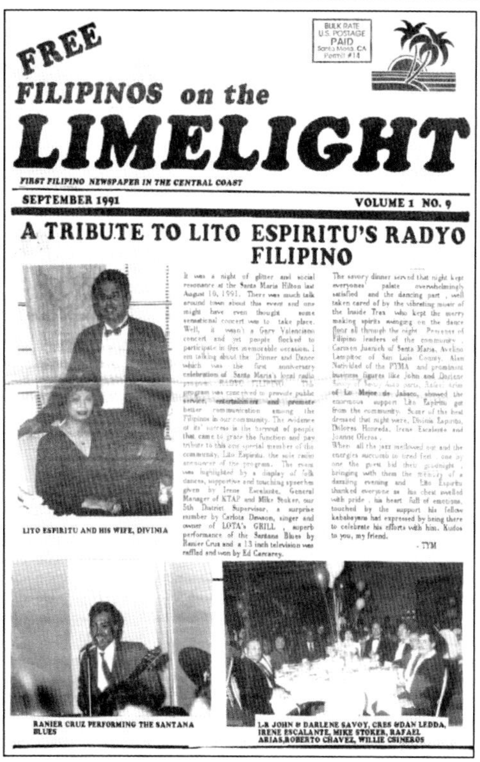

FREE

BULK RATE
U.S. POSTAGE
PAID
Santa Maria, CA
Permit #14

FILIPINOS on the LIMELIGHT

FIRST FILIPINO NEWSPAPER IN THE CENTRAL COAST

SEPTEMBER 1991 VOLUME 1 NO. 9

A TRIBUTE TO LITO ESPIRITU'S RADYO FILIPINO

LITO ESPIRITU AND HIS WIFE, DIVINIA

It was a night of glitter and social resonance at the Santa Maria Hilton last August 10, 1991. There was much talk around town about this event and one might have even thought some sensational concert was to take place. Well, it wasn't a Gary Valenciano concert and yet people flocked to participate in this memorable occasion. I am talking about the Dinner and Dance which was the first anniversary celebration of Santa Maria's local radio program RADYO FILIPINO. The program was conceived to provide public service, entertainment and promote better communication among the Filipinos in our community. The evidence of its' success is the turnout of people that came to grace the function and pay tribute to this one special member of the community, Lito Espiritu, the sole radio announcer of the program. The event was highlighted by a display of folk dances, supportive and touching speeches given by Irene Escalante, General Manager of KTAP and Mike Stoker, our 5th District Supervisor, a surprise number by Carlota Dawson, singer and owner of LOTA's GRILL, superb performance of the Santana Blues by Ranier Cruz and a 13 inch television was raffled and won by Ed Carcarey.

The savory dinner served that night kept everyones' palate overwhelmingly satisfied and the dancing part, well taken cared of by the vibrating music of the Inside Trax who kept the merry making spirits swinging on the dance floor all through the night. Presence of Filipino leaders of the community, Carmen Juanich of Santa Maria, Avelino Lampitoc of San Luis County, Alan Natividad of the FYMA and prominent business figures like John and Darlene Savoy of Savoy Auto parts, Rafael Arias of Lo Mejor de Jalisco, showed the enormous support Lito Espiritu got from the community. Some of the best dressed that night were, Divinia Espiritu, Dolores Honreda, Irene Escalante and Joanne Olcros.

When all the jazz mellowed out and the energies succumb to tired feet, one by one the guest bid their goodnight, bringing with them the memory of a dazzling evening and Lito Espiritu thanked everyone as his chest swelled with pride, his heart full of emotions, touched by the support his fellow kababayans had expressed by being there to celebrate his efforts with him. Kudos to you, my friend.

- TYM

RANIER CRUZ PERFORMING THE SANTANA BLUES

L-R JOHN & DARLENE SAVOY, CRES &DAN LEDDA, IRENE ESCALANTE, MIKE STOKER, RAFAEL ARIAS,ROBERTO CHAVEZ, WILLIE CSINEROS

Filipinos on the Limelight was the first Filipino newspaper in the Central Coast. Started in 1991, the *Limelight* was published monthly and circulated in Santa Maria, Lompoc, San Luis Obispo, Los Osos, Oxnard, and the 5 Cities Area, comprised of Arroyo Grande, Oceano, Grover Beach, Pismo Beach, and Shell Beach. (Courtesy of Delia and Sid Cabran.)

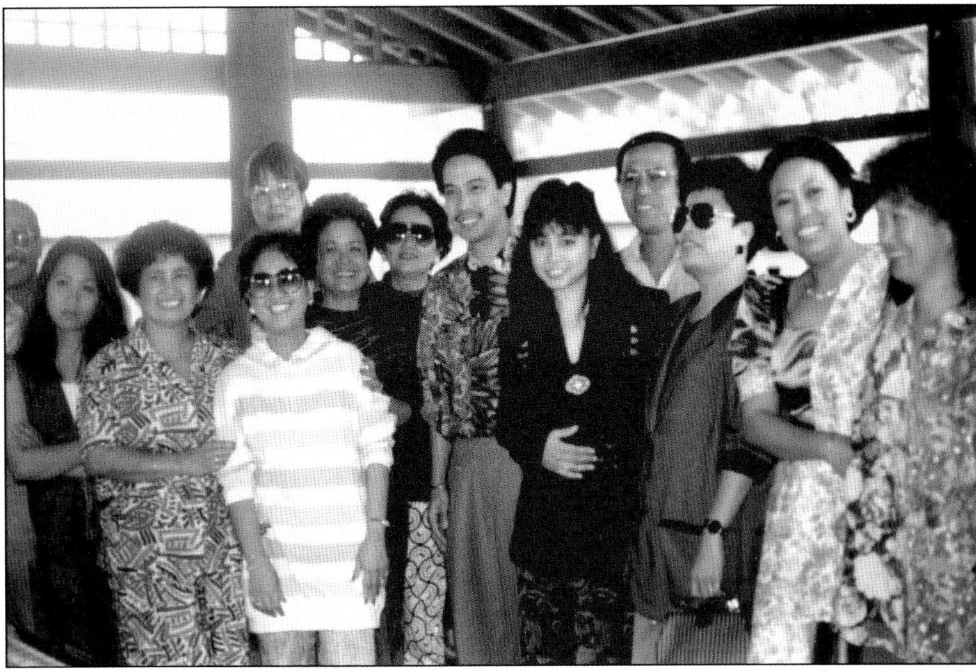

Members of the Cavite Association of Ventura County pose with Filipino singer Hajji Alejandro in 1991 in Oxnard. Cavitenos held festivities at the Oxnard College Estates Park with Hajji Alejandro headlining and Ninette Tenza from the musical group The Flashbacks. (Courtesy of Delia and Sid Cabran.)

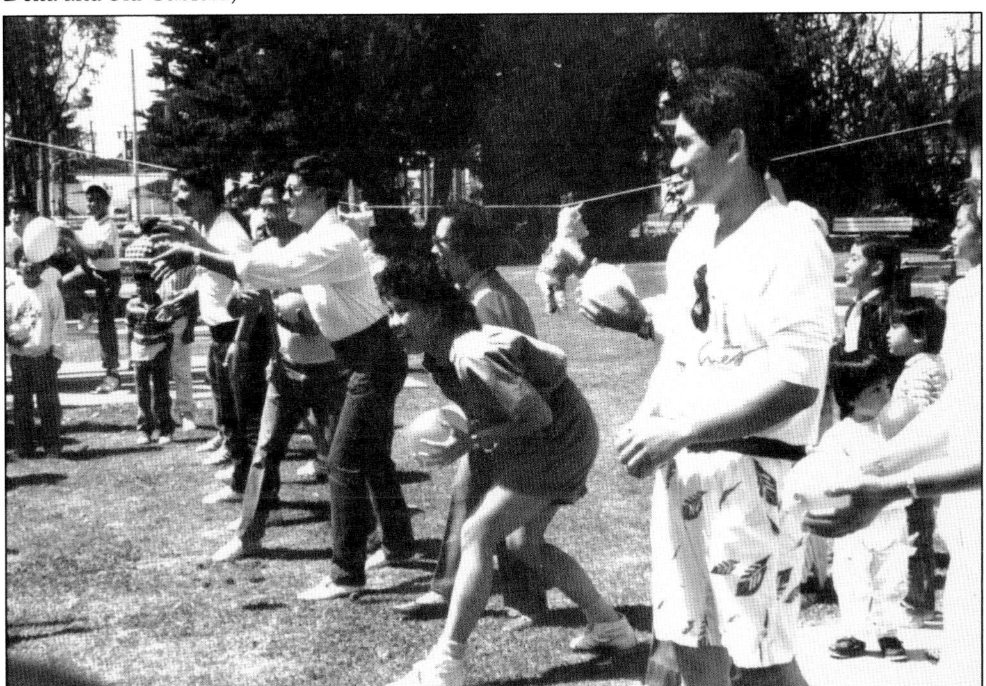

The PINOYS Easter Picnic was held in 1987 at the Navy Base at Port Hueneme. Families enjoyed the day's events, which included food, games, and festivities. (Courtesy of the Peter Villanueva.)

CHANGE WITH TONY V. GREY

Are you ready for a refreshing change to the Oxnard City Council?
Isn't it time to elect someone......

- **Who will be the voice of the people.**
- **Who will listen to the people's concerns.**
- **Who will take action on your behalf.**

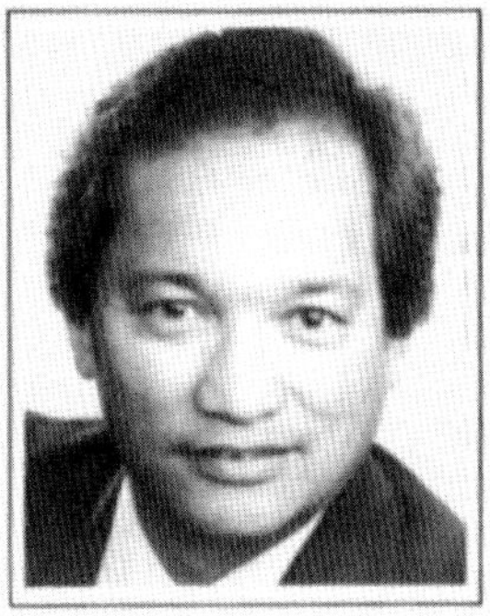

Who is the man that wants to represent YOU on Oxnard's City Council? Who is TONY V. GREY? He is a SUPPLY SYSTEMS ANALYST in the Federal Government. Born in the Philippines. Retired Navy Master Chief Petty Officer (E-9). Oxnard Military Citizen of the Year in 1981.

His education includes, BS in Accounting, University of La Verne, California; Member, Alpha Gamma Sigma Honor Society. His Civic and Community Involvements are, Member Ventura County Civil Service Commission, 5th District; Air Pollution Control District Citizen Advisory Committee, 1981-82; Ventura County Community College District Citizen Advisory Committee on Minority Affairs, 1982-83; Filipino American Community of Ventura County, Inc.; Oxnard Noontimers LIONS Club; NAACP; Federal Managers Association; Ventura County Council, U.S. Navy League; Deputy Grand Knight, Knights of Columbus Oxnard Council 750; Board of Director, Filipino American Political Association, Mexican American Chamber of Commerce.

IT IS TIME TO ELECT ANTONIO V. "TONY" GREY!!!

A man who will represent only one special interest...you, the citizens of Oxnard.

HE WILL:

- **ESTABLISH MORE EFFECTIVE LINES OF COMMUNICATIONS BETWEEN THE CITIZENS AND THE CITY COUNCIL.**
- **PROMOTE UTILIZATION OF OXNARD'S GREATEST RESOURCE...PEOPLE!!!**
- **STRIVE TO IMPROVE THE QUALITY OF LIFE.**
  SUPPORT RENT STABILIZATION
- **SUPPORT ANTI-CRIME AND PUBLIC SAFETY PROGRAMS.**
- **INITIATE A POLICY OF SOUND FISCAL MANAGEMENT.**
  REVIEW THE NEED FOR UTILITY TAX
- **STRIVE FOR LONG RANGE ECONOMIC DEVELOPMENT.**
  PROMOTE SMALL BUSINESS AND CLEAN INDUSTRIES
- **SUPPORT CONTROLLED GROWTH WITH THE INTENT OF PRESERVING OUR GREEN BELT (AGRICULTURAL LANDS), INLAND PARKS AND RECREATION AREAS, AND COASTAL BEACHES**

TONY V. GREY will return your city government to you.

TONY GREY is your man for the city council.

Paid for by the Committee To Elect Tony V. Grey. (805) 985-2217

Pictured is a campaign advertisement from Tony V. Grey's first run for Oxnard City Council in 1984. Grey campaigned and ran three times for office calling for greater Filipino-American political unity and a voice in policy making, government representation, and political clout. His column called "The Grey Spot" in *Kapitbahay*, a Filipino American publication, echoed the same themes and addressed community related concerns. (Courtesy of Tony V. Grey.)

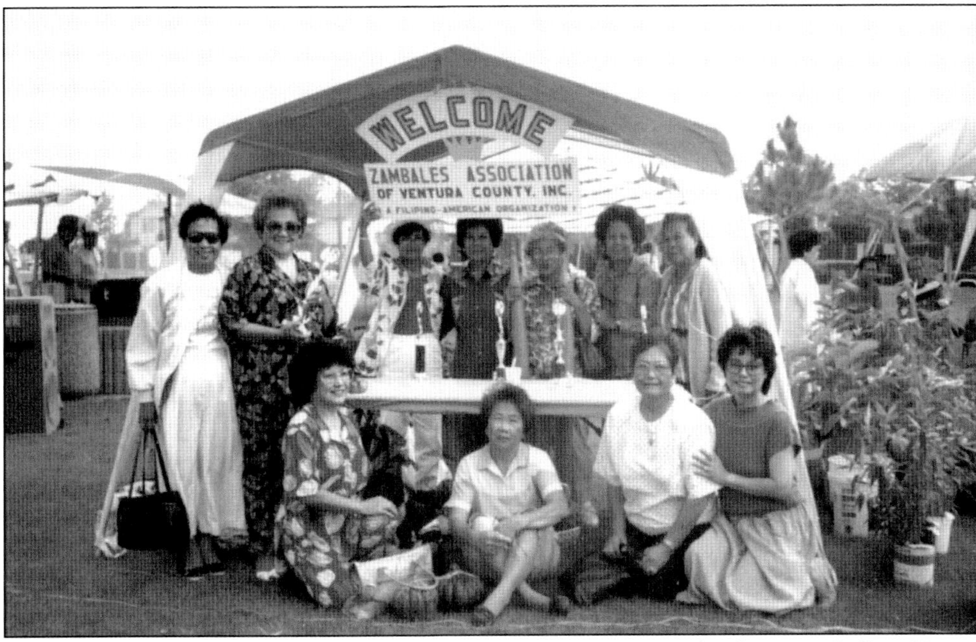

The Zambales Association of Ventura County hosts a plant auction fundraiser at College Estates Park in Oxnard on August 19, 1990. (Courtesy of Vicky Barretto.)

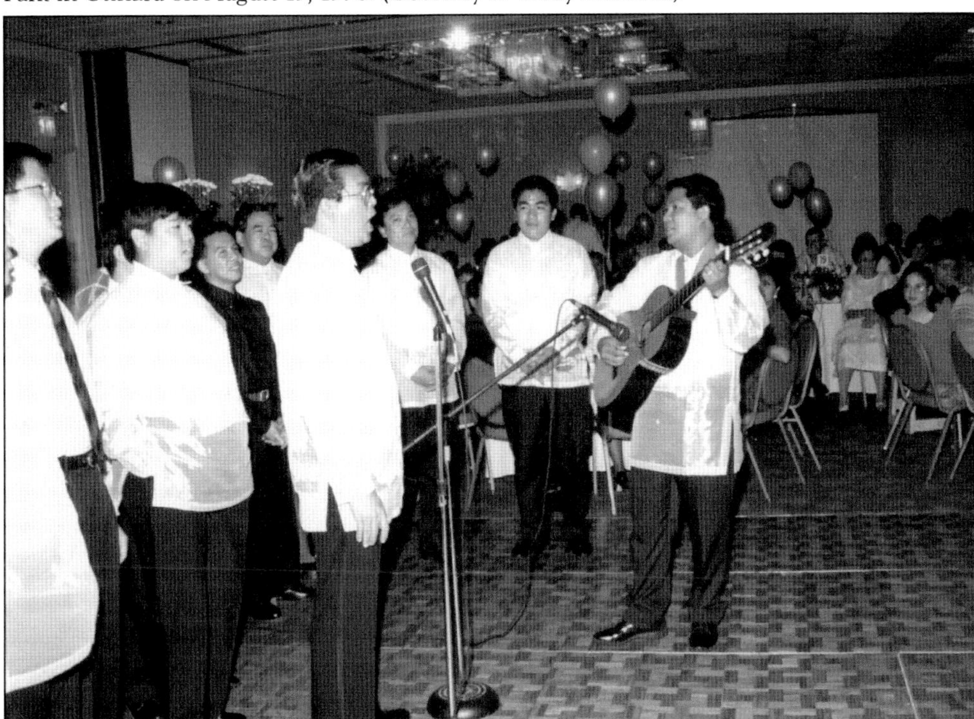
The Philippine Patron of Arts organizes performances every two years, and in 1996 members sponsored the University of the Philippines Madrigal Singers. This photograph shows the University of the Philippines Madrigal Singers performing at the 25th anniversary reception of Chief Deputy Dante Honorico and his wife, Ellen, in Camarillo. (Courtesy of Ellen and Dante Honorico.)

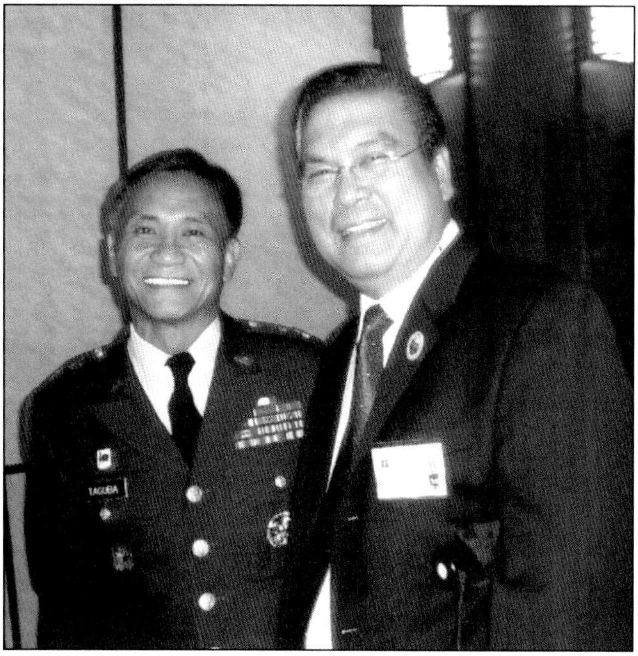

Some of Chief Deputy Dante Honorico's achievements include serving as inaugural chairman of the Ventura County Sherriff's Department Minority Relations Committee (1991) and receiving the Leadership Award from the National Association of Asian Peace Officers (1995) as well as the Americanism Medal from the Daughters of the American Revolution (1999). Pictured in 2003 in Washington, DC, are Honorico and Gen. Antonio Taguba, author of the Taguba Report regarding the detainees at Abu Ghraib in Iraq. (Courtesy of Ellen and Dante Honorico.)

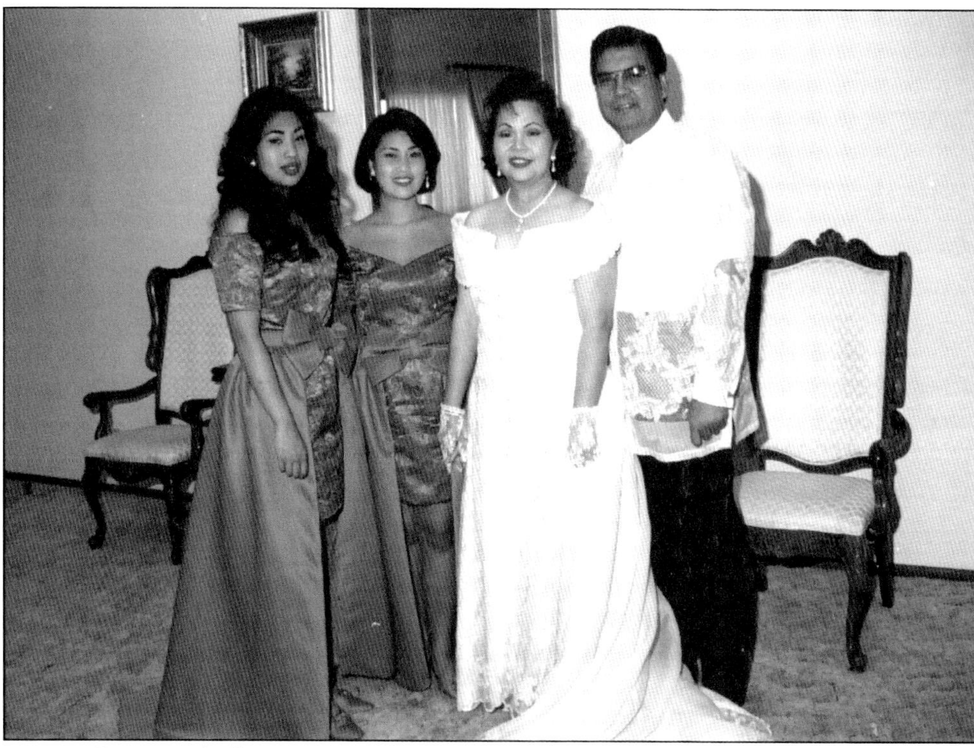

In 1996, Dante and Ellen Honorico celebrate their 25th anniversary at the United Methodist church in Camarillo. The Honoricos were part of the third wave of Filipino immigration that included professionals. Ellen was a registered nurse and Dante a college graduate when they immigrated in 1975. They have two daughters, Genevieve and Abigail. (Courtesy of Ellen and Dante Honorico.)

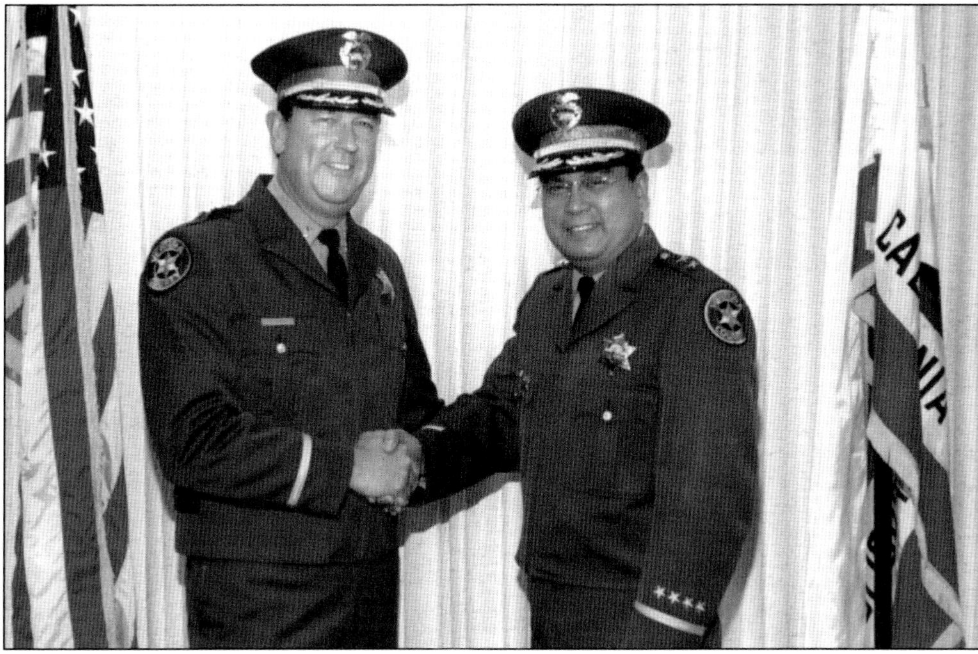

In 1997, Dante Honorico was selected and promoted to chief deputy at the Ventura County Sheriff's Department, replacing retiring chief deputy Don Lanquist. Honorico is the highest-ranking Filipino in law enforcement in Ventura County. He joined the sheriff's department in 1976 and holds a bachelor's degree in business administration from Lyceum of the Philippines University and a master's degree in public administration from California Lutheran University. (Courtesy of Ellen and Dante Honorico.)

Commander picked to fill No. 3 post at sheriff's department

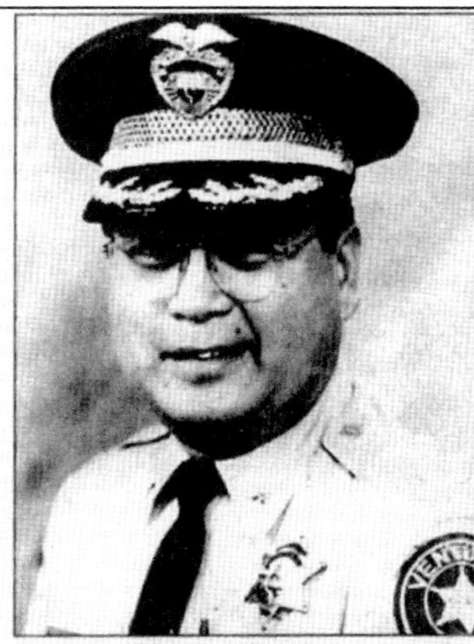

Dante Honorico
Rises through ranks

By Jesse Hiestand
Daily News Staff Writer

VENTURA — Ventura County Sheriff's Cmdr. Dante Honorico, a Filipino immigrant who rose through the ranks from patrol deputy to a top administrator, is set to move into the department's No. 3 spot next month.

Honorico will be promoted to chief deputy June 29, replacing retiring Chief Deputy Don Lanquist, officials said.

"I have profound respect for Chief Honorico's ability as a leader, not only in the Sheriff's Department, but also in the community of Ventura County that we serve," Sheriff Larry Carpenter said in a prepared statement.

Honorico came to the United States from the Philippines in 1975. He joined the Sheriff's Department a year later and started out as a deputy assigned to work in the jails, Capt. Mark Ball said.

During the past two decades, Honorico served in every division of the department, from patrol duty to helping lead construction of the Todd Road Jail.

He was the first chairman of the department's Employee Relations Committee, which tackled internal labor issues.

Honorico, of Camarillo remains a leader in the Filipino-American Council of Ventura County.

With the promotion, Honorico will become one of the department's four chief deputies who answer to the sheriff and undersheriff.

It is likely he will take over the support services division, Ball said. The three other chief deputies handle detention services and policing in western and eastern Ventura County.

Lanquist, the retiring chief deputy, is in charge of detention services, Ball said.

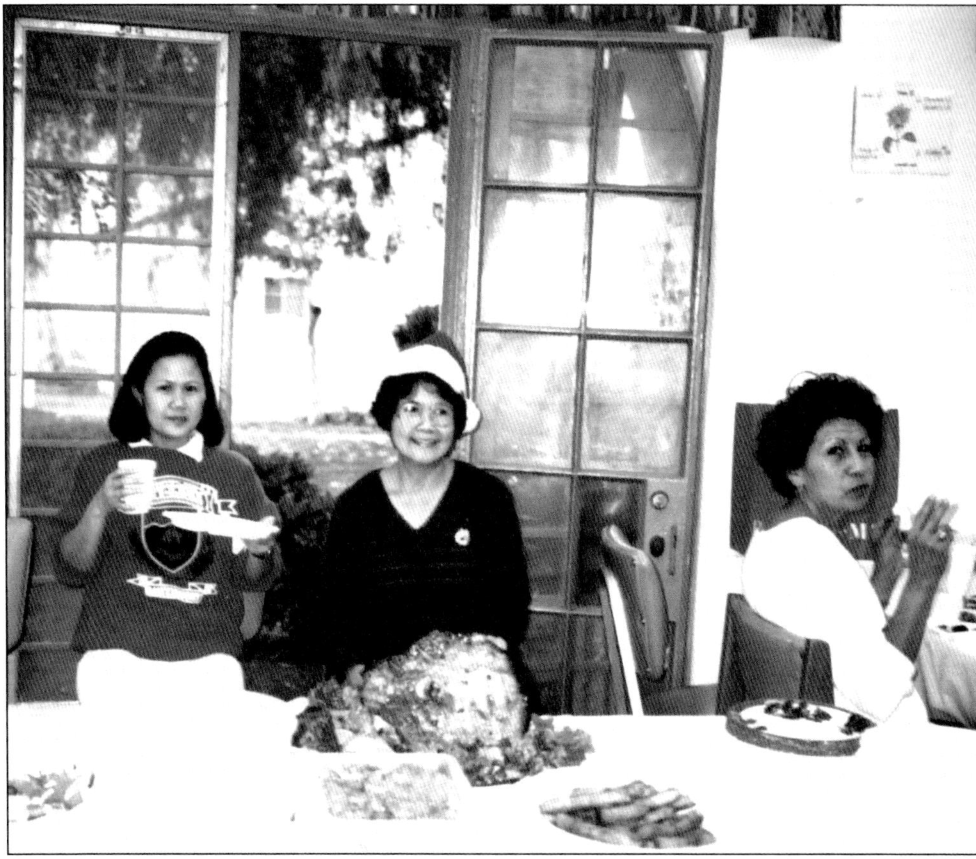

Linda Caldejon, Delia Cabran, and Ester Estrada enjoy themselves at the 1996 Christmas party at Camarillo State Hospital. In 1997, the hospital closed its doors, and in 2002, the hospital complex was transformed into California State University Channel Islands, Ventura County's first public university. The signature red French doors, courtyards, and Spanish Revival architecture still remain today throughout the campus. (Courtesy of Delia and Sid Cabran.)

Camarillo State Employees

Send their love on Valentines Day

To:	From:	To:	From:
Eder	Jane Saqui	Gani	Josie Sabalerio
Roy	Ofelia Biascan	Jun	Linda Caldejon
Zoe	Job Decolongan	Doming	Lina Tolentino
Vilma Capina	Joe William	Amor	Juanita Tolentino
Gus	Edna Guanio	Nicole & Evelyn	Mar Manansala
Shay Cleveland	Ruth Preston	Lando	Ramona Taylan
Family and Friends	Monica Reyes	Jay	Violy Orense
Urbano	Jacinta Real	Sid	Del Cabran

Many Filipino nurses, technicians, and caregivers worked at the Camarillo State Hospital until it closed its doors in 1997. This greeting of love on Valentine's Day is from Camarillo State Hospital employees to their spouses and loved ones. It appeared in the Valentine issue of *Kapitbahay* in February 1993. (Courtesy of Delia and Sid Cabran.)

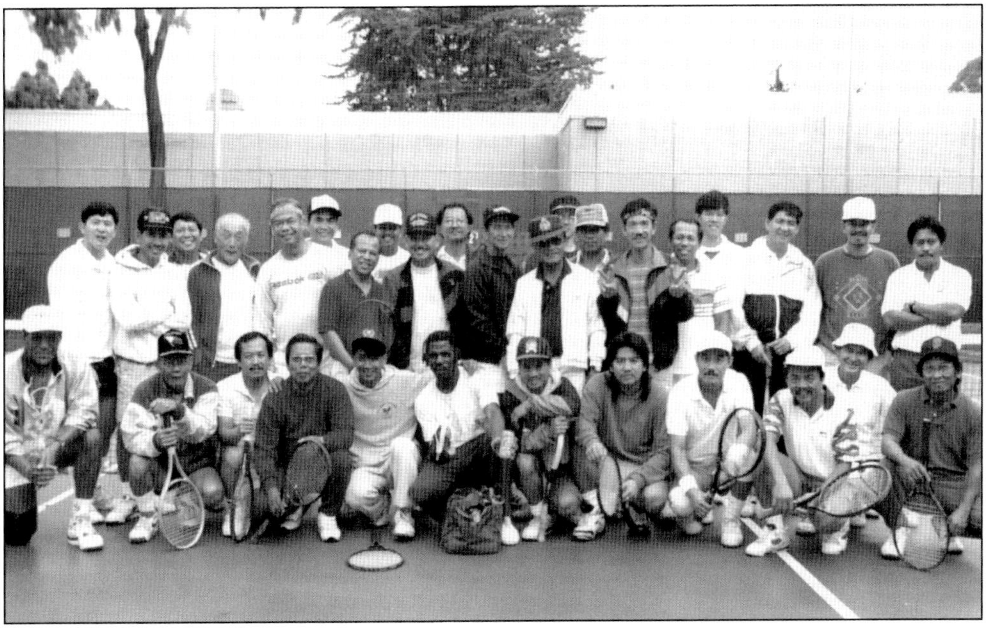

For years, Filipinos in the community gathered to play tennis every Saturday and Sunday morning at Channel Islands High School (CIHS) until the 1990s. This impromptu photograph was taken on one such occasion. Once CIHS closed its gates on weekends, Filipinos started playing at Miranda Park in Port Hueneme. (Courtesy of Irene and Eduardo Austria.)

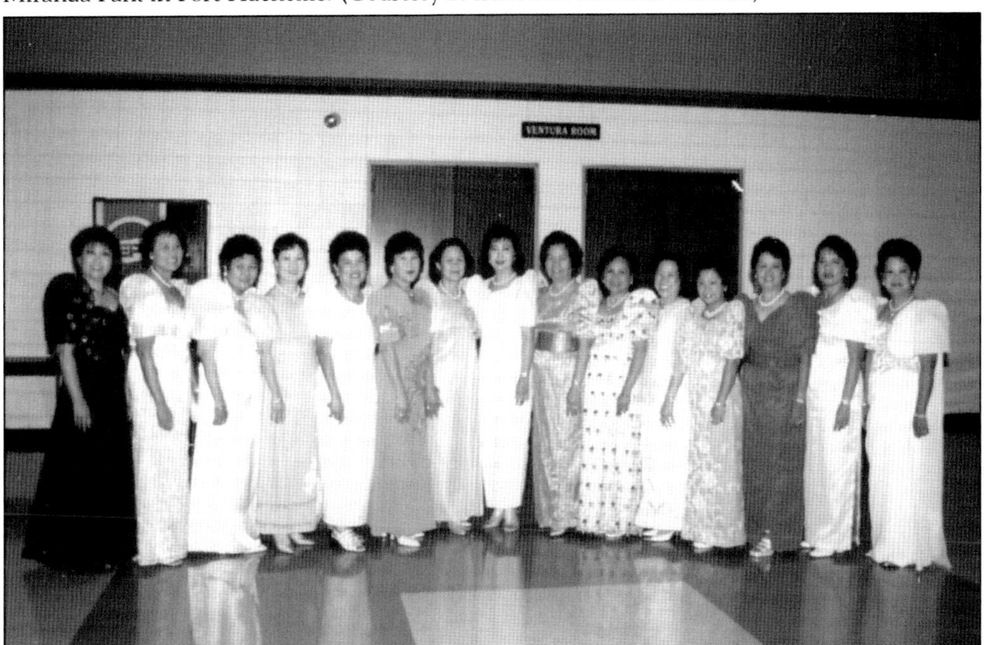

The Ladies Auxiliary of the Filipino American Military Retired Club pose at the annual Maria Clara Debutante's Ball at the Oxnard Performing Arts Center in 1999. The first Maria Clara Debutante's Ball was in 1979, and since then, it has been the major fundraiser for the Ladies Auxiliary. The debutantes participate in tea with their mothers and cotillion with their selected escorts. (Courtesy of Nellie and John Obispo.)

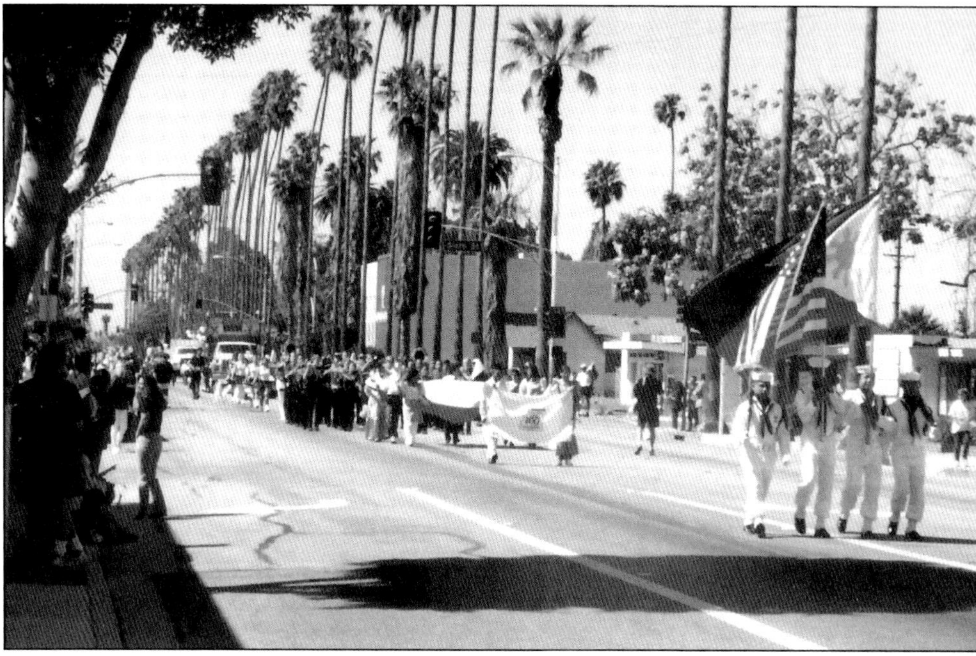

In 1998, the Filipino community celebrated the 100th anniversary of Philippine Independence with festivities throughout the week, including a parade complete with color guard, a marching band, and a 30-car motorcade traveling through downtown. Festivities continued at Plaza Park in Oxnard. The *L.A. Times* reported an estimated 6,000 people in attendance, the largest-ever Filipino gathering to date in Ventura County. (Courtesy of Augie Castaneda Jr.)

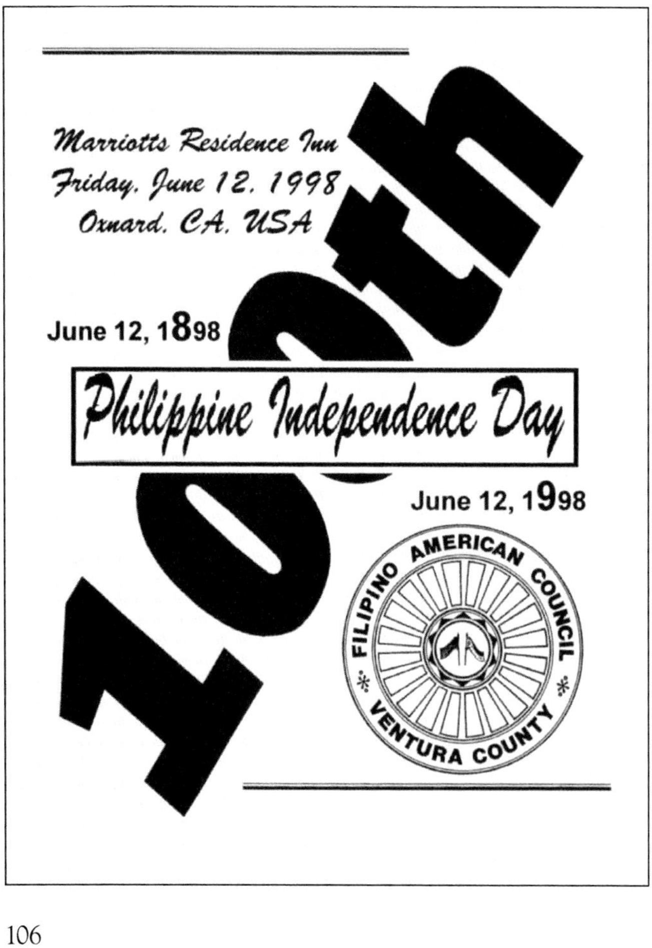

The weeklong 100th anniversary of Philippine Independence celebration concluded with a dinner and program on Friday, June 12, 1998, at the Marriott Residence Inn. (Courtesy of Irene and Eduardo Austria.)

The Filipino American Seniors float is pictured during the Philippine Centennial Parade in 1998. Vicky Barretto stands next to Manuel Lopez, mayor of Oxnard. (Courtesy of Vicky Barretto.)

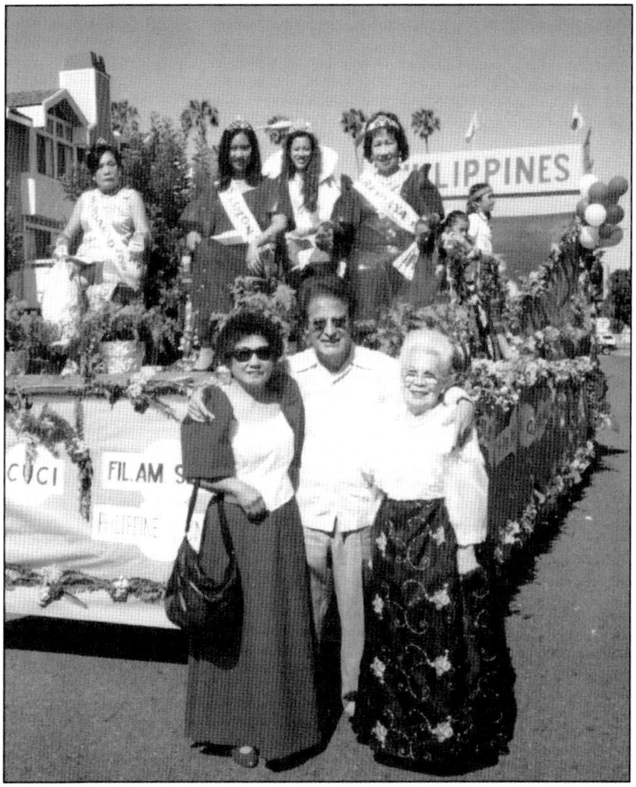

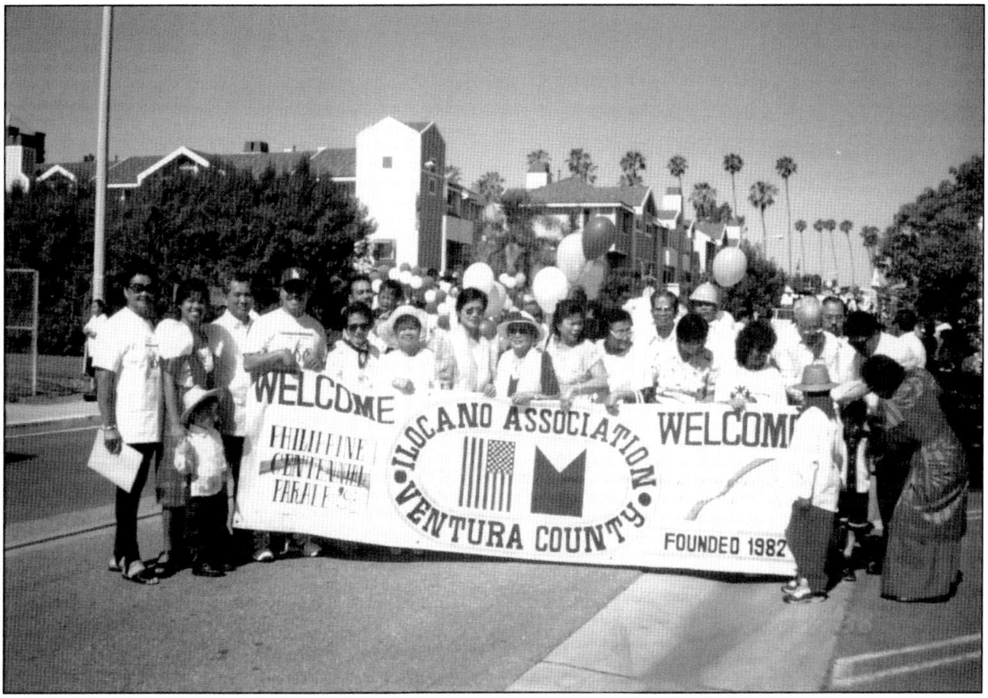

Members of the Ilocano Association of Ventura County pose with their banner during the Philippine Centennial Parade. (Courtesy of Cathy and Jim Ines.)

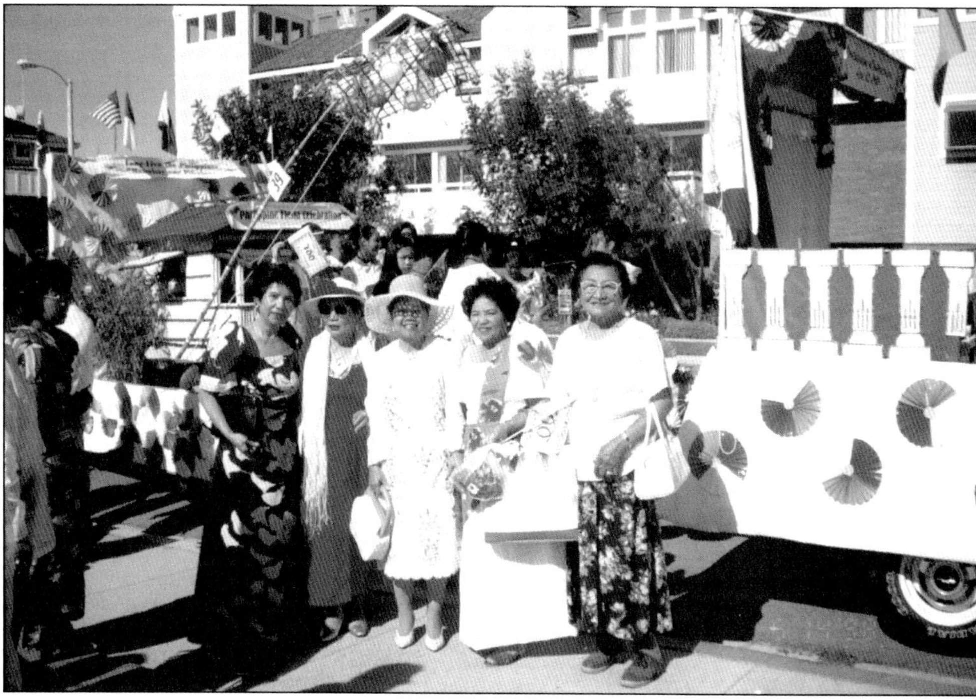

Ladies stand in front of floats during the 1998 Philippine Centennial Parade in Oxnard. Below, this float reads, "The struggle for freedom." (Above, courtesy of Cathy and Jim Ines; below, courtesy of Augie Castaneda Jr.)

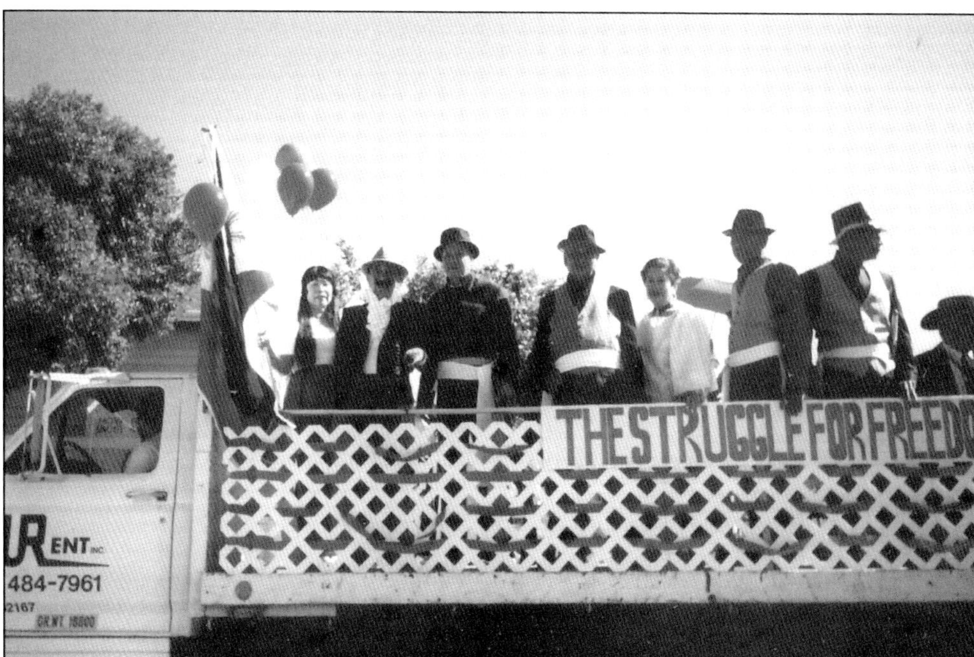

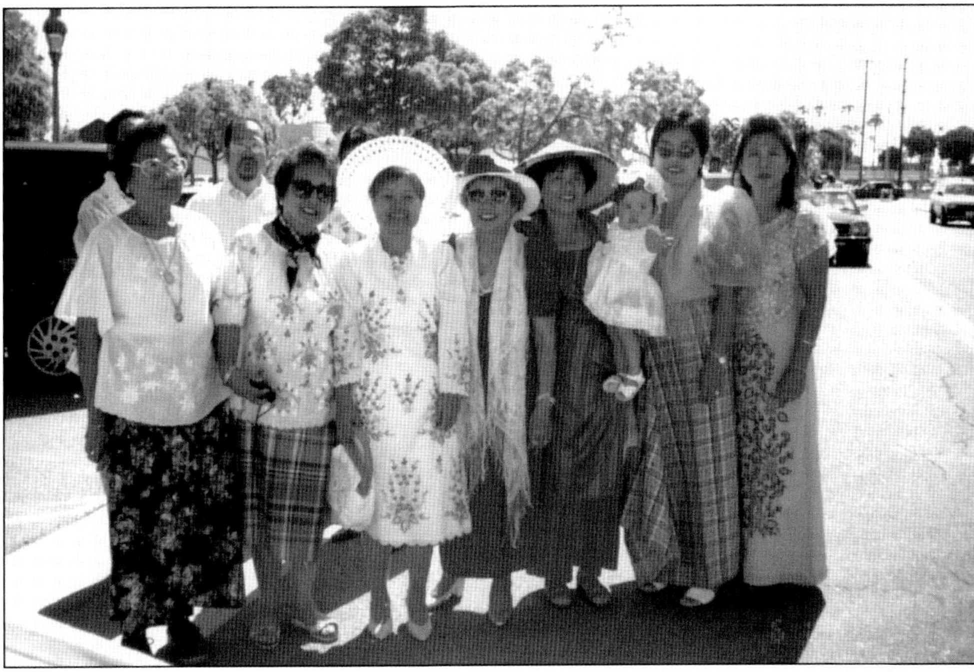

Ladies are dressed in colorful dresses from different regions of the Philippines for the 100th anniversary of Philippine Independence celebration. (Courtesy of Cathy and Jim Ines.)

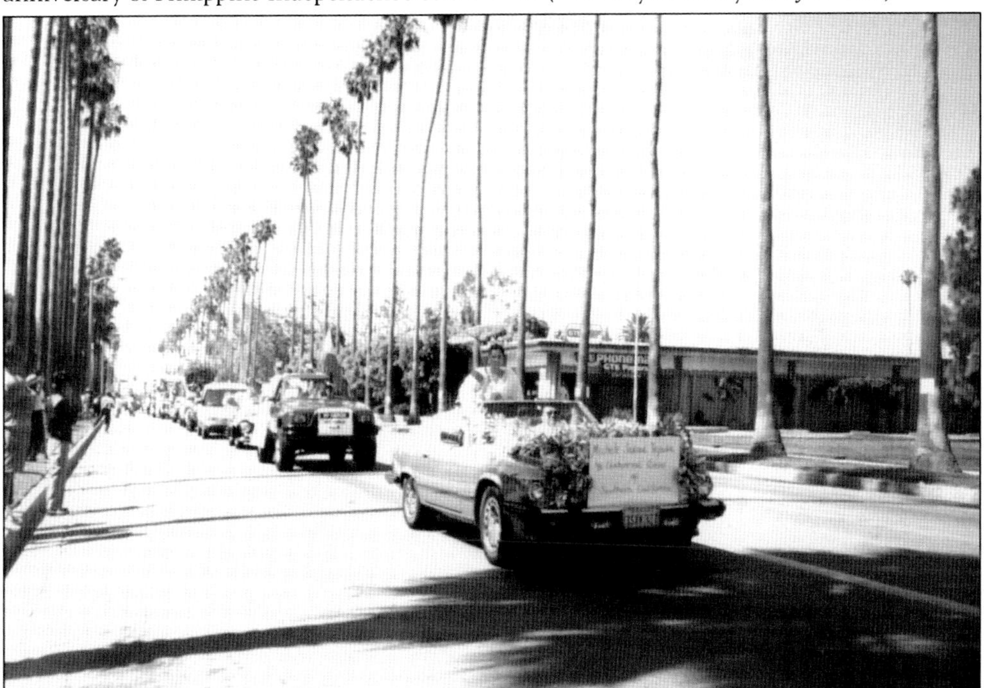

Here is a glimpse of the 30-car motorcade at the 100th anniversary of Philippine Independence celebration. The first car carries Michele Tajada, the 1998 centennial queen, while the second carries P.P. Garcia, a crewmember of the USS *Pueblo* and also a POW of the Korean War. (Courtesy of Tony V. Grey.)

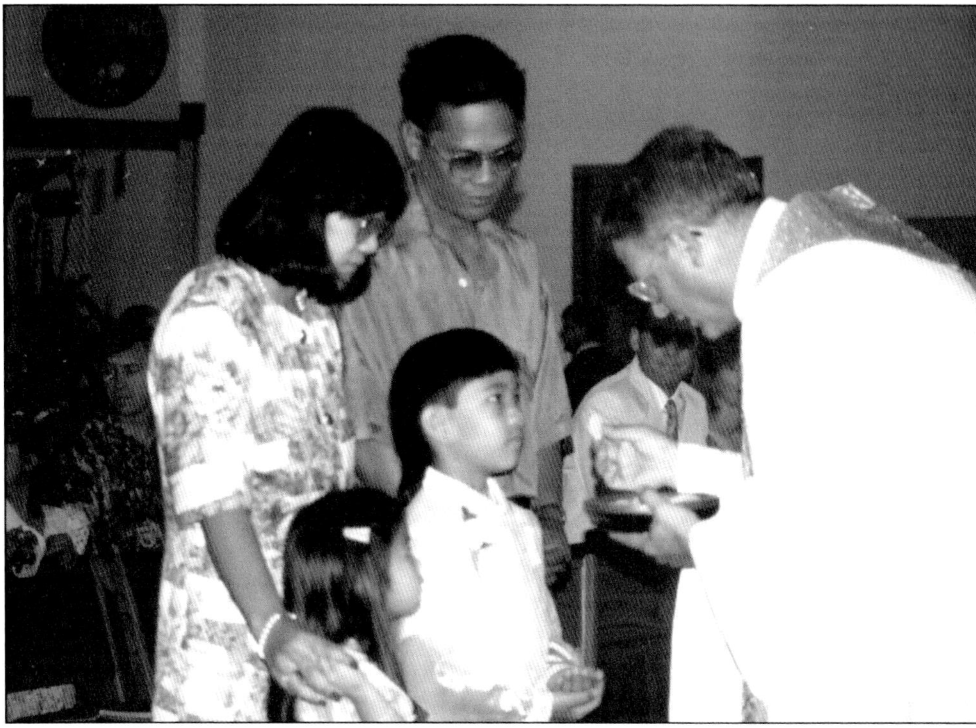

Eight-year-old Ariel Sarreal takes his First Communion at St. Joseph the Worker Church at Port Hueneme Naval Base Ventura County in 1993. Supporting him are his five-year-old sister, Adrianne; his father, Alejandro; and his mother, Rosalina. (Courtesy of Rosalina and Alejandro Sarreal.)

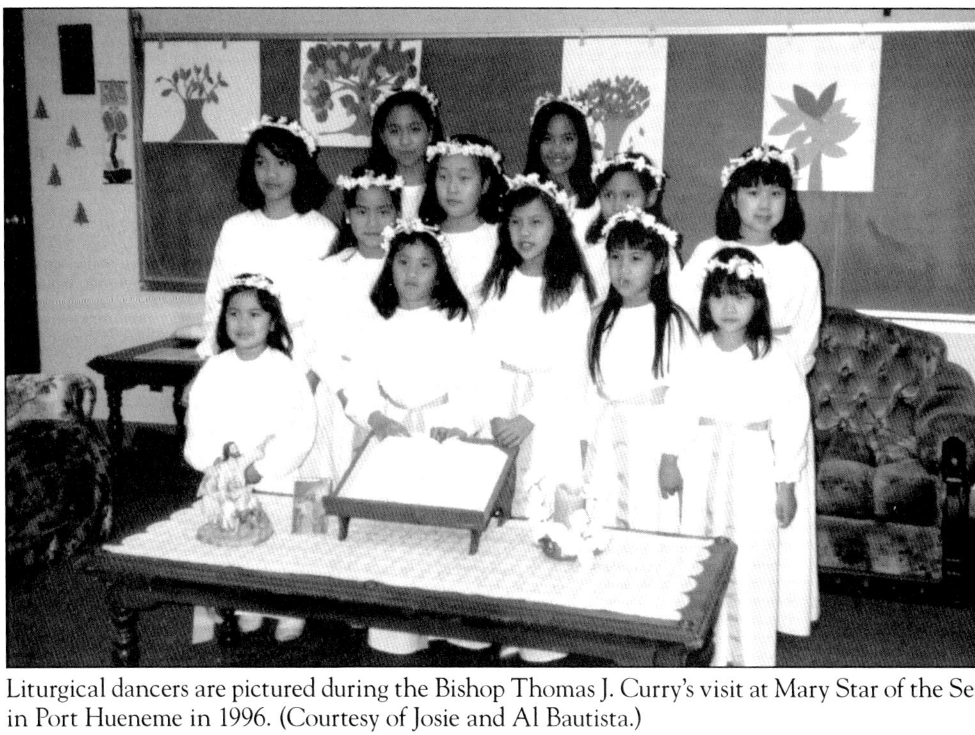

Liturgical dancers are pictured during the Bishop Thomas J. Curry's visit at Mary Star of the Sea in Port Hueneme in 1996. (Courtesy of Josie and Al Bautista.)

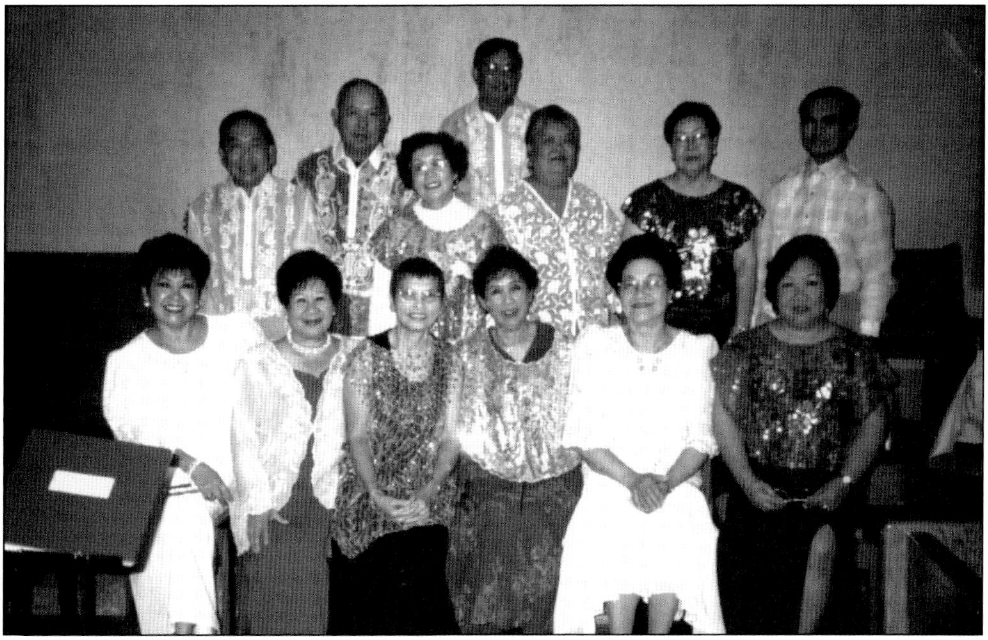

Members of the Simbang Gabi Choir at Mary Star of the Sea Church are, from left to right, (first row) Evelyn Besine, Marylou Gajardo, Coring Mercado, Marcy Matatquin, Incarnation Galler, and Gina Libao; (second row) Chris Mariano, Bert Calimlim, Cora Victoria, Fernando Bugayong, Venny Lim, Ched Aquino, and Rene Guarin. (Courtesy of Vic R. and Coring G. Mercado.)

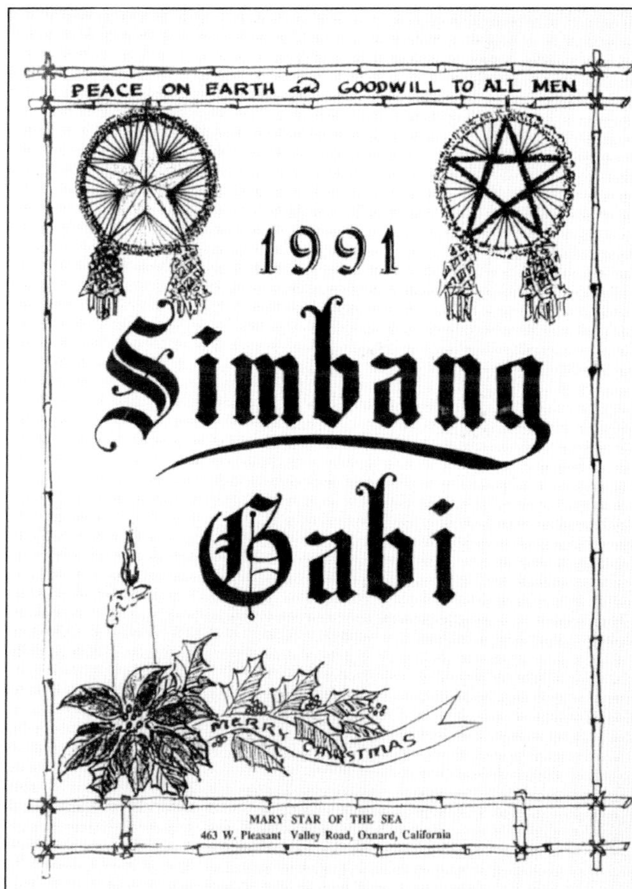

Simbang Gabi is a Filipino Christmas tradition that involves attending a series of nine masses at dawn from December 16 to December 24. In 1989, priest Gerald Cosagayon and Vic Mercado started the Simbang Gabi Christmas at Mary Star of the Sea, which is the only parish in the county that still celebrates all nine days. (Courtesy of Irene and Eduardo Austria.)

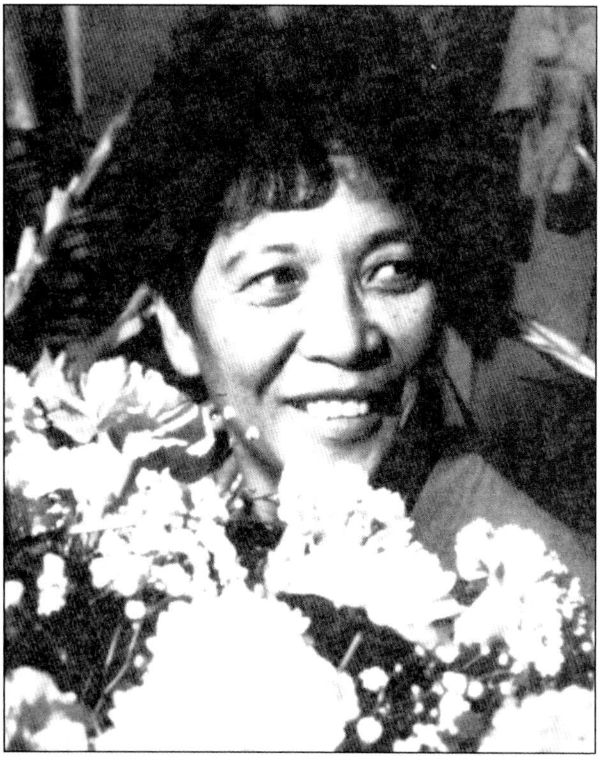

In May 1992, Pope John Paul II conferred on Josie Bautista the papal award *Pro Ecclesia et Pontifice*, translated "For Church and Pope," also known as the "Cross of Honor," a tradition that dates back to 1888. Josie was awarded for her outstanding service in the ecclesiastical community. (Courtesy of Josie and Al Bautista.)

The Collar Guard of the San Buenaventura Assembly of the Knights of Columbus gather for the ground breaking of the new Mary Star of the Sea in Port Hueneme in April 1996, with the Dedication Reception scheduled for August 2, 1997. Those pictured are, from left to right, Tony Hernandez, Vic Mercado, Bishop Thomas J. Curry, Ralph Leon, and Bruce Archer. (Courtesy of Vic R. and Coring G. Mercado.)

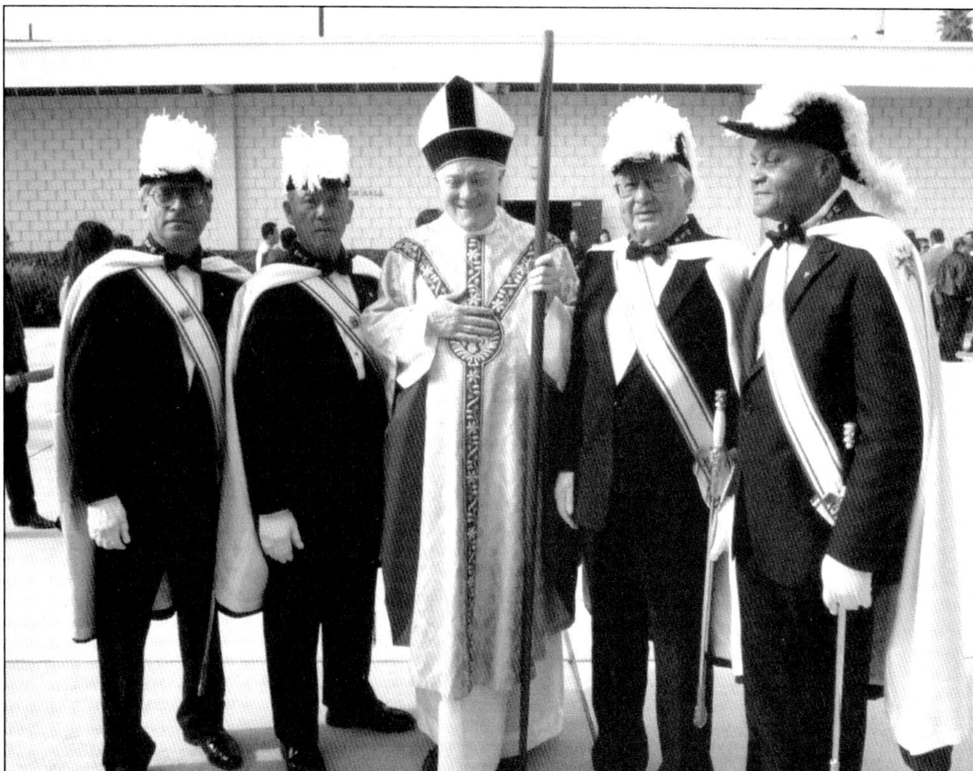

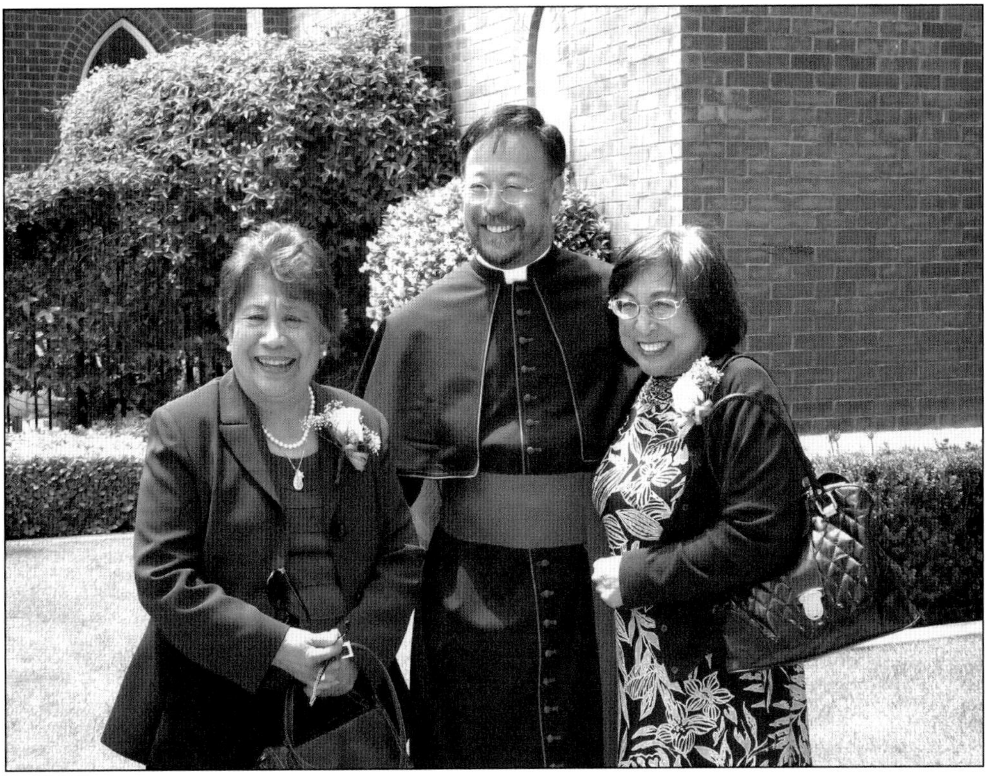

Monsignor Jon Marajucon stands with his mother, Nina Marajucon (left), and his *ninang* (godmother), Marjorie "Bets" Andrade (right). Monsignor Marajucon has had a pilot's license for the past 22 years. His home parish is Santa Clara Church at 323 South E Street in Oxnard. Nina Marajocon and her late husband, Fel Marajucon, were active members of the FCVCI and the Filipino community since the early 1950s. (Courtesy of Jon Marajucon.)

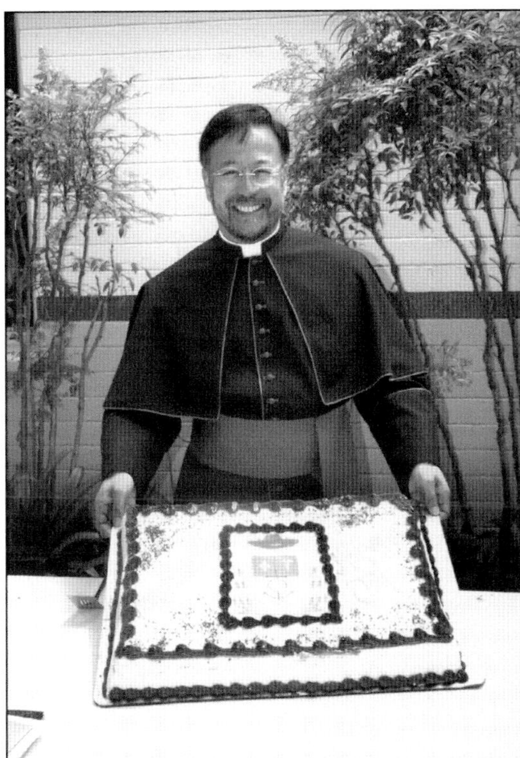

In February 2010, Jon Marajucon was named monsignor by Pope Benedict XVI. Mgr. Jon Marajucon is a product of local Catholic school education. He attended St. Anthony Elementary School (1972), Santa Clara High School (1976), and earned his master's in education from Loyola Marymount University, and a master in divinity from St. John's Seminary in Camarillo, California. (Courtesy of Jon Marajucon.)

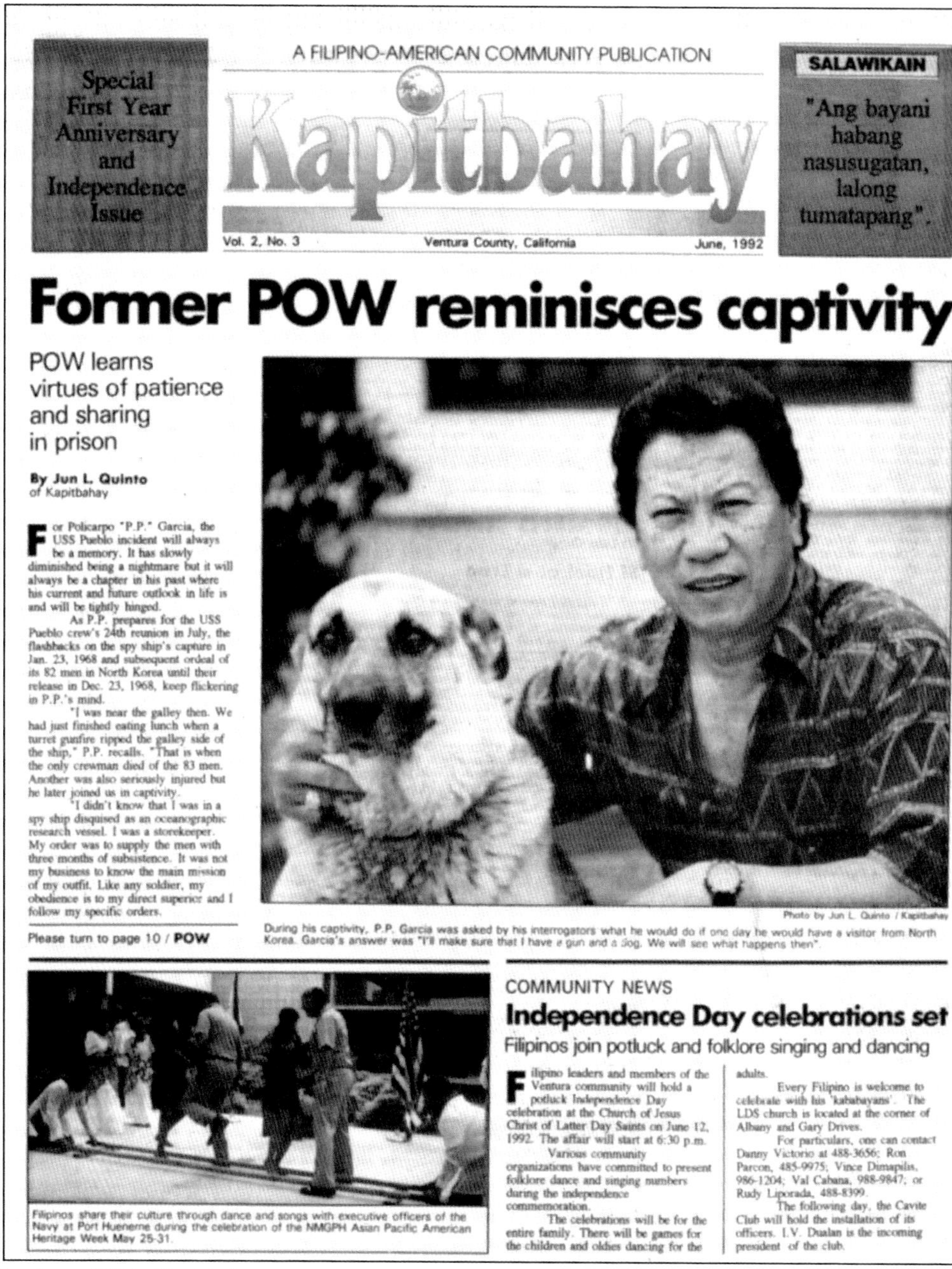

Special First Year Anniversary and Independence Issue

A FILIPINO-AMERICAN COMMUNITY PUBLICATION

Kapitbahay

Vol. 2, No. 3 Ventura County, California June, 1992

SALAWIKAIN

"Ang bayani habang nasusugatan, lalong tumatapang".

Former POW reminisces captivity

POW learns virtues of patience and sharing in prison

By Jun L. Quinto
of Kapitbahay

For Policarpo "P.P." Garcia, the USS Pueblo incident will always be a memory. It has slowly diminished being a nightmare but it will always be a chapter in his past where his current and future outlook in life is and will be tightly hinged.

As P.P. prepares for the USS Pueblo crew's 24th reunion in July, the flashbacks on the spy ship's capture in Jan. 23, 1968 and subsequent ordeal of its 82 men in North Korea until their release in Dec. 23, 1968, keep flickering in P.P.'s mind.

"I was near the galley then. We had just finished eating lunch when a turret gunfire ripped the galley side of the ship," P.P. recalls. "That is when the only crewman died of the 83 men. Another was also seriously injured but he later joined us in captivity.

"I didn't know that I was in a spy ship disguised as an oceanographic research vessel. I was a storekeeper. My order was to supply the men with three months of subsistence. It was not my business to know the main mission of my outfit. Like any soldier, my obedience is to my direct superior and I follow my specific orders.

Please turn to page 10 / **POW**

Photo by Jun L. Quinto / Kapitbahay

During his captivity, P.P. Garcia was asked by his interrogators what he would do if one day he would have a visitor from North Korea. Garcia's answer was "I'll make sure that I have a gun and a dog. We will see what happens then".

Filipinos share their culture through dance and songs with executive officers of the Navy at Port Hueneme during the celebration of the NMGPH Asian Pacific American Heritage Week May 25-31.

COMMUNITY NEWS

Independence Day celebrations set

Filipinos join potluck and folklore singing and dancing

Filipino leaders and members of the Ventura community will hold a potluck Independence Day celebration at the Church of Jesus Christ of Latter Day Saints on June 12, 1992. The affair will start at 6:30 p.m.

Various community organizations have committed to present folklore dance and singing numbers during the independence commemoration.

The celebrations will be for the entire family. There will be games for the children and oldies dancing for the adults.

Every Filipino is welcome to celebrate with his 'kababayans'. The LDS church is located at the corner of Albany and Gary Drives.

For particulars, one can contact Danny Victorio at 488-3656; Ron Parcon, 485-9975; Vince Dimapilis, 986-1204; Val Cabana, 988-9847; or Rudy Liporada, 488-8399.

The following day, the Cavite Club will hold the installation of its officers. I.V. Dualan is the incoming president of the club.

In June 1992, *Kapitbahay* commemorates its one-year anniversary with an issue dedicated to independence featuring former Korean War POW Policarpo "P.P." Garcia, a storekeeper on board the USS *Pueblo*, who was captured on January 23, 1968, along with 82 men, and later released on December 23, 1968. Garcia was one of the original owners of Pilipinas Bakery on 3640 Saviers Road in Oxnard. (Courtesy of Delia and Sid Cabran.)

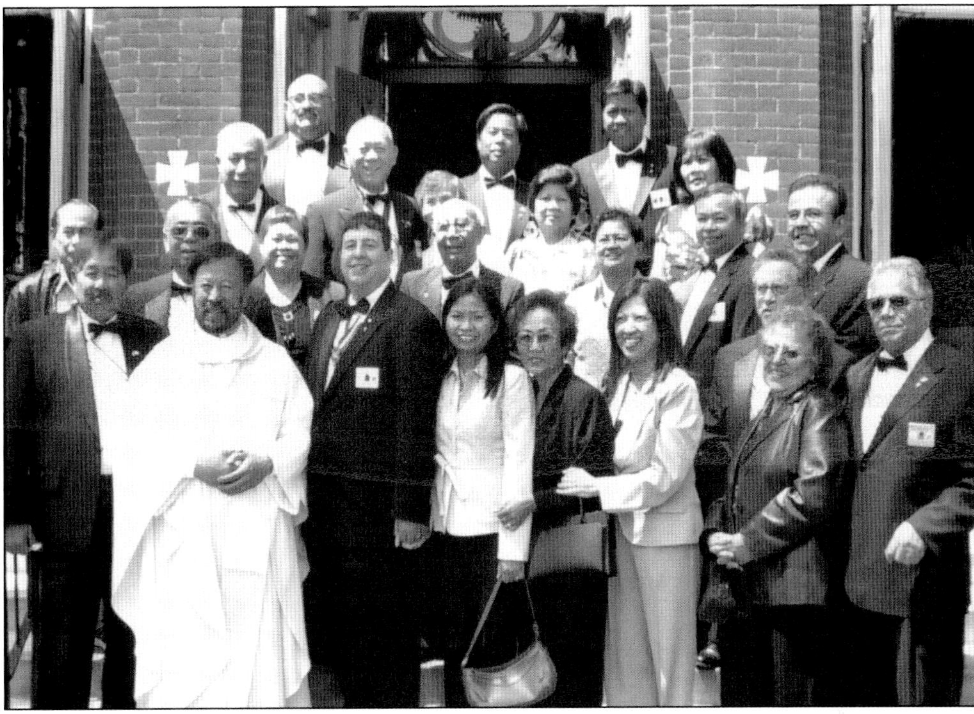

Mgr. Jon Marajucon and the Knights of Columbus are pictured after the Installation of new officers in front of Santa Clara Church in Oxnard. (Courtesy of Vic R. and Coring G. Mercado.)

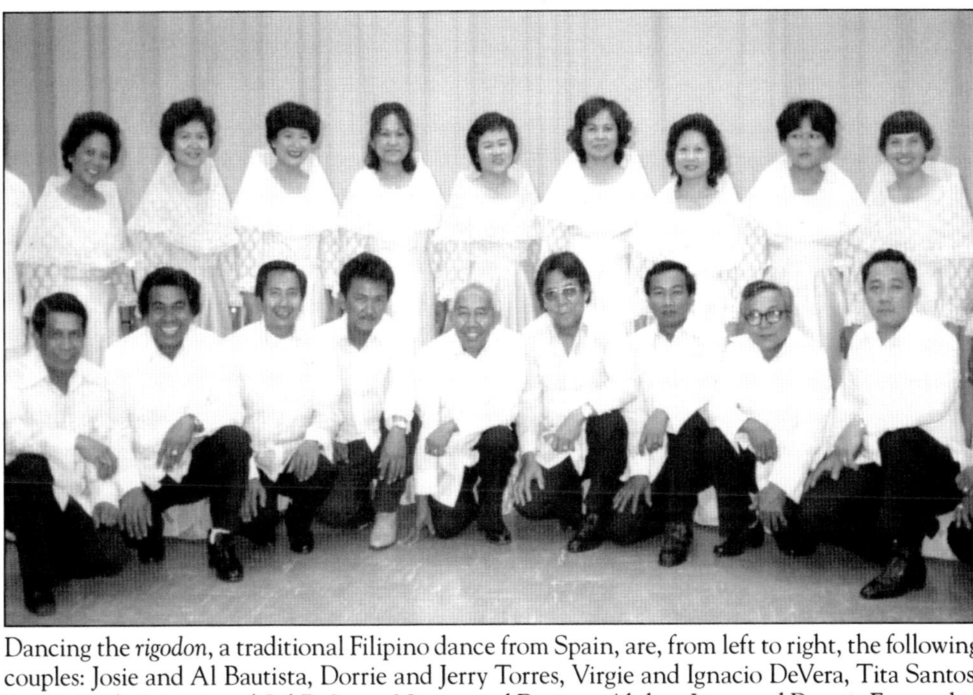

Dancing the *rigodon*, a traditional Filipino dance from Spain, are, from left to right, the following couples: Josie and Al Bautista, Dorrie and Jerry Torres, Virgie and Ignacio DeVera, Tita Santos, Canonizaola, Loring and Sal DeLeon, Norvie and Doming Abdon, Lucy and Dennis Fernandez, Cinoy and Pete Villanueva, and Coring and Vic Mercado. (Courtesy of Vic R. and Coring G. Mercado.)

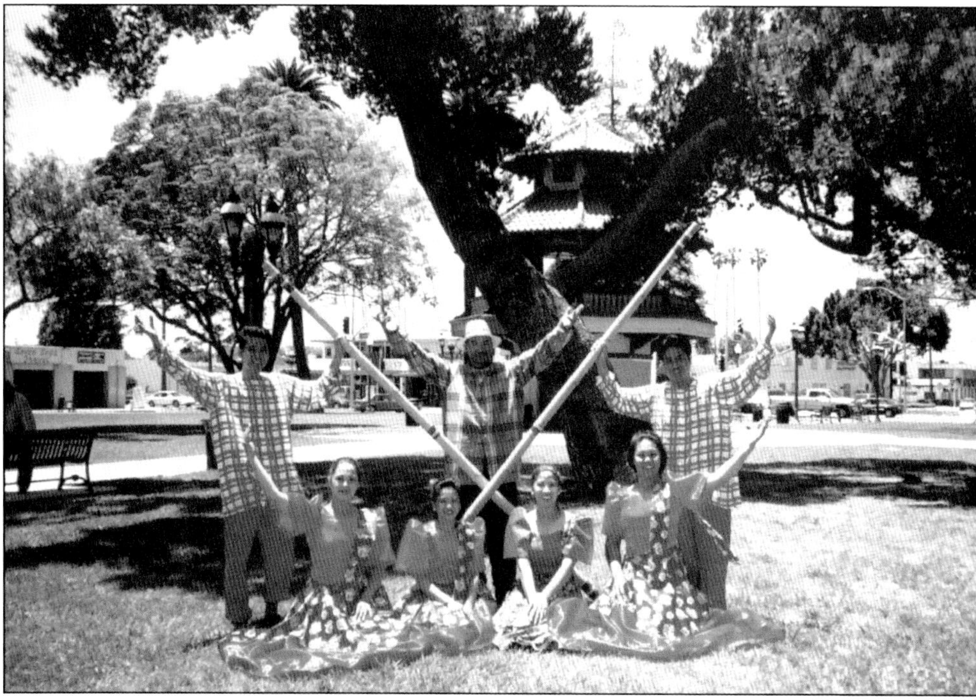

In Oxnard, Sonya Armadilla leads the dance group Salin-Lahi, which means "generations." Sonya teaches dance and prepares all the young people for the Filipino American community performances. This photograph was taken at the Plaza in Oxnard. (Courtesy of Vicky Barretto.)

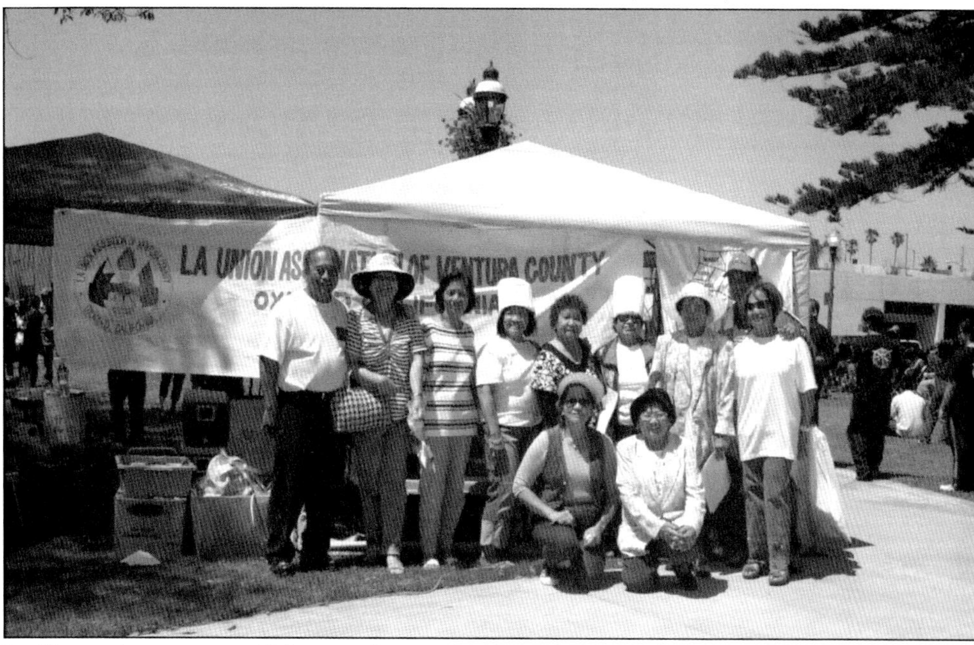

La Union Association of Ventura County has been helping Filipino community members for many years. Past president Gregory Morla established a scholarship that provides funding for scholars to attend school in the Philippines. Since its inception, 17 graduates have matriculated. (Courtesy of Charleen Morla.)

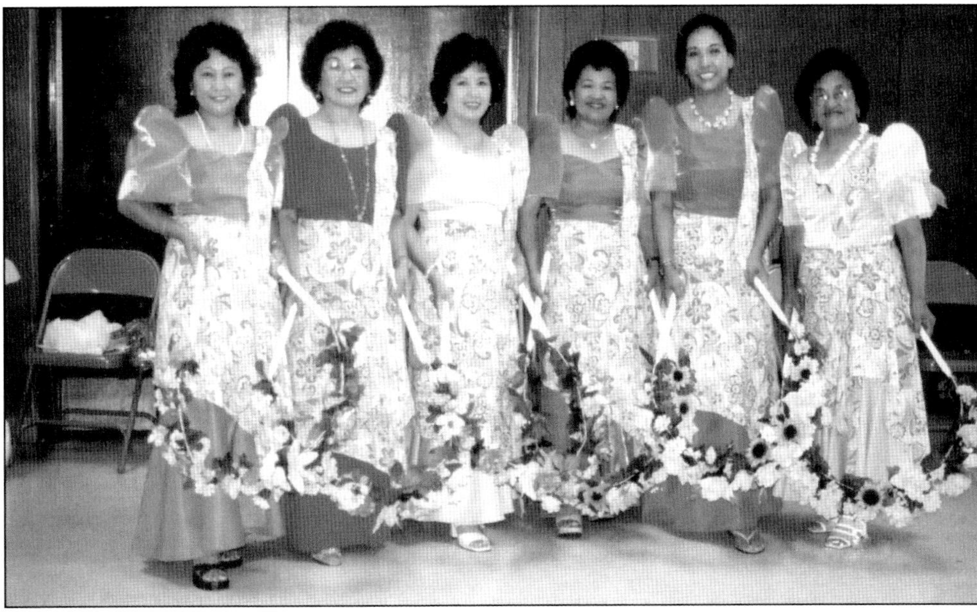

The Zambales Association of Ventura County ladies are dressed for a dance performance in the 1990s. Pictured from left to right are Josie Farala, Vicky Barretto, Annie Retome, Angie Basila, unidentified, and Fe Cayabyab. (Courtesy of Vicky Barretto.)

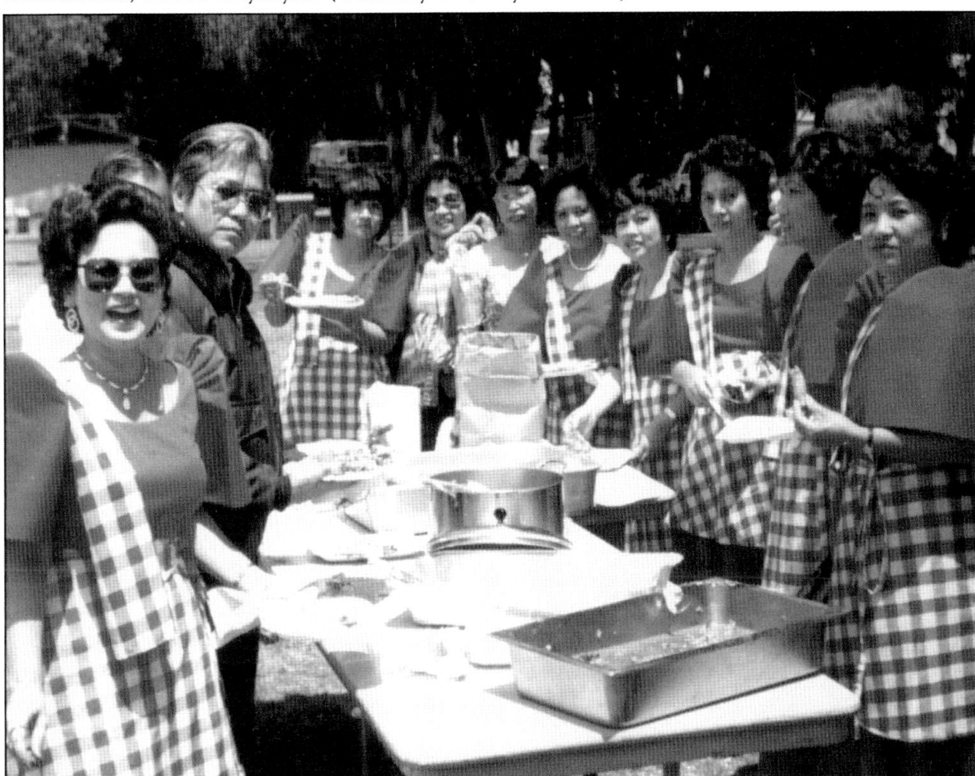

Members of the Filipino American Military Retired Club Ladies Auxiliary are shown at the Pacific Island event at Point Mugu in the 1980s. (Courtesy of Josie and Al Bautista.)

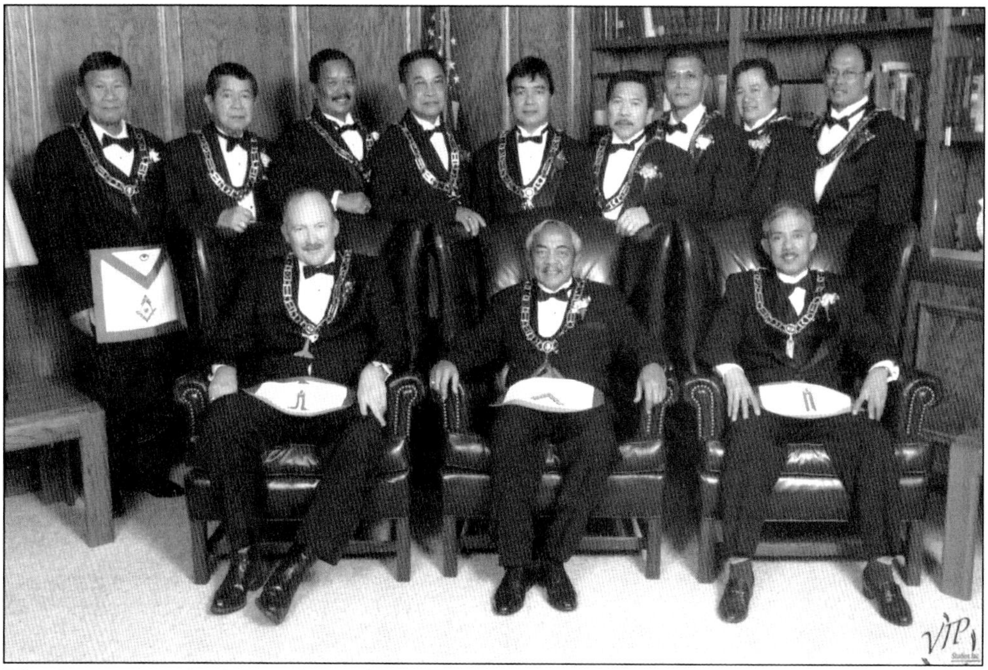

The Anacapa Lodge 710 in Oxnard was founded in 1950 and celebrated its 50th anniversary in 2000, under the leadership of Grand Master Eduardo Austria. Pictured from left to right are (first row) Larry Miller, Eduardo Austria, and Juanito Borreta; (second row) Gregorio Sagmaquen, Pepito Salazar, Victor Maxion, Emberto Guiang, Alfredo Antonio, Aresenio Briones, Roman Ladaw, Rodrigo Vertudez, and Wilfredo Dumaop. (Courtesy of Irene and Eduardo Austria.)

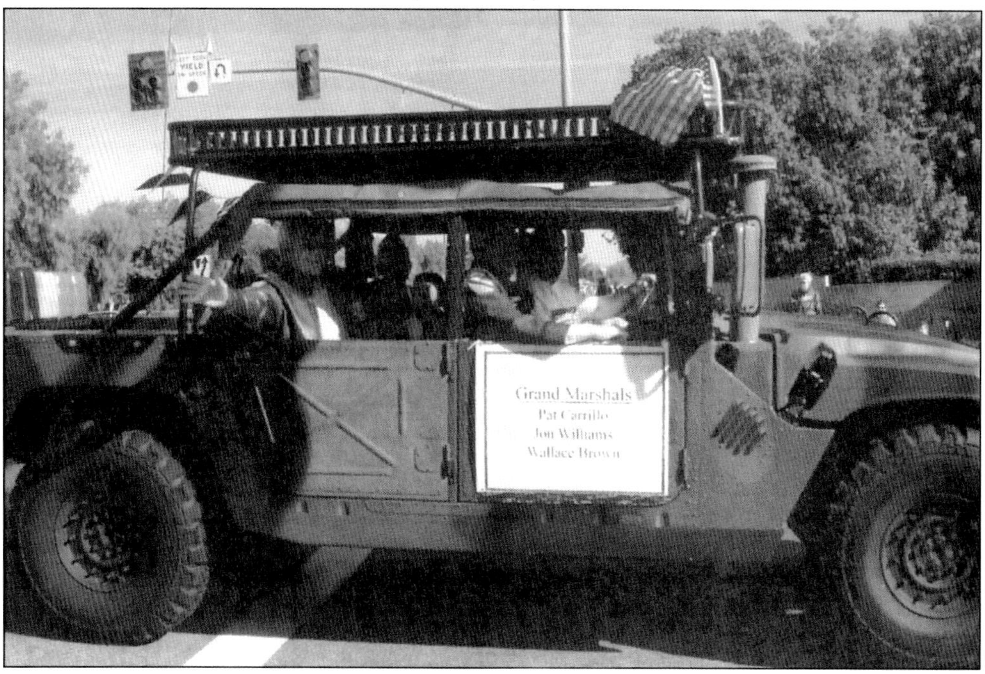

Pat Carrillo was one of the featured grand marshals at the Camarillo Christmas Parade, which honored veterans in 2003. (Courtesy of Julia Carrillo Macasieb.)

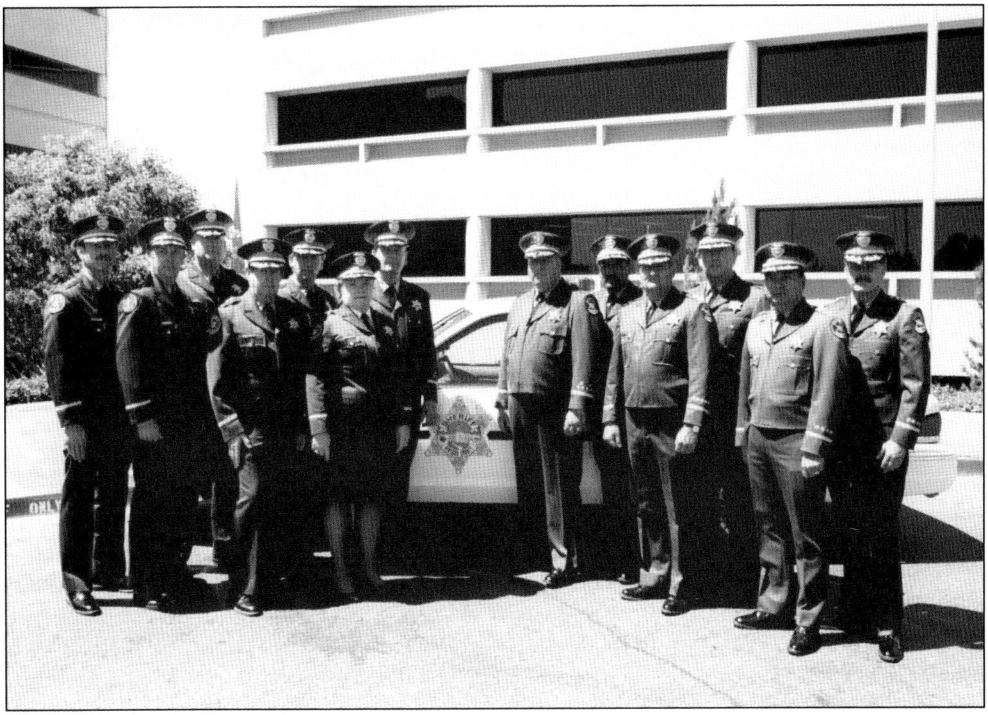

The Command Staff at the Ventura County Sherriff's Department is pictured in 1998 with Chief Deputy Dante Honorico, second from the far right. (Courtesy of Ellen and Dante Honorico.)

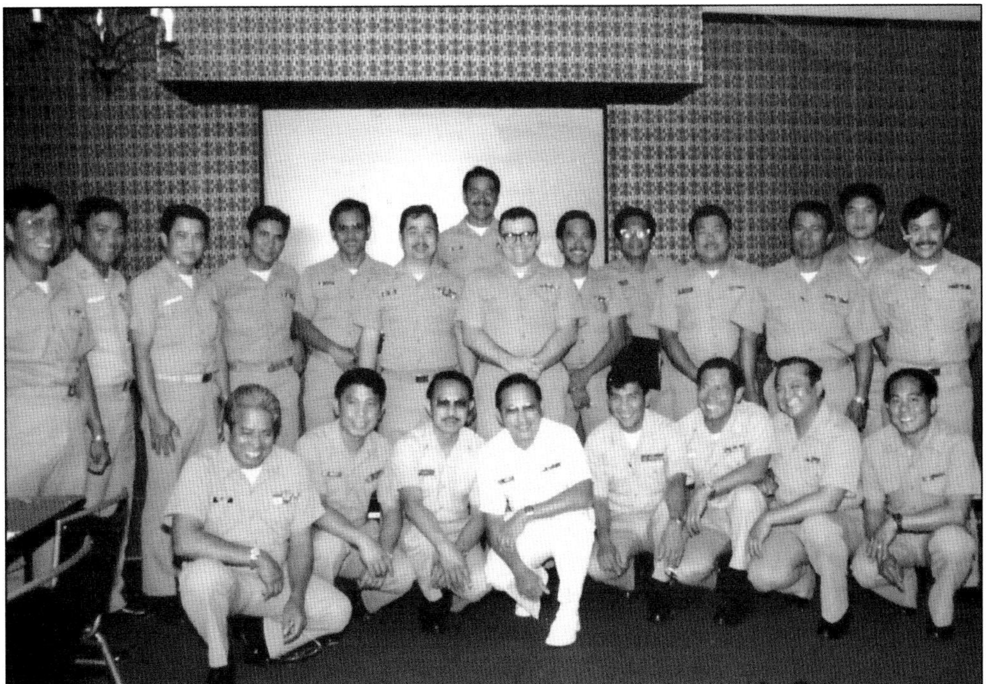

The Chief Petty Officer Club take an impromptu group shot at Navy Base Ventura County at Port Hueneme in June 1981. (Courtesy of Cathy and Jim Ines.)

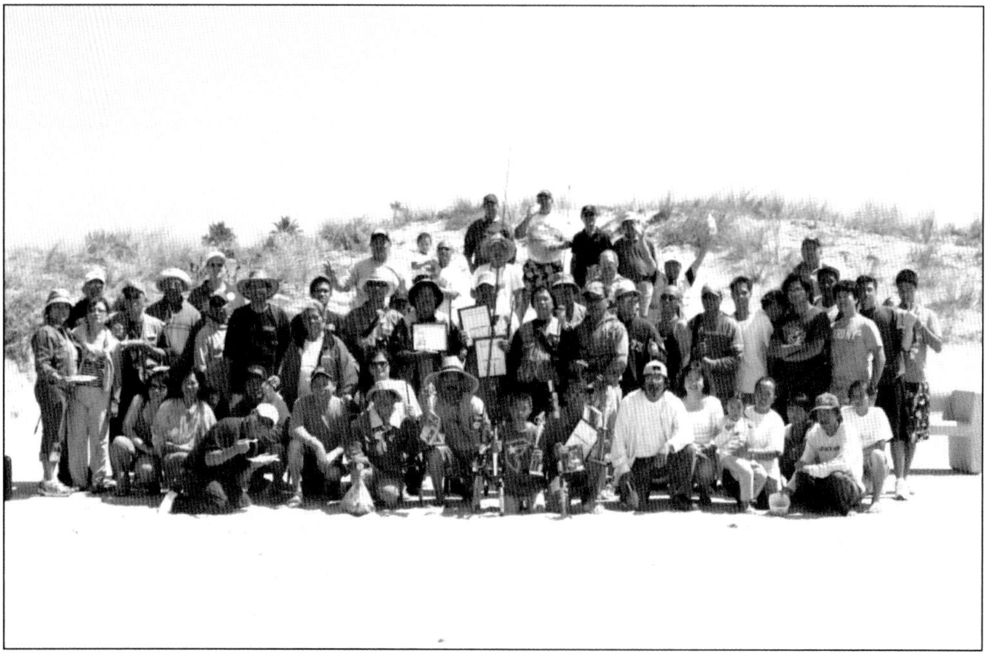

The Visayan Association of Ventura County sponsored the Second Annual Fishing Derby in 2008 to raise funds for the Philippine Center of Oxnard. (Courtesy of Charleen Morla.)

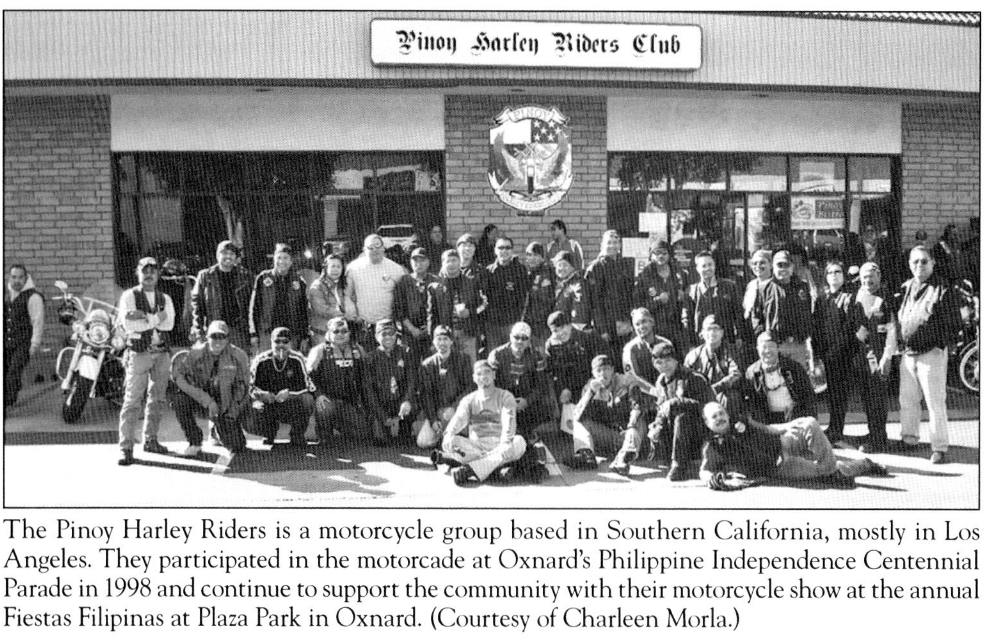

The Pinoy Harley Riders is a motorcycle group based in Southern California, mostly in Los Angeles. They participated in the motorcade at Oxnard's Philippine Independence Centennial Parade in 1998 and continue to support the community with their motorcycle show at the annual Fiestas Filipinas at Plaza Park in Oxnard. (Courtesy of Charleen Morla.)

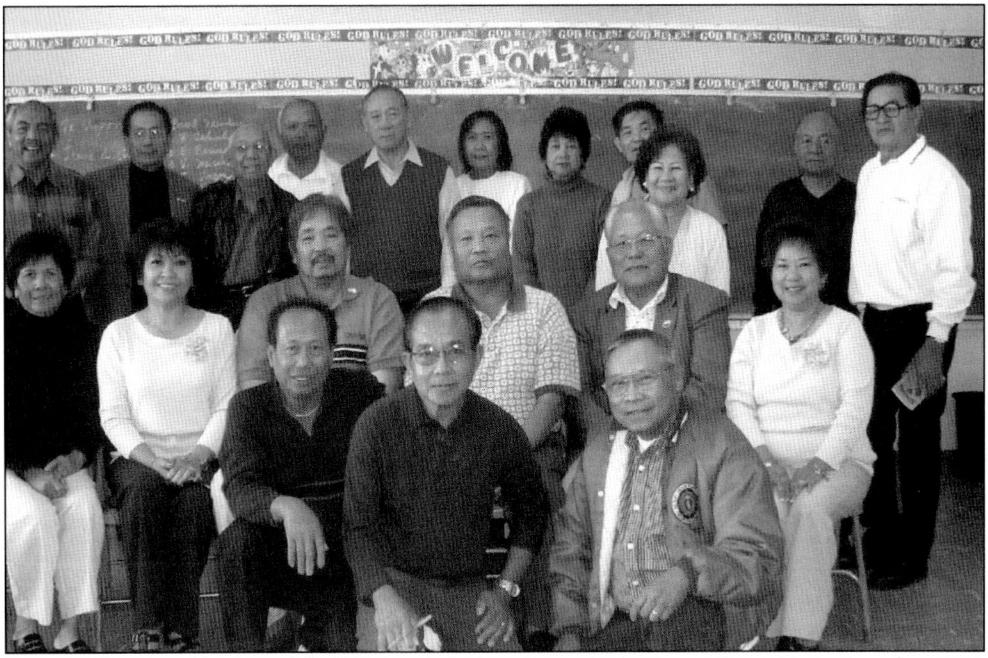

Past presidents and leaders of the Filipino American organizations pose for a picture in a classroom at Mary Star of the Sea Church in Oxnard. Pictured from left to right are (third row) Eduardo Austria, Iggy DeVera, unidentified, Burt Calimlim, Vic Mercado, Irene Austria, three unidentified people, Bernie Basila, and Armando Bautista; (second row) Fe Vinzon, Evelyn Besina, Danny Flores, Bert Gan, Toots Vinzon, and Cora Ortiguerra; (first row) unidentified, Pol Barcena, and Roger Santos. (Courtesy of Vic R. and Coring G. Mercado.)

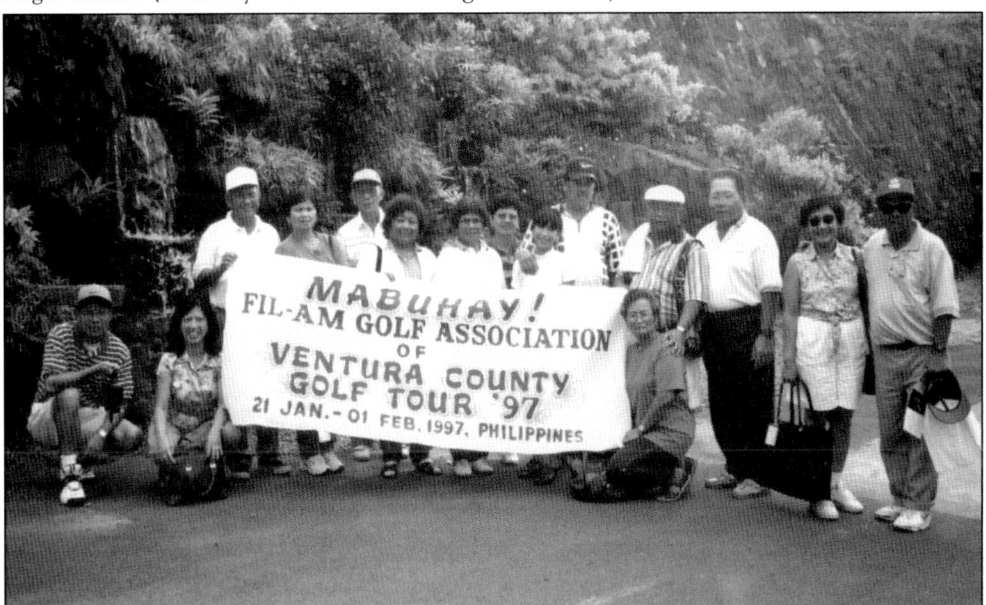

The Filipino American Golf Association of Ventura County usually plays at the NBVC Port Hueneme Golf Course or at the River Ridge Golf Club in Oxnard. They pose together here during a 1997 Philippine Islands tour. (Courtesy of Fe and Toots Vinzon.)

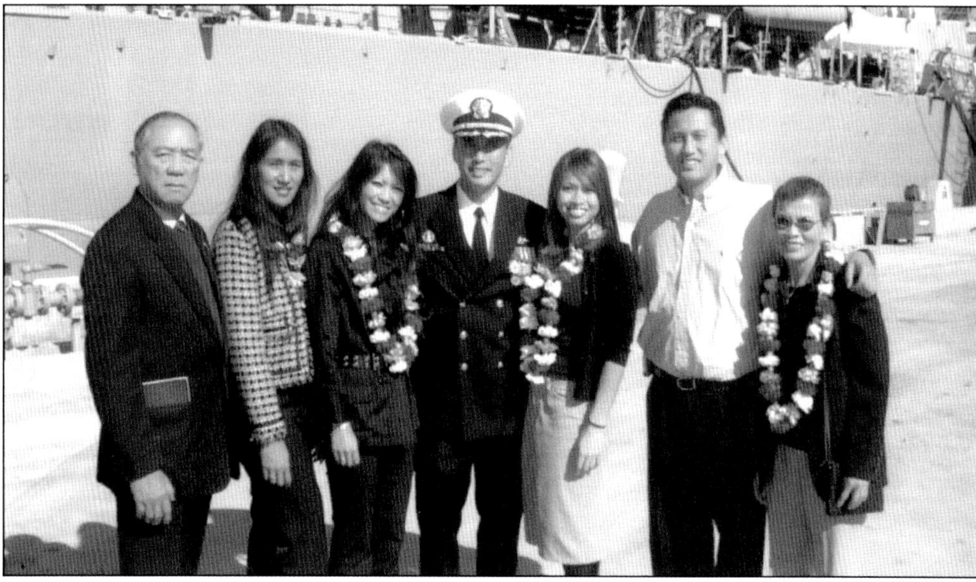

Vic and Coring Mercado have five children, Helen, Elsie, Victorino, Erwin, and Kristine. Four attended Channel Islands High School while the youngest attended Santa Clara High School. They are all college graduates with degrees from University of California, Los Angeles; California State University, Northridge; California Polytechnic State University San Luis Obispo; San Diego State University; Pepperdine University; Whittier Law School; and the US Naval Academy. In this picture, Capt. Victorino G. Mercado, Commanding Officer of the USS Decatur (DDG73), a guided missile destroyer, is pictured with his family after a change of command ceremony. (Courtesy of Vic R. and Coring G. Mercado.)

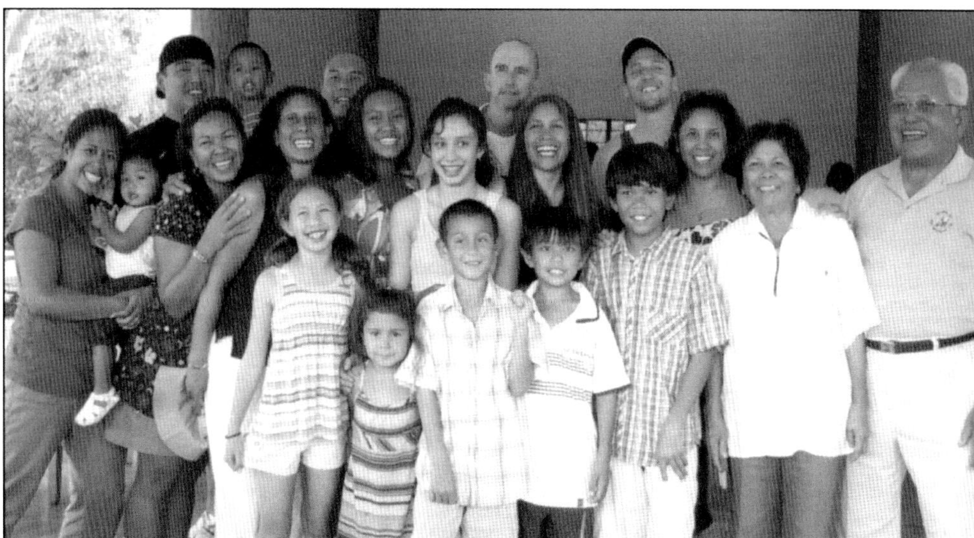

Fe and Toots Vinzon have six children, Noel, Jennifer, Daisy, Liberty, Delila, and Diana. They grew up at 1224 Callas Drive and attended Channel Islands High School in Oxnard. All Vinzons are college graduates and earned degrees from University of California, Los Angeles; California State University, Northridge; and the US Naval Academy. This photograph was taken in 2008 when the entire Vinzon clan traveled to the Philippines for family vacation. (Courtesy of Fe and Toots Vinzon.)

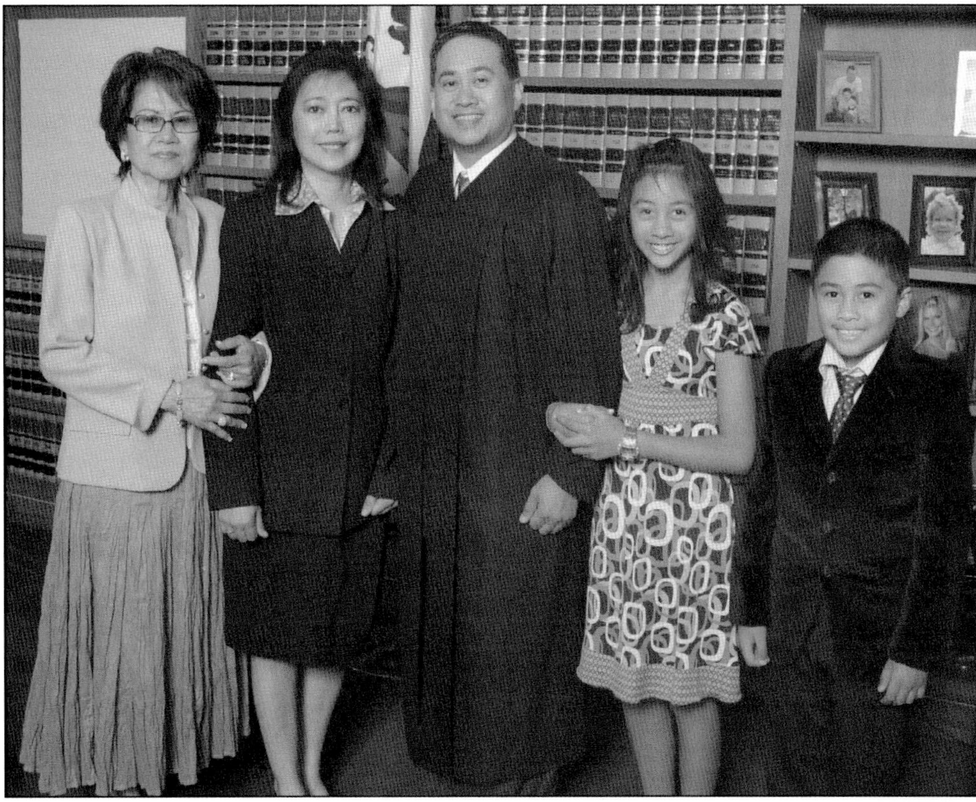

In October 2008, Governor Schwarzenegger appointed Judge Bernie LaForteza as a judge of the superior court, Los Angeles County, North District, where he is assigned to preside over criminal matters, including jury trials. A graduate of Channel Islands High School (1979), UCLA (1984), and University of California Hastings College of Law (1990), LaForteza practiced in Los Angeles County first as a Deputy Public Defender, then later as a Deputy District Attorney before his appointment to the bench. Son of Virginia LaForteza and the late Floro LaForteza, Bernie is married to Marie, and they have two children, Alexandra (age 12) and Daniel (age 10). (Courtesy of Marie and Bernie LaForteza.)

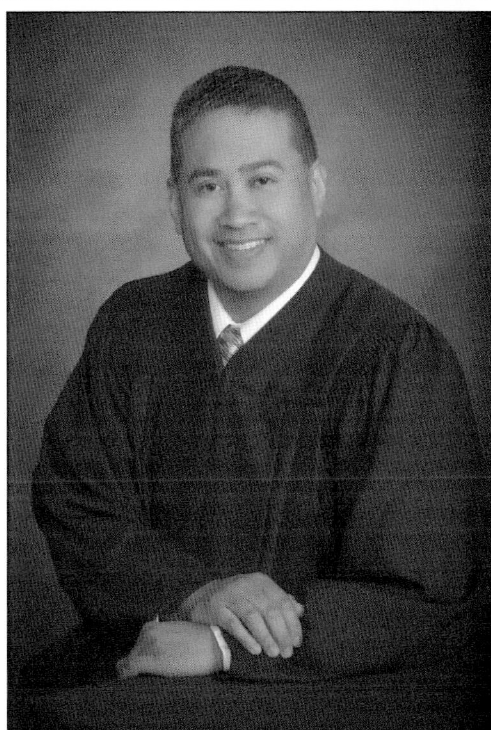

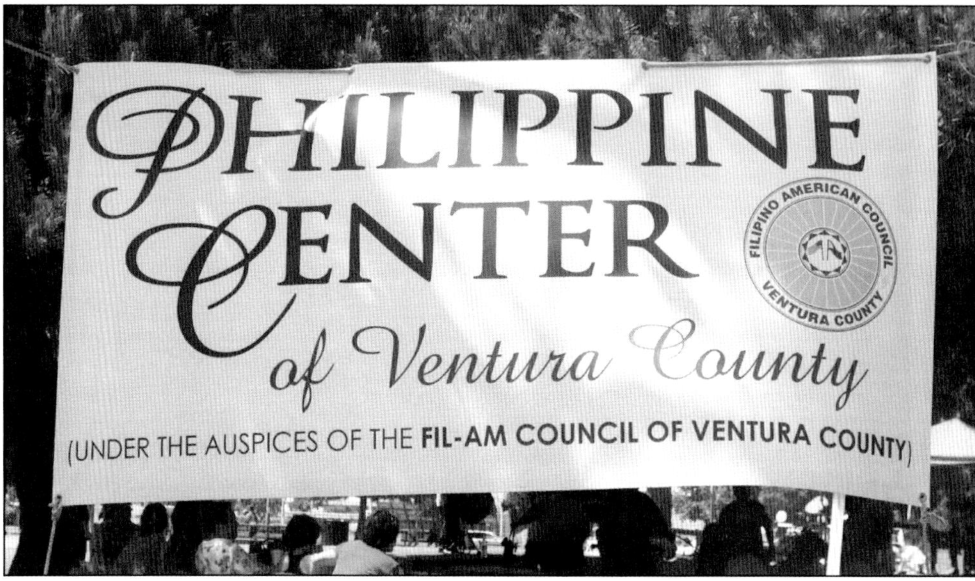

The Philippine Center of Ventura County is going into its third year with the long-term fundraising goal to purchase a building with multipurpose space for meetings and events. The Center envisions offering classes, resources, and services for the community. Currently, the Philippine Center's fundraising campaign includes its annual Benefit Dinner, Valentine's Dance, Golf Tournament, and Santacruzan. Other Filipino organizations under the Filipino American Council have been collaborating and donating proceeds from their own fundraisers to support the Center. (Courtesy of Charleen Morla.)

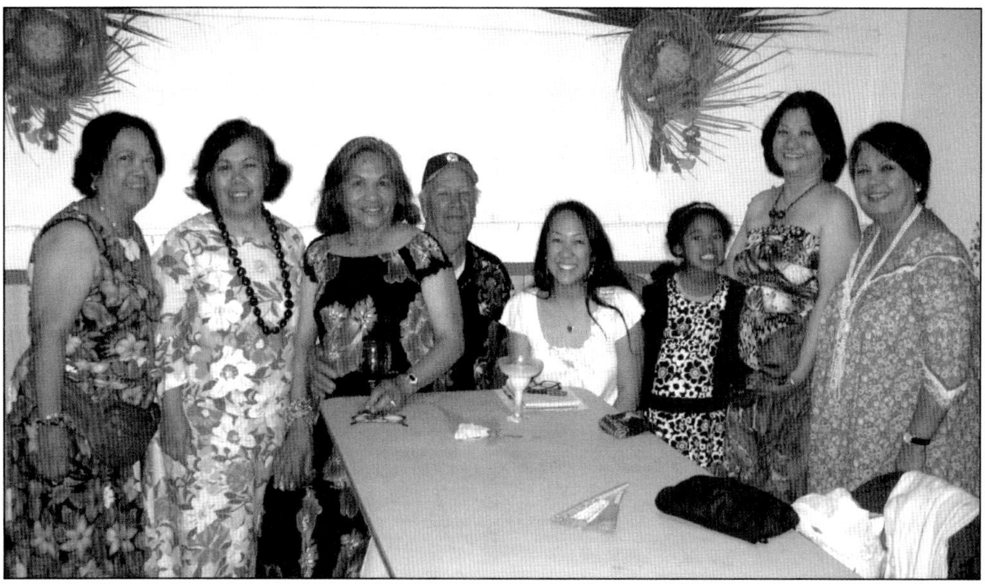

Bill Coleman was a teenager in the 1950s and grew up with the Dacayanas in La Conchita del Mar. In 1963, Coleman bought land in Carpinteria and began farming where he continues to live and farm today. The Coleman Family Farm is run by Bill, his wife Delia, and son Romeo. They specialize in organic Asian vegetables, salad and cooking greens, and sell their produce at the Santa Monica and Oxnard College Farmers Markets. Bill Coleman is seated (center) with his wife Delia (left) sitting on his lap.

Filipino Community of Ventura County Inc.'s 50th anniversary program: 1931–1981 took place on Valentine's Day, February 14, 1981. The FCVCI is the oldest of the 26 organizations under today's Filipino American Council. The year this book is publishing, 2011, marks a very special 80th anniversary for FCVCI. (Courtesy of Irene and Eduardo Austria.)

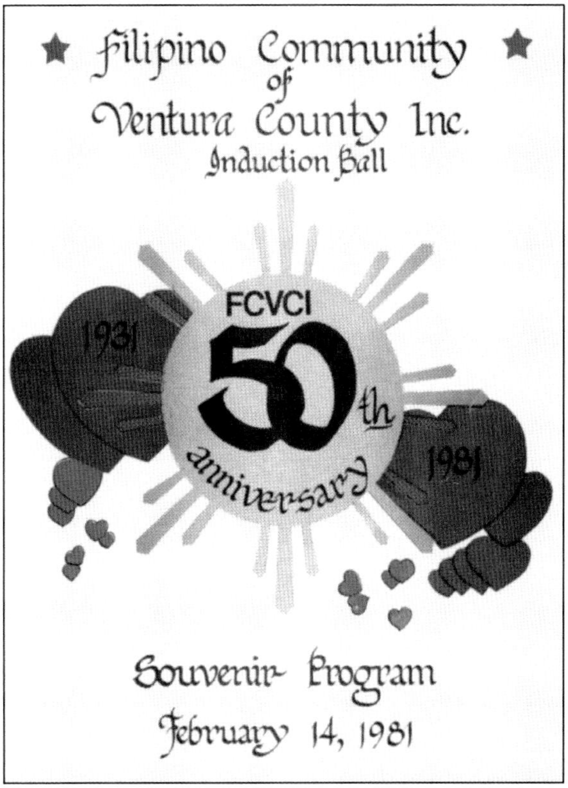

The image below was taken in the summer of 2010 during a special visit of old friends (and cousins) at the Talaugon home in Santa Paula. From left to right are (first row) Elaine Alpenia, Federico (Dick) Talaugon Jr., and Jack Alpenia; (second row) Claudia Matthews, Johnny Cruz, and Nora Talaugon.

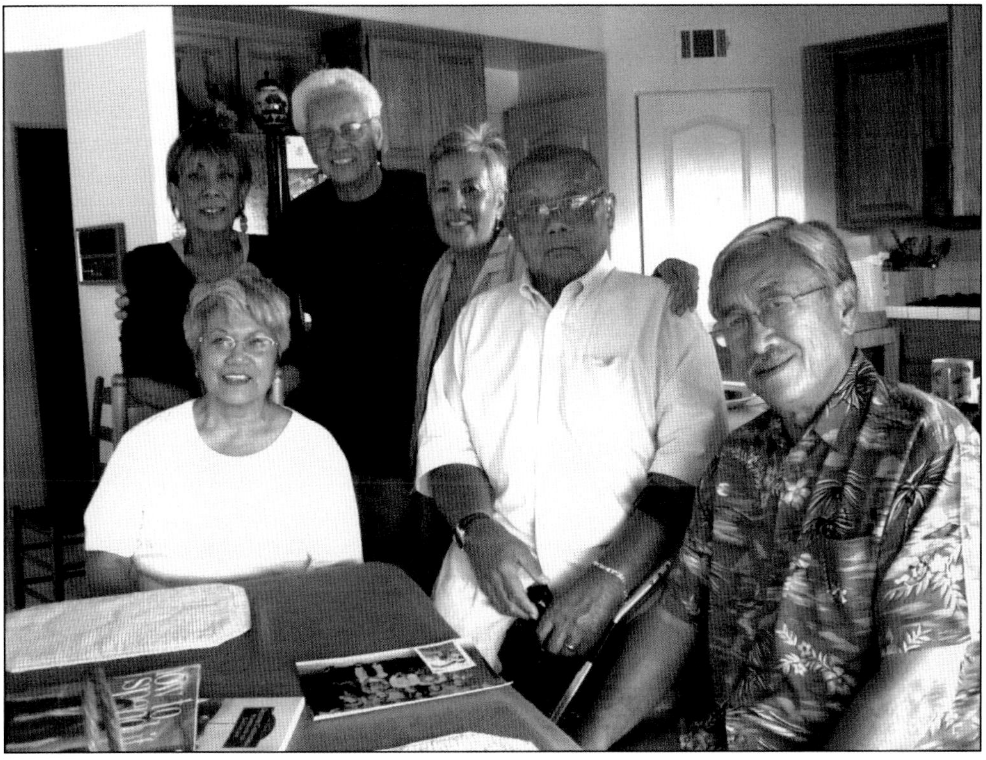

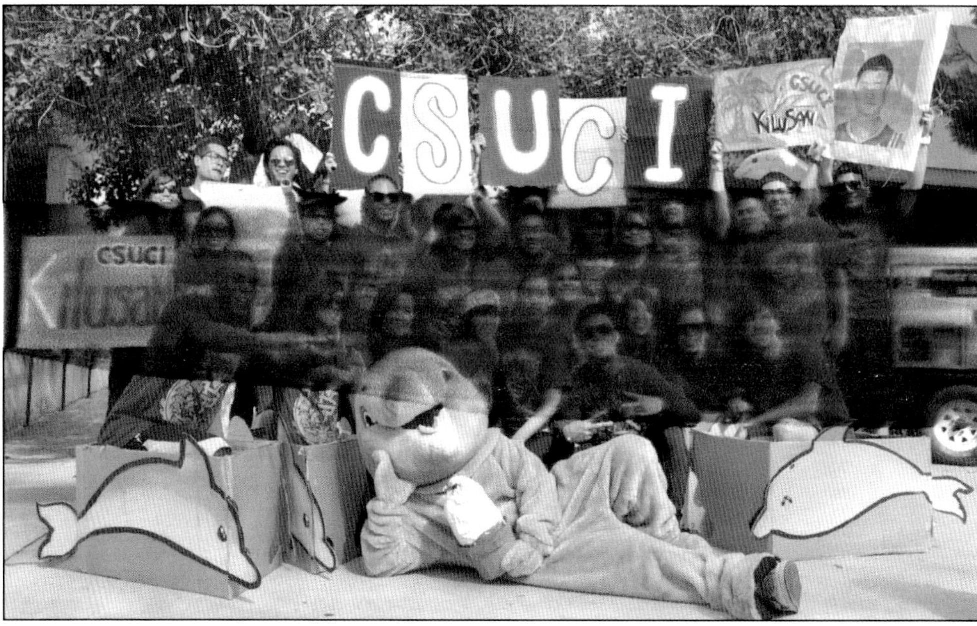

Kilusan Pilipino at California State University Channel Islands (KP-CI) is a student club established during the spring of 2010. Kilusan Pilipino's mission is to promote Filipino culture to the Channel Island campus, Ventura County community, family, and friends. Pictured here are KP members at their first Friendship Games, the largest Filipino American collegiate event. It is a 25-year tradition held at California State University Fullerton, where over 30 clubs come together to show their school spirit, share Filipino pride, and compete in games.

Bibliography

Barrios, Oscar. "Pat Carrillo, Filipino American Profile." *Kapitbahay*, October 1994, 6.

Borah, Eloisa Gomez. "Americans of Filipino Descent: FAQs." http://personal.anderson.ucla.edu/eloisa.borah/filfaqs.htm.

Daily, Stanley. *Camarillo and Other Remembrances.* Camarillo, CA: U Build a Book, 2007.

Fabros, Alex S. "California and Second World War: California's Filipino Infantry." http://www.militarymuseum.org/Filipino.html.

Filipino American National Historical Society California Central Coast Chapter. "PI Market Pismo Beach, California." *Stories, Legends, and Memories*, InstantPublisher.com.

"Filipino Boys, Students at Hueneme." *Oxnard Courier*, November 27, 1903.

"Filipino Farewell Party at Hueneme." *Oxnard Courier*, June 24, 1904.

"Filipino Leader Dela Rosa Dies." *The Press-Courier*, August 20, 1982, 2.

Fleming, Leonard N. "Filipinos See Need to Boost Political Clout Activism." *Los Angeles Times*, August 29, 1993, 1.

"No Longer the Value but the Promise." *Kapitbahay*, March–April 2004.

Reynolds, Helen. "Filipino Community Reveres Leader." *PC: The Weekly Magazine of Ventura County*, April 19, 1981, 3–5.

"275 Acres in Fine Peas on Arneill Ranch." *Oxnard Courier*, January 7, 1929.

Index

Abarca, Darlene, 63, 86, 88
Alpenia, 17, 20, 21, 125
antimiscegenation laws, 9, 23, 36
Arneill Ranch, 8, 22, 51
Austria, Eduardo, 7, 83, 118, 121
Babauta, 47, 49
Bagay, Aquilino, 27, 43, 57
Barretto, 7, 50–52, 57, 61, 107, 117
Bautista, 7, 40, 59, 67, 82, 86, 96, 112, 115, 121
Caballeros De Dimas-Alang, 16, 23, 26, 38, 39
Carrillo, 7, 55–57, 60, 61, 67, 70, 71, 118
Castaneda, 7, 27–29, 43, 44, 54, 55, 57, 65–67, 72, 73, 80, 81, 97
Colonia, 31, 42
Dacayana, 17, 20, 21, 124
Daily, 7, 22
Dela Rosa, 7, 11, 14, 24, 25, 27, 29 33, 41, 46, 54, 56, 57
DeLeon, Celistino, 86, 88, 94
Doctolero 14, 24, 27
Filipino American Military Retired Club, 95, 105, 117
Filipino Community of Ventura County Inc., 9, 23, 54-61, 66, 67, 71, 93–96, 113, 125
Garcia, P.P., 109, 114
Gaynor Ranch, 15, 17, 44
Grey, 7, 47–49, 53, 62, 78, 79, 87, 97, 100
Hamoja Housing, 28, 48, 53
Honorico, 7, 65, 101–103, 119
Ines, 7, 10, 13, 24, 25, 27, 30, 31, 42, 45, 54, 68, 83
Jacobe, 15, 19, 75
Jordan Lodge 604, 16, 23, 24, 26, 27
Kapitbahay, 93, 100, 104, 114
Knights of Columbus, 97, 112, 115
LaForteza, Bernie, 92, 123
Legionarios Del Trabajo, 16, 23, 24, 26, 27
Macasieb, 7, 81
Majarucon, 7, 57, 113, 115
Mary Star of the Sea, 94, 110–112, 121
Mercado, 7, 85–86, 90, 91, 94, 96, 97, 111, 112, 115, 121, 122
Montayre, 15, 74, 75
Obispo, 7, 64, 84
Ocean View Farm, 8, 45
Omo, 7, 10, 24–29, 32–36, 38, 56, 62, 68
Personnel for Improvement in the Naval Organization and Yeoman's Services (PINOYS), 86, 88, 93, 99
Philippine Centennial Parade, 106–109, 120
Philippine Day, 32–34, 37
Sarreal, 7, 87, 88, 110
Simon, Julian, 24, 25, 27, 56, 57, 66
Springville Ranch, 8, 13, 31, 50, 51
Talaugon, 7, 9, 11, 12, 15, 17–19, 21, 43, 44, 125
Tayag, 7, 92
Torres, Tom, 50, 51
Ventura, 13, 24, 25, 43
Vinzon, 76, 77, 86, 88, 89, 96, 97, 121, 122
Yabes, 24–26

For a complete index, please visit www.elnoratayag.com.

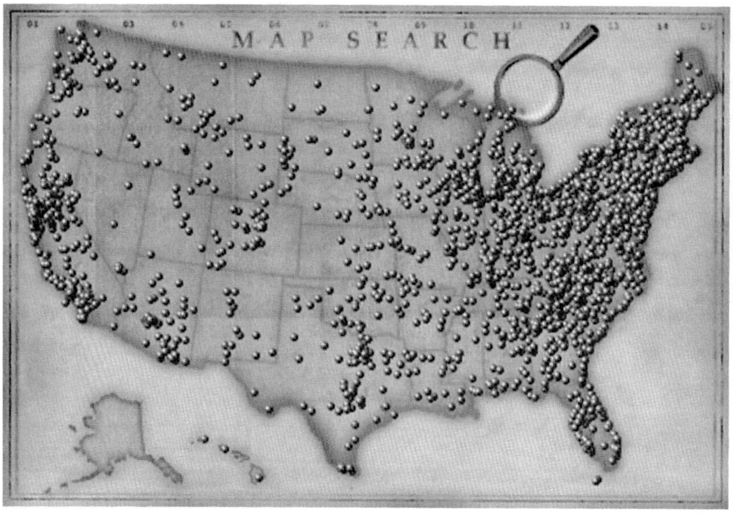
MAP SEARCH